THE IMPORTANCE OF BEING ERNEST

The Life of Actor Jim Varney

(Stuff that Vern doesn't even know)

JUSTIN LLOYD

Copyright © 2013 Justin Lloyd
All rights reserved.

Book Cover Design by Luisa Trujillo

Front Cover Photo Courtesy of Joe Liles
Back Cover Photo of Jim Varney Courtesy of Rob Neuhauser

ISBN: 1492746312
ISBN 13: 9781492746317

For Greta Kathleen, Talia Jane and Eden Cecelia

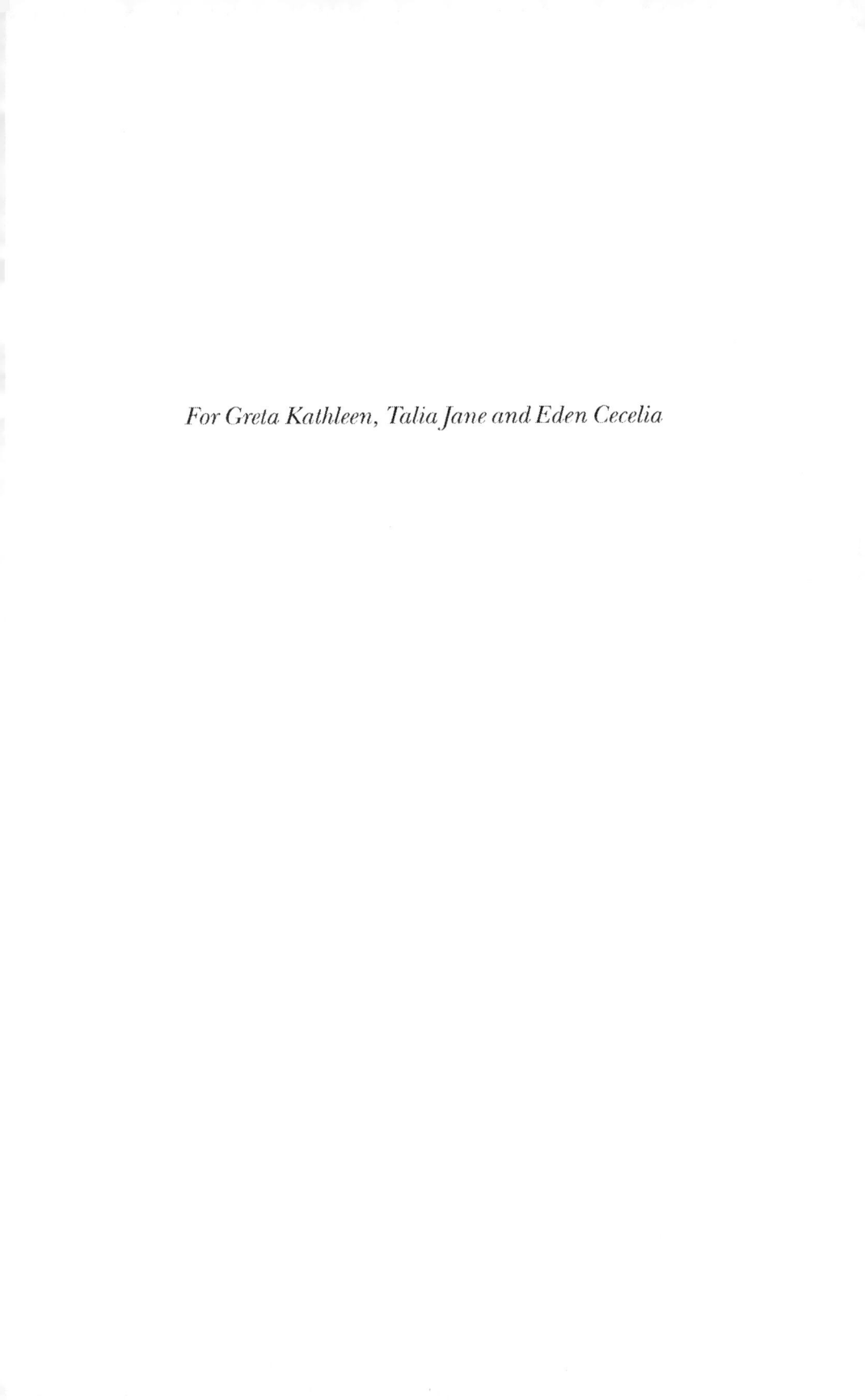

TABLE OF CONTENTS

PREFACE..1

Chapter 1   SHOTGUN WEDDING.........................5

Chapter 2   THE BEGINNING..........................7

Chapter 3   WATCHING TV...........................21

Chapter 4   DISCOVERING THE THEATER...............25

Chapter 5   ANNE, HER MOTHER AND THE
FINER THINGS..........................31

Chapter 6   THE VARNEY PARKERS....................37

Chapter 7   HIGH SCHOOL YEARS.....................39

Chapter 8   LEAVING LEXINGTON.....................47

Chapter 9   FINDING GLORY WITH CHERRY.............65

Chapter 10 STRIKING IT RICH IN CALIFORNIA........79

Chapter 11 BECOMING VERN'S FAVORITE NEIGHBOR....97

Chapter 12 THE SECRET OF ERNEST'S SUCCESS.......113

Chapter 13 GLOOM BEAMS, HEARTBREAK AND A
LITTLE LUCK..........................141

Chapter 14 ERNEST IN THE MOVIES.................153

Chapter 15 PLUVIO...............................167

Chapter 16 HOBO STEW............................171

Chapter 17 HANDGUN WEDDING 175

Chapter 18 SAVING CHRISTMAS 179

Chapter 19 THE LINE BLURS BETWEEN JIM
                  AND ERNEST 187

Chapter 20 "HEY VERN!" 197

Chapter 21 BLUE JEANS AND T-SHIRT MAN. 203

Chapter 22 BUCKMASTERS & BUBBA 207

Chapter 23 A HILLBILLY OF AN OZARK KIND 211

Chapter 24 SLINKY DOG 219

Chapter 25 THE END OF A "GREAT ADVENTURE" 229

NOTES 243

ACKNOWLEDGEMENTS 289

PREFACE

Jim Varney was my uncle – the younger brother of my mother, Sandra. Most people know him by the iconic Ernest P. Worrell character he portrayed in thousands of commercials, nearly a dozen movies and a Saturday-morning TV show.

But to me, he was Uncle Jim, the multi-talented sensation of our family. You never knew a room was dark until he lit it up. I actually don't believe he had an "off" switch. There weren't enough hours in the day for Jim to soak up all that life had to offer. Whether he was collecting antiques or poring over Civil War history, acting or writing songs, Jim was a full-on participant in countless pursuits.

Jim was a loving brother, a devoted son and an amazing uncle. In any other family I would have been considered "the funny one." But in our family, Jim left me in the dust. And he was so talented, I was just happy to have a front-row seat during his visits. He was also smart, caring and had a DeLorean. What more could a young nephew ask for? In addition, like everyone, Jim had his personal heartbreaks and his internal struggles. Despite the simpleton he portrayed as Ernest, in his soul Jim was an artist of incredible diversity. And when he died in 2000, a light went out not only for his fans but for my family.

THE IMPORTANCE OF BEING ERNEST:
THE LIFE OF ACTOR JIM VARNEY

I was compelled to write this book because I knew much more about Jim's life remained to be told than was out there in popular culture. I wanted Jim's fans to truly know who he was. I could rely on someone else to tell the story of one of the most notable people in my family's history, or I could (deep breath) attempt it myself. To numerous people, Jim *was* Ernest. And love Ernest or hate him, the truth is that Jim brought something special to the character that made Ernest unforgettable in the same way Charlie Chaplin embodied The Little Tramp.

Jim's trajectory to stardom was not unlike that of many other famous actors and celebrities. He was the class clown who dropped out of high school. He moved away to follow his acting dreams and struggled and starved in New York before heading to Los Angeles to try and break into television. Despite landing some promising roles and appearing on "Johnny Carson," nothing ever really gelled for Jim in Southern California. He became intimate with failure and rejection.

Finally, in 1980 at the age of 31, during one of the lowest points in his life, Jim's career took an unexpected turn. A small Nashville ad agency created a character to advertise a theme park in Kentucky. The character, Ernest, would bring Jim fame, fortune and countless opportunities. At the same time, Ernest ultimately became his identity onscreen and off, and that proved difficult for Jim to overcome when he tried to expand as an actor. Still, with roles such as Jed Clampett in the movie version of "The Beverly Hillbillies" and (being the voice of) Slinky Dog in the groundbreaking animated film "Toy Story," Jim persevered.

Although Jim was only 50 when he died, he brought laughter and entertainment to more people than he could have ever imagined. Luckily for the world, much of Jim's work was captured on film for future generations to discover.

PREFACE

In this book I have attempted to offer the most comprehensive account of Jim's life as possible within the means available to me. My goal has been to provide the insight of a family member coupled with the objectivity of a journalist. I have combed through hundreds of newspapers, magazines and online sources. Numerous people who played significant roles in Jim's story had never spoken to the media. Interviewing many of them, including my own family members, enabled me to capture the essence of who Jim was in addition to the uncle I knew and loved. In the end, I believe I have painted a more complete picture of Jim than has been done before. (A comprehensive list of my sources can be found in the Notes section at the end of this book.)

My goal has been accuracy and a 360-degree view of Jim. Yet despite my best efforts, I was unable to reach everyone mentioned in the book. I had to rely on other sources to reconstruct the past. Every attempt has been made to be accurate and respectful of those I was unable to interview, as well as protect their privacy as much as possible while still including the impact they had on Jim's life.

Writing this book has taken over five years. It has been one of the most challenging tasks I have ever undertaken. Yet every struggle along the way – and there have been many – has been worth it. I feel honored to be in the position to share the story of a man who meant so much to so many. I hope that I have created a work that pays proper tribute to Jim's legacy, one he would be proud of were he still here.

Justin Lloyd, Versailles, Kentucky, August 2013

CHAPTER ONE

SHOTGUN WEDDING

Two young bridesmaids, 12 and 14, enter the living room of their modest Kentucky home. The bride, their older sister, follows. They all make their way to a makeshift altar where a young minister awaits. Now comes the groom, followed by the bride's much younger brother, pressing ... is that a shotgun to the groom's back? Yes, it is. Yet the bride and groom are surprisingly cheerful as they exchange vows, a contrast to the bride's grief-stricken mother sitting on a nearby sofa wringing her tear-soaked handkerchief into a small bowl.

The little brother carrying the toy shotgun is 7-year-old Jim Varney, who will one day become the 20th century pop-culture phenomenon known as "Ernest." The wedding is actually a 45-second silent home movie filmed in 1956, appropriately titled "Shotgun Wedding." The actors were members of the McChord and Varney families, connected by James Varney Sr. and his sister Iona McChord. Jim's cousin Ed McChord filmed the ceremony.

Jim's mother arguably stole the show with her melodramatic cameo. Her early days performing in church plays had made her an obvious choice to portray the bride's mother. The fact that the girl playing the bride was her real-life daughter seemed to enhance her Method acting approach. It was fitting that her part involved the exaggerated use of a prop. In the slapstick brand of humor that would come to define her son's acting career, the ability to draw laughs from the simplest of items would be an integral part of his appeal. "Shotgun Wedding" remains a timeless reminder of the humor in the Varney family, while revealing one of the many ways they cultivated Jim's passion for entertaining.

CHAPTER TWO

THE BEGINNING

The names that Jim answered to throughout his life were as varied as the characters he portrayed: Jimmy, Jimbo, Bo, Elvis, Dylan, Ernest, Vern and the "Hey Vern" guy. His two wives and close friends simply called him Varney.

Jim was named after his father, James Albert Varney Sr., who was born in the small coal-mining town of Norton, Va., on Jan. 1, 1910. Big Jim was the fourth of eight children and the firstborn son of a coal miner named Andrew Varney and his second wife, Rena. Andrew and Rena had moved from Andrew's hometown of Varney, W. Va., to Norton to find employment just after their oldest child, Roxie, was born. By the time James Sr. was about 15, his father had moved everyone 100 miles northeast back to Varney. (Author's note: I could not find a definitive link in my research between the town's name and Jim's ancestry, although there may very well be one.)

Varney is a small, unincorporated town located in Mingo County. The town of Matewan (just southwest of Varney) is also located in Mingo. Matewan, across the border of eastern Kentucky along the banks of the Tug Fork River, was still dealing with the aftermath of the famous "Matewan Massacre" when James Sr. was coming of age. The incident, which took place in 1920, was a shootout between a group of striking coal miners employed by the Stone Mountain Coal Company, local lawmen sympathetic to their plight and mine detectives hired to evict the miners from their company-owned houses. (John Sayles' critically acclaimed 1987 film "Matewan" brought to life this violent episode while illuminating the oppression endured by early Appalachian coal miners.)

The Mingo County area is also notable for serving as the backdrop for much of the Hatfield-McCoy feud of the late 1800s. The Varneys were linked to the Hatfield family by blood and marriage. Andrew Varney's first cousin was Levisa Chafin, the wife of William Anderson "Devil Anse" Hatfield. John Henderson Varney, Andrew's uncle, married Devil Anse's sister, Martha Hatfield. Larkin and Andrew were two of their sons. Although Jim's grandfather wasn't known to have directly participated in the feud, his cousins Larkin and Andrew did. (Larkin – sometimes referred to as "Lark" – was portrayed by actor Noah Taylor in the popular Hatfields & McCoys movie starring Kevin Costner that aired on The History Channel in 2012.)

THE BEGINNING

JIM'S ROOTS STRETCH BACK TO THE HATFIELDS
THE VARNEYS WERE LINKED TO THE FEUDING FAMILY BY BLOOD AND MARRIAGE

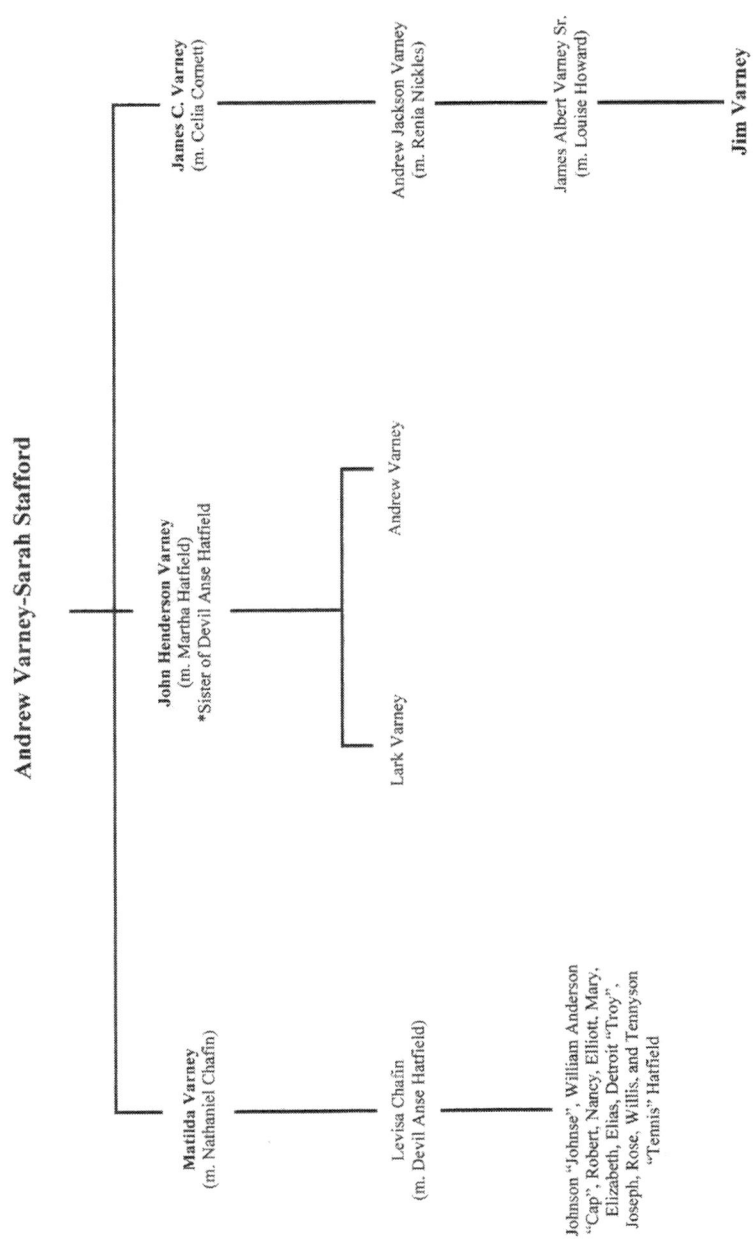

THE IMPORTANCE OF BEING ERNEST:
THE LIFE OF ACTOR JIM VARNEY

For whatever reason, Jim and his sisters were never made aware of their strong family connection to the Hatfields. They did grow up hearing stories about Grandfather Andrew Varney hunting squirrel with members of the Hatfields, but that was the extent of their knowledge. Perhaps Jim's father was not even fully aware of the family connection himself since it wasn't exactly something his parents would want to boast about during the years following the bloody feud. What shaped the children's view of their father's upbringing even more (besides old family stories) was the one family trip they took to West Virginia in the early 1950s. Jim's sister Jake vividly remembers the visit:

"A 1949 green Plymouth was our second car. It wasn't new and it wasn't air-conditioned, but few cars were at that time. It had gray upholstery and enough room for all six of us if Jim sat on Mama's lap.

"Daddy wanted to take us all to West Virginia to see his family, some of whom he hadn't seen since he left to join the Army in 1931.

"We went in the summer (of 1952), just before school started when Jim was 2. It would be a trip of about 10 hours, with frequent stops to gas stations, not to use the bathroom but to wash our faces and hose vomit off the car.

"To say it was a miserable trip would be to put it mildly. We all got carsick and vomited out of the windows. The car was like an oven, and the road was one curve after another through the mountains of eastern Kentucky.

"We visited several of Daddy's elderly aunts, some cousins and their families. They still called Daddy 'Ab,' a shortened version of his middle name Albert. For the most part, they were miners. We saw living conditions far below our own.

THE BEGINNING

"Daddy's family was fairly well educated and had more than most, but those who got their education and moved back to West Virginia couldn't find work not connected to coal mining.

"The drive back from West Virginia was not as traumatic as the ride there. It rained for most of the way home. We cracked the car windows, and the car was much cooler. We pulled into our home in Bluegrass Park, a government housing project, and thought we were rich.

"We never went to West Virginia again as a family, though Mama and Daddy visited (Daddy's) nephew often. Jim never realized the life we might have had if Daddy had stayed in West Virginia.

"Jim jokingly told people he was a 'Hill William (instead of a hillbilly).' He was from a large city, far away from a hill of any sort. (Yet) he admired mountain people and let everyone believe he was one of them."

Coal mining defined much of Appalachian life in the early 1900s as the region's precious resources brought in big coal companies. Unfortunately, the ease with which a young man could find a coal-mining job was offset by its dangers. Jim's father experienced this firsthand when he began working for the Red Jacket Coal Company in Mingo County at 16. His younger brother, Sam, soon joined him, as the responsibility for providing for much of the family's income fell on their shoulders. Their father was unable to work after suffering a chest injury during a mine cave-in.

After five years at the mine with only a 5-cent raise, bringing his wage to 55 cents an hour, James Sr. decided he had had enough and quit the mine in 1931 after a chance meeting with an Army recruiter at the local mine store.

Before long, Jim's father was looking out upon the sunny beaches of Hawaii, where he would be stationed for the next three years. It must have felt like a million miles away from the depths of the West Virginia coal mines, where sunlight and fresh air were nonexistent. James Sr. made sure a portion of his Army checks were mailed back to West Virginia to support his family. He also kept up his correspondence with many of his siblings, including sisters Iona and Cecelia who had moved to Lexington, Ky. Cecelia's letters soon included an extra page or two from a new (and single) sister-in-law named Louise Howard; the correspondence made her brother eager to visit the city that Cecelia now called home.

Jim's mother, Nancy Louise Howard, grew up the youngest of five in a farming community in Winchester, Ky., just east of Lexington. The acting in Jim's blood most likely came from his mother. Years before her son found worldwide fame with Ernest, Louise entertained members of the Macedonia Christian Church in Lexington, acting in various plays as a teenager. In the Family Register section of a Bible that Louise purchased in 1986, she recalled one of these plays. Just below the entry of her baptism date, she wrote, "Had the lead in 'Backwoods School of 1849' at church, it was fun."

A few years before Louise joined the church, her family made a short move from Winchester to the outskirts of Lexington to the horse farm known as Hamburg Place. There, her father, James Howard, worked as a horseman and gardener for John E. Madden, the world-renowned horse breeder. John Madden trained five Kentucky Derby winners on the Lexington farm (today the land is the site of a thriving commercial development, still called Hamburg Place). Along with his primary duties, James Howard assisted in other projects on the storied horse farm such as the construction of a horse cemetery.

Louise's mother, Annie "Belle" Howard, would outlive her husband by almost 25 years. Known as "Granny" to the Varney children, she was the only grandparent Jim and his sisters would ever know. She was a tiny woman, barely five feet tall, but one of the most capable women they ever knew. Even in her early 60s, with her husband retired, she entered the workforce as a presser in a Laundromat.

Although Jim and his sisters had only one grandparent in their lives, they enjoyed a close relationship with a number of aunts and uncles living in Lexington. Louise's two sisters lived in town: Sally and Betty. Betty actually lived on the same street as Jim's family on two separate occasions. James Sr.'s sister Iona, deaf from a childhood illness, had settled in Lexington with her husband, Winfield (they met at a deaf school). Iona and Winfield had three sons: Win, Jack and Ed. (Although none were deaf, they all signed as if it was a second language. Ed, the youngest, could sign so fast that he was nicknamed "Fast Eddie.")

None of Jim's relatives played a more significant role in Jim's life than the aunt and uncle who brought the Howard and Varney families together. Louise's older brother, Everett, worked in Lexington as a painter and dabbled in everything from plasterwork to the tasks associated with a finishing carpenter. His work could be seen in many of the finer homes in Lexington, as well as in local theaters and downtown office buildings. It was in one of those theaters that he met James Sr.'s sister Cecelia. She had moved to Lexington with her first husband's family. She met Everett shortly after her husband's death. Everett and Cecelia married in 1928 and were in Lexington when the Great Depression arrived. During those tough times they lived for a few years with Everett's parents at Hamburg Place.

Cecelia got along well with Everett's family and became close friends with Louise. Cecelia mentioned to Louise that her younger brother was serving in the Army. The more Cecelia talked about

James, the more intrigued Louise became. She began writing him letters that Cecelia included in the envelopes of her own correspondence. James Sr. wrote back to Louise, and before long the two were keeping in touch on a regular basis and counting the days until they could meet. That day finally came in the summer of 1934 when James Sr. finished his three-year tour in Hawaii. The first time Louise saw him she was standing anxiously at the train station waiting for his arrival home. Cecelia helped point her brother out among the crowd of passengers. Not only was James Sr. tall and broad-shouldered, when he smiled his white teeth reminded Louise of a model in a Pepsodent toothpaste advertisement.

Jim Varney's future parents spent the summer getting better acquainted before James Sr. was shipped overseas for another tour. He spent the next three years in the Philippines, where he eventually reached the rank of corporal. He and Louise continued to correspond and eventually married shortly after he returned to Lexington in 1938.

Within the first five years of their marriage, Louise gave birth to two girls, Jo Gail and Janice Ann (who came to be known as Jake). Meanwhile, James Sr. found employment as a ward attendant at the Veterans Administration Hospital in Lexington. Louise stayed home raising the girls. The Varneys settled into a small residence in Bluegrass Park around 1940. They would stay 14 years. Opened in 1938, Bluegrass Park was one of Lexington's first low-cost housing projects, and many other military families lived there.

In March 1944, just as Louise learned she was pregnant with their third daughter, Sandra (or Sandy as she came to be called), James Sr. returned to active service. He was assigned to Camp Barkeley, outside of Abilene, Texas, where he guarded German prisoners at the POW camp. When World War II ended roughly a

THE BEGINNING

year later, James Sr. returned home to his family and his job at the hospital.

A few years later, Louise finally gave birth to a son. James Albert Varney Jr. was born on June 15, 1949, at Good Samaritan Hospital in Lexington. Dr. A.J. Whitehouse helped bring Jim into the world. (Whitehouse would become a local legend for delivering thousands of babies over 50 years.) After three daughters, James Sr. was ready to welcome a son into the fold.

Although not exactly tiny, Jim hardly resembled the 15-pound giant his father claimed to have been as a newborn. Louise was so convinced she had been carrying another girl that she had actually made a dress for the baby to wear home. Perhaps to help distinguish his name from the one he shared with his father, the family called the new arrival Jimbo and sometimes "Bo" for short. All of Jim's sisters were excited to have a little brother, and each would have a role in helping to raise him. The baby became their new toy, and they never tired of playing with him. Often called a "little sponge," Jim's ability to retain so much of what he read or heard amazed the family. It was not only the amount he retained that impressed them but the early age at which it began. Sandy swears that Jim could read portions of their elementary schoolbooks before he was 3.

The constant attention Jim received from his sisters would prove to be all the more important as he battled asthma from an early age. He had so much trouble breathing that he would occasionally break blood vessels in his eyes. When he was outside playing and experienced an attack, one of his sisters was usually there to see that he went inside to recover. His mother stayed up many nights with him, sometimes holding his sleepy head over a vaporizer. The aroma of Vick's often filled the house in fall and winter, while the thermostat stayed turned up an extra notch to keep him warm. Jim became all too familiar with the "rules" of his condition, which made him long for spring and summer when many of his symptoms subsided. Unfortunately, the only treatment available then was a shot administered by a doctor (who came to the house). The doctor told Jim's parents that he would outgrow his asthma but would probably have problems with his lungs. True to the doctor's word, the episodes grew farther apart as Jim matured. As far as anyone knows, he never had to use an inhaler.

Because of Jim's asthma, his parents discussed the possibility of Big Jim transferring to another VA hospital located in a warmer climate. James Sr. had worked his way up to a physical-therapist position while taking on additional duties that included organizing recreational activities and serving as a barber. But since his main specialty was so specific, options were limited. One opportunity they considered was in Palo Alto, Calif. The children all wanted to go, but in the end their mother could not bear to leave Lexington and her family. She decided to leave things as they were, hoping that Jim would get better.

Along with his job and family obligations, Jim's father was extremely involved in the local community. Having boxed as a young man, including earning a title while stationed in Hawaii, he was able to find work as a referee at many Golden Gloves tournaments held in Lexington. He also worked as a parking-lot attendant at the Keeneland racetrack during the spring and fall meets. Through his involvement with the VA, he participated in many of their volunteer activities and was active in his local Masonic lodge.

Despite the extra money his side jobs brought in, Jim's father could not provide for his kids in the way that he wanted. He did manage, however, to use the resources available to him to keep them entertained and physically active. With the VA Hospital's permission, he regularly brought recreational equipment home for

THE BEGINNING

his children to use. James Sr. made sure that even his daughters learned the skills essential to boxing. This included proficiency on the speed bag, where Jo Gail quickly became known as the most dangerous. Jim's father refereed boxing matches between the kids and their friends. He enjoyed the time spent with the neighborhood kids throughout Jim's childhood. Many of them have fond memories today of "Mr. Varney" and credit him with teaching them good sportsmanship.

The VA also let James Sr. bring his kids to swim in their indoor heated pools. He preferred to do this on Sunday afternoons just after the pools were cleaned. The children had the water to themselves for hours. Jake and Sandy remember swimming there during winter, looking out the windows and watching the snow fall.

Jim's father was successful in teaching all the children to swim except for Jim. Although he wanted to please his father, Jim always panicked as soon as his head began to go under water. His sisters tried but never succeeded in helping him overcome his fear.

Jim's father didn't always need equipment or a pool to whip his kids into shape. Many mornings before he went to school, Jim and his sisters were led through a multitude of exercises that included push-ups, sit-ups and jumping jacks. Although it was not always easy keeping up with his older sisters, Jim's fitness level greatly improved over time. That helped control his asthma and added muscle to his thin frame.

Jim's father enjoyed many other activities with his children. He demonstrated card tricks and participated in games such as checkers and chess. With the entire family joining in, these games could become competitive. Bingo was played for nickels and dimes, and that was considered "high stakes."

As Jim grew older, he began to take an interest in the items his father had acquired while stationed in Hawaii and the Philippines.

THE IMPORTANCE OF BEING ERNEST: THE LIFE OF ACTOR JIM VARNEY

This is where his lifelong fascination with knives, swords and watches began. Jim soaked up every detail of the workmanship and the history of each item. This time also gave him the opportunity to connect with his father in ways he never could around athletics.

Jim also pursued his own interests. He sang, danced and mimicked characters he watched on TV. The ease with which Jim could pick up on the accent and mannerisms of a person carried over to musical instruments. Sister Jake remembers buying Jim a harmonica when he was around 8 years old. Jim immediately began playing a Stephen Foster tune called "Ring Ring the Banjo." Surprised, Jake asked Jim how he could play the song so well. Jim told her he had heard the song somewhere and was just playing it back the way he remembered. A few years later he showed the same natural ability on an Appalachian dulcimer he purchased.

Before long, it was not only family he entertained but any neighborhood friends and classmates who showed Jim attention. Some, like neighbor Sonny Wilson, joined Jim in various routines. Years later, Jim credited Sonny for helping him develop his comedic abilities. Jim recalled once, "Sonny was a real cut up. He'd wear weird things, put on weird hats. He and I were like the Marx Brothers."

Through the years, the dinner table served as a sounding board for Jim and his sisters. There, everyone traded interesting stories that were often very funny. The Varney kids were encouraged to share anything they thought entertaining. But the kids' tales rarely topped their father's, which included experiences from his childhood, the Army and his job at the VA.

Of all his father's stories, the tales of growing up in the mountains seemed to capture Jim's imagination the most. Although raised in the suburbs of Lexington, Jim came to identify strongly with the Varney's mountain heritage. This is partly because it was so inextricably linked to the father he admired so much.

THE BEGINNING

It's interesting to note that Jim's Ernest character became another hillbilly caricature that was commercialized and parodied in much the same way many of his Hatfield and Varney ancestors were portrayed. Because of this, it can be said that throughout modern American history, a handful of closely related Varneys have been largely responsible for some of the most popular representations of the stereotypical hillbilly.

The communities in which Jim's father was raised endured many hardships due to poverty, demanding work and limited resources. Yet they were also places where family, fellowship, music and laughter sustained a person almost as much as a warm meal. Over time, Jim learned how to effortlessly channel many of the colorful residents of these mountain hollers into his own unique characters.

The absurdity of Jim's character "Lloyd Worrell," whose family pretends to eat supper, is such an example. The idea of a poor, starving family could not be more heartbreaking, but to watch Jim portray a man who slices into an imaginary steak while marveling over a weight-gaining son was endlessly entertaining.

In addition to his father's influence, Jim drew some of his future material from other adults in the family. Jim's mother was a teetotaler, most likely as a result of watching alcohol ruin the lives of uncles and cousins. The second husband of one of Louise's older sisters was believed to be an alcoholic. From observing this uncle, young Jim saw firsthand how someone drunk behaved.

When Jim's oldest sister, Jo Gail, graduated from high school, the family hosted a party for her friends and family. Jim's father purchased non-alcoholic sparkling wine for the younger crowd. Eight-year-old Jim drank a few glasses and then proceeded to convince everyone that he was "drunk," staggering around and slurring his words. He kept it up for hours. He told his father that he had "had enough" and would have to "sober up" before posing for any pictures. Everyone was entertained by his antics. This early imitation helped shape various winos Jim portrayed years later in stand-up routines.

Although Jim's mother never had a problem with alcohol, she had other problems that were just as serious. From Jim's early childhood to well into his teenage years, he and his sisters watched her battle depression and hypochondria. To the neighbors, she was the model housewife who excelled at cooking and homemaking. But inside their home, the children saw a nervous person who exhibited signs of obsessive compulsiveness (mopping the floor repeatedly and getting distraught if a dessert didn't turn out just the way she wanted). She constantly complained about various ailments and sought refuge in bed. When their father was at work, the children sometimes felt abandoned.

During these times Jim had his sisters to keep an eye on him. None was more vigilant than Jo Gail. She, as much as Jim's mother, raised the youngest three kids. While Jo Gail was easygoing, that didn't stop her from going after any of her siblings if she felt it necessary. When Jim got into trouble, he would plead with his other sisters not to tell Jo Gail. He didn't mind as much if his mother found out since she did little to punish him.

CHAPTER THREE

WATCHING TV

Jim was growing up in a time when television was beginning to replace radio as the major form of household entertainment. Because of this, he received increasing exposure to the acting world. After the family purchased their first television, Jim would sit in front of it for hours. Popular TV characters during this time included cowboys such as Hopalong Cassidy and The Lone Ranger. Jim enjoyed dressing up as his cowboy heroes when playing with his toy guns, as well as wearing homemade capes while pretending to be Superman.

One TV program Jim rarely missed was a children's show called "The Magic Forest." It aired on Louisville's WAVE Channel 5 and had a signal strong enough to be picked up in Lexington. Host "Uncle Ed" Kallay would sit on a tree stump in the magic forest and talk to his puppet friends while playing cartoons and silent movies. One of the show's major sponsors was "The Ranch House," a Louisville hamburger restaurant whose signature item was the "Ranch Burger." Jim often begged his parents to take him there, but a 70-mile trip for a burger was out of the question.

If a certain TV show had a sponsor, Jim wholeheartedly believed he and his family were supposed to use their product. Sweetheart Soap was among the products that Jim asked his mother to buy.

THE IMPORTANCE OF BEING ERNEST:
THE LIFE OF ACTOR JIM VARNEY

She told him that it was somewhat fragrant, and his father probably wouldn't like it. Jim answered, "Well, the lady on TV said we should use it, so Daddy will just have to get used to it."

One sponsor's product that he had a little more success in convincing his mother to buy was a Fifth Avenue candy bar. Jim made sure to have one ready to eat before the show it sponsored aired. That way, he could enjoy it along with the people on TV during the commercial break.

Comedic actors who would go on to become legends were all over the TV dial when Jim was growing up, influencing and shaping him, from Sid Caesar to Laurel and Hardy. As an adult, Jim referred to comedian Sid Caesar's "Your Show of Shows" as the "Saturday Night Live" of its time.

A TV special that captured Jim's imagination, perhaps more than any other during his childhood, was "Peter Pan." The version he saw starred Mary Martin and aired live in 1955. Right before it came on, Jim was asking everyone in the house questions such as, "How is Peter Pan going to be able to fly?" and "Who will be tiny enough to play Tinker Bell?" When the production came on Jim was enthralled, sitting spellbound in front of the television the entire time.

After the show ended, Jim ran into his bedroom and started crying. When his mother asked him what was wrong, he told her that he was sad that it was over. Yet because of the show Jim developed a fear of anything that resembled a hook, based on the infamous metal limb of Peter Pan's nemesis, Dr. Hook. James Sr. couldn't resist teasing Jim about it. He sometimes told Jim that a hook was hanging outside the bedroom door or somewhere in the closet. A few years later, Jim actually had a classmate with a father who had a hook for a hand. Jim and the boy were playing together at school one day waiting to be picked up. When the boy's father came into the classroom, he noticed that Jim was afraid. He asked Jim if had ever seen a real hook hand. Jim replied that he hadn't. The man proceeded to show him all the things he could do with it and explained how he had lost his real hand (family legend has it that the loss was due to a war injury). When Jim came home he talked about the experience for days. That seemed to cure his fear. It wasn't always easy, but Jim was growing up.

CHAPTER FOUR

DISCOVERING THE THEATER

The curiosity and imagination Jim possessed served him well as he entertained friends and family, but those skills rarely translated to success in the classroom. He found his schoolwork repetitive and dull, with little to hold his attention. He often got caught up in other things he found more interesting, such as colorful classmates.

Although his grades never reflected it, Jim was extremely intelligent and constantly reading above grade level. Yet he was rarely motivated enough to do the work required to take advantage of his abilities. He preferred browsing through encyclopedias over working on assignments. By the time Jim was in second grade, his family had accumulated the entire Funk and Wagnalls Encyclopedia collection from a local supermarket promotion. Sandy remembers Jim surprising her once with an obscure fact, and when she asked him how he knew it, he pointed to the encyclopedias, saying, "From those books over there." Years later in grade school, Jim stood up in the middle of class and began talking about how the Egyptians embalmed people. In gruesome detail he described how long hooks were used to pull the brain out through the nose. The teacher was not amused. The only subject that confounded Jim was math. Whenever he talked about his struggles with math as an adult, he said he was missing the math gene.

THE IMPORTANCE OF BEING ERNEST:
THE LIFE OF ACTOR JIM VARNEY

Being an avid reader at such an early age, Jim was knowledgeable on many subjects, in part because of the National Geographic magazines his father brought home from work for the kids. Along with the encyclopedias, they satisfied Jim's thirst for knowledge, to the detriment of his schoolwork. During the times when Jim was confined indoors recovering from an asthma attack, reading helped pass the time, along with TV.

When Jim was 8 years old, his sister Jake read an ad in the paper for auditions at Children's Theatre in Lexington. She asked Jim if he wanted to go. When the big day came, he and Jake rode the bus to the Carriage House, which housed Children's Theatre. When they arrived, close to 40 children, ages 8 to 16, were waiting to be interviewed. The young assistant director, Mary Warner Ford, introduced herself. (Author's note: Today, she is Mary Polites.) Ford was initially interested in Jim's sister, but Jake informed her that Jim was the one trying out. Ford handed him a script and was impressed enough with his performance to accept him.

Children's Theatre soon allowed Jim to put on display much of the potential his family saw in him. His first role was Abraham Lincoln's childhood friend, Abner, in the play, "Abe Lincoln – New Salem Days." In no time Jim was consistently landing starring roles such as Prince Charming in "Sleeping Beauty" and Scrooge in "A Christmas Carol." Not only did the theater ignite Jim's passion for acting, it began to instill in him a sense of purpose.

Ford was a pivotal influence on Jim's acting career. She was a high school student serving as assistant director under Fred Sliter when Jim first joined Children's Theatre. In 1959 she took over as director while attending the University of Kentucky and serving as resident student director for the U.K. Theatre. Her many years with Jim at Children's Theatre gave him a solid start to learning his craft.

DISCOVERING THE THEATER

Looking back, Mary Polites (nee Ford) says that he probably had more potential as a character actor than anyone she had ever seen. Yet she wasn't sure if it would come to fruition. "I knew he had the talent, but not the discipline," she says. Jim often missed rehearsals and sometimes argued with her about his blocking – the positioning and movement of actors onstage.

Jack Pattie, a well-known Lexington radio personality today, was a few years younger than Jim when the two acted together in Children's Theatre. This was around the time Jim was entering his teenage years and becoming what Pattie describes as "edgy" for the times. Jim enjoyed sneaking up to the third floor of the Carriage House to smoke cigarettes. One time, he tried to teach Pattie how to French inhale.

Despite Jim's popularity in Children's Theatre, Pattie says he never noticed an ounce of ego. Jim was usually the center of attention, onstage and off. During rehearsal breaks, he often entertained the other children with his impressions and tricks. Jim was amused at Pattie's rendition of a Cinderella spoof called "Rindercella" that Pattie had memorized. The spoof, known as a spoonerism, exchanged many letters in the words of the story for comedic effect. (Actor/comedian Archie Campbell performed a memorable rendition of it years later on "Hee Haw" during one his popular barbershop sketches.) It always made Pattie feel cool when Jim would be in the middle of entertaining a small group and would call Pattie over to recite it.

By the time Jim was 10 years old, his family had moved out of Bluegrass Park and into the suburbs. Even though the neighboring families were more spread out, Jim was still able to make new friends. Next door lived a family with a house full of boys. Jim was a few years older than the youngest son and was constantly amazed by the bad language the kid seemed to get away with using. Jim enjoyed riding bikes and playing baseball with the boys next door. During one of their many baseball games, Jim chased after a pop fly. As he reached up for the catch, he missed and the ball smashed into his top lip. He knew it wasn't good when he felt something crack. His lip swelled with blood, filling the spaces between his teeth. Jim ran home holding his bleeding mouth. The dentist's X-rays showed that Jim had fractured one of his front teeth and another one right next to it. The dentist pulled both and inserted a small plate with two teeth attached to fit into the roof of Jim's mouth. Louise feared that it might affect his smile as he grew older.

Eventually, Jim got used to the plate. It never affected his speech, and few people ever noticed it. Once Jim became an adult, he had a permanent bridge made. It was only noticeable in close-ups and bright light. As a kid, it was a relatively minor setback compared to how he would come to feel about his looks as an adult and how they might limit his potential as an actor.

Even at a young age, Jim had his sights set on performing. He had become well aware of Hollywood and Broadway from browsing newspapers and magazines at the library. He lived near a street called Hollywood Drive, and the neighborhood itself was called Hollywood. Jim often saw the city bus drive down his street with "HOLLYWOOD" listed as its destination. Young Jim knew that movie stars lived in Hollywood and asked Jake one time if she could take him on the bus to see them.

Another source of entertainment for Jim during this time came from the Baptist church he attended with sister Sandy. When the family was living in Bluegrass Park they all attended a nearby Christian Church. After the family moved away, the drive to the church became too long, and they stopped attending. Soon after moving into their new home, Jim and Sandy would catch a bus on Sundays to attend a nearby Baptist church. The pastor there was charismatic, and often Jim would get more caught up in his delivery than the message.

With his growing love of acting it was no surprise that Halloween became one of Jim's favorite holidays. The Varney kids all enjoyed creating their own unique costumes for trick-or-treating. Through the years Jim dressed up as everything from a cowboy to a clown. Sandy remembers him fooling other kids by dressing up and talking like an old lady, hunched over and wearing a hat as he passed out candy from their door.

CHAPTER FIVE

ANNE, HER MOTHER AND THE FINER THINGS

When Jim was around 13, he met a girl who would become one of his first girlfriends and eventually, a lifelong friend. One day, Jim and a buddy were running down the street from the bus stop to rehearsal at Children's Theatre in the pouring rain. Anne Lambert's big house was just around the corner. From her porch she saw the two boys running, and she yelled for them to come up to dry off. They told her where they were headed, and she mentioned that her mother had been an actress in New York. All of a sudden, the friendly girl about their age became a lot more interesting to the boys.

After Lambert introduced Jim to her mother, Jane, he became captivated with stories of her acting career. He began spending more and more time at the Lambert house. Anne Lambert remembers Jim being much more interested in her mother than her at first. Along with stories about working in the theater, Jane Lambert also taught Jim such manners as dining etiquette. Jake believes that she saw Jim was a "diamond in the rough" who needed polishing.

Anne Lambert and Jim dated for a short time in high school. They loved going to the movies. Lambert recalls seeing "Becket," starring Peter O' Toole and Richard Burton, with Jim in the spring of 1964. To Lambert's amazement, after the movie, Jim gave dead-on impersonations of the two leading men. The movie became one of his all-time favorites.

Jim also loved to watch Sean Connery in the five Bond films released from the time Jim was 13 to 18. Jim was impressed with how refined Connery was as Bond, as well how he used his good looks and suave demeanor to attract the most beautiful girls. Bond girls may have been out of Jim's reach, but he discovered that a Rolex similar to Bond's was not as elusive. The most affordable Rolex he could find was $125, a lot of money at that time and especially for a teenager. He made a deal with a local jeweler to buy it on a payment plan. Jim asked the jeweler to engrave "007" on the back. He wore that watch for years. As an adult, whenever he gave someone a watch (which was often) it was usually a Rolex.

In addition, Jim admired a lesser-known actor to American audiences: France's Jean-Paul Belmondo. In contrast to Connery, Jim probably identified more with Belmondo's unconventional good looks. If there was one real negative about Jim's love of acting during his teenage years it was that he became more and more critical of his appearance. Compared to his favorite actors such as Connery and O'Toole, Jim's large nose and wide mouth were just not up to par. And physically, he had the skinnier build of his mother, not the boxer's frame of his father. He was already thinking about how his looks would affect the types of roles he would be offered as an adult. Even though Jim desperately wanted to be the hero who got the girl, he thought he would probably be cast as the villain. He seemed resigned to the fact that he would be limited to the small screen, playing in series such as "Playhouse 90" and the "Hallmark Hall Of Fame."

ANNE, HER MOTHER AND THE FINER THINGS

Jim's preoccupation with his looks worsened as he entered puberty and, like many kids, endured his share of acne. Mary Warner Ford tried to tell him that a character actor such as himself would never need to worry about having movie-idol looks. She thought he was handsome enough in his own right, although Jim never saw that when comparing himself to others.

Jake once asked Jim a riddle where a person must decide if they would rather have beauty, wealth or fame. By choosing one, you could never attain the others. Jim didn't hesitate for a second. Beauty, he replied. With that choice, Jake reminded him that he would never be rich or famous. Jim said he didn't care. But then he added that there should be another choice. Jim said that if love was one of the options he would choose that. Jake thought it was an unusual response for a 14-year-old.

Jim spent a fair amount of free time by himself in his early to mid-teens. Since his mother never learned to drive and his father was at work, he would either walk or ride the bus. One place he loved to frequent was a cigar store downtown on Main Street. He would buy magazines, cigarettes and the occasional cigar or pipe. Jim began smoking Marlboros around 13. He called them "Marleybarleys." Occasionally he bought Benson & Hedges, perhaps because they were considered more of an upscale brand.

Jim couldn't afford many of the things he wanted as a teenager. But when he did save up the cash, he enjoyed spending it on items that gave him a taste of how the upper class lived, such as gourmet cheeses, chocolates and English toffee. He liked to talk about his knowledge of these finer things, such as how the English referred to gumdrops as wine gums. Not even a simple candy treat was beyond the reach of his historical knowledge.

As far as clothing, Jim loved the feel of cashmere. Although he couldn't afford a cashmere coat, he did find a way to scrape up enough money for a scarf. He always said that he had "expensive feet," because cheap shoes were often painful for him to wear. He loved anything made of leather and enjoyed wearing soft leather loafers and boots.

Jim's interest in jewelry and knives continued to grow in his teenage years. He kept a cigar box in his bedroom full of all types of jewelry and trinkets that he had collected and received as gifts. He loved to go through the box, almost as if he was studying some of the pieces for the first time. He would read up on their characteristics until he could talk at length about each one. For example, he would tell you about how one of his railroad wristwatches had a lever to set the time. As an adult, Jim created what he called a "curiosity table" at his home in Tennessee. The big round oak table in his den was covered with dozens of items such as old coins, telescopes, gears, knives and so on. He invited anyone visiting to inspect the items, and he would explain what made them unique.

Jim loved giving jewelry as a gift almost as much as he did buying it for himself. Starting as a teenager, he would give almost every female he knew a watch, and the present always included a lesson on how to operate and care for it. He found many vintage watches in pawnshops and secondhand stores. When he found an old watch that caught his eye he would bring it home, polish it up and buy a new band for it. He loved bringing to life a piece whose value he felt someone else had overlooked.

As an adult, Jim had jeweler's loupes (magnifiers) attached to a pair of glasses. A pronounced crease would appear between Jim's eyes when he inspected something. His intense curiosity would almost convince you he was a visitor from another planet. He would marvel for hours at the workmanship of Swiss watches and the detail in hand-etched coins. He didn't collect something for its value as much as he did out of admiration for the craftspeople who had made it. He could spend hours cleaning and polishing pieces in his collection. It was a calming pastime.

Beginning as a teenager, Jim enjoyed wearing a variety of pieces of jewelry, including a signet ring given to him by his father. For most of his adult life there were about six pieces he consistently wore: a small loop earring, a silver chain bracelet, a Celtic cross necklace, numerous rings (one of which displayed the thespian masks) and his stainless-steel Rolex. Some of these pieces were even visible when he was dressed as Ernest. His jewelry represented his many interests while reflecting the diversity of his personality.

CHAPTER SIX

THE VARNEY PARKERS

One particular photograph of Jim and his father has always been a family favorite. In it, Jim is about 15. He leans back against a car while standing next to his father in a parking lot. They both wear hats with the word "PARKING" inscribed across the front.

To bring in more income, James Sr. formed a small business parking cars that the family affectionately referred to as "The Varney Parkers." Along with Jim and his father, the "Parkers" usually consisted of Jim's cousins Ed, Win and Jack McChord, as well as many of their friends, including some of Jack's college buddies.

Starting the little business seemed like a logical choice to James Sr. after working as a parking attendant at Keeneland during the racing season. He had business cards printed up and started handing them out. When someone called, he would decide how many men he would need for the job and then figure $5 per man. Wedding receptions brought in their biggest business. In addition to tips, delicious leftovers often came with the job.

When Jim started working with the guys he was too young to drive so he would direct parkers into their spots. During the event the men hung out by the cars, cracking jokes and listening to James Sr. tell stories. Of course Jack, Win and Ed respected their uncle immensely and in many ways saw him as larger than life. His stories never failed to captivate them, whether they were about his boxing exploits or tales of the gigantic pythons he had encountered in the Philippines. Ed would later recall a particularly memorable story where, as a teenager working in the mines, his Uncle Jim had gotten into an argument with another teenage boy. The boy left and soon returned with his father. The story goes that James Sr. ended up whipping them both. Despite his humble beginnings as a teenage coal miner with a ninth-grade education, Jim's father demonstrated to the young men that in life, anything was possible.

CHAPTER SEVEN

HIGH SCHOOL YEARS

By the time Jim entered Lafayette High School, he had been acting for almost eight years. From home movies to Children's Theatre, Jim was ready to take his acting to the next level. Soon he'd leave an indelible mark on Lafayette, a big school where it was easy to get lost in the crowd.

Jim immediately began taking advantage of the Speech and Drama courses. This is where he met drama teacher Thelma Beeler. Her association with Jim would ultimately help cement her status as one of the top drama teachers in Kentucky. Her long tenure and passion for teaching eventually led to Lafayette's auditorium being named in her honor in 1976.

Beeler spotted something unique in Jim immediately. Perhaps sensing his need for extra guidance, she seemed to take on a motherly role in his life. Jim's other teachers were not as impressed as they grew increasingly frustrated at his lack of enthusiasm and attendance. Beeler occasionally stepped in to make sure he was keeping his grades up enough to stay on the drama team. One such episode involved an incomplete English assignment that threatened to prevent Jim from competing in a district drama competition. Beeler arranged for Jim to make up the assignment after school. She remembered years later, "Jim wrote a better paper than many of the students who had been working on it for three weeks." A few times when Jim had to stay after school to finish an assignment, Beeler brought him home. Jim later recalled, "She hung in there with me, and we won drama awards left and right."

The summer following Jim's junior year provided an important opportunity. It was July 1966. The University of Kentucky's Centennial Players' Summer Theatre was preparing for "A Midsummer Night's Dream." The project involved hiring professional actors to work with college and high school ones. The plays were held at the Guignol Theatre on the university's campus. The college actor set to play the part of Puck dropped out just weeks before the performance after accepting a professorship elsewhere. The play's director went through all his contacts and eventually took a chance on Jim on the word of Mary Warner Ford at Children's Theatre. Ironically, Ford had been unsuccessful at convincing Jim to play the part of Puck in a Lexington Children's Theatre performance of "Dream" not long before the second opportunity arose.

It was Jim's most difficult role to date. He spent weeks at the university rehearsing and memorizing his lines. He later confessed, "I had to just about live with a script in my hands." He came home late with green makeup still visible behind his ears and around his eyes. He didn't say too much about the play to the family, only that they should all come see it.

One of the professional actors in the play who was just beginning what would become a brilliant career as a character actor was 31-year-old M. Emmet Walsh. Walsh has long been entertaining audiences with diverse character roles such as Dr. Joseph Dolan (Dr. Jellyfinger) in "Fletch" and the corrupt Detective Visser in "Blood Simple."

HIGH SCHOOL YEARS

"Dream" became one of Centennial's most impressive productions of the summer. Critic Mary Agnes Barnes of the Lexington Herald-Leader wrote of the opening-night performance, "The audience responded very warmly." In what may have been a foreshadowing of Jim's career, she noted, "This production relies heavily on slapstick." But it was clear that Jim had opening-night jitters. When Barnes singled out individual performances, she observed, "Jim Varney, as Puck, talked much too fast."

But when Jim's parents attended the performance, they couldn't help but overhear the compliments whispered about Jim in the audience. Jim's father had once imagined himself hearing admiring comments while watching Jim play football or basketball. So seeing Jim excel onstage had to be gratifying. At 17, Jim could now claim his first professional acting experience.

In addition to Jim's young age, something else had the crowd gossiping – Jim's clothing, or lack of it. With his entire body covered in green paint, the small loincloth of the same color he wore made him appear nearly nude when the lighting was turned down. He later joked, "I was the most nude actor they'd ever had in Lexington."

Jim's thirst for performing now became so great that he began to experiment beyond the stage. In local college hangouts, such as the Nexus coffeehouse, he stepped up to the microphone and introduced many of the comical characters he had created. He told jokes and entertaining stories about his grandmother's Ford Mustang and a character named the Orange Kool-Aid Kid. He also performed impressions of famous actors such as Richard Burton and John Wayne. Much of this material he used again to win one of his high-school talent shows.

Another local performer, Jerry Morse, was a student teacher at Jim's high school. Morse played flamenco music at some of the same venues where Jim performed. Jim later used some advice Morse offered about Jim's acting ambitions: "You *are* an actor, and now you have to figure out how to get paid for it."

Just as Jim didn't represent the typical student, he rarely dressed like one either. Many of his clothes reflected the rebellious spirit of the 1960s. One of his favorite accessories was a sleeveless blue-jean jacket. He constantly wore black, along with Beatle boots. Black was an easy color for him to pick out since he was colorblind. He went from white socks as a young child to black socks as a teenager. His sisters often helped him out, especially if he was dressing for a special occasion.

In addition to Jim's clothing, his long hair and pierced ear gave him a unique look. His father and Mary Warner Ford of Children's Theatre were not fans of either one. When it came to his hair, it wasn't so much the length that bothered Ford as it was the fact that it appeared Jim never touched a comb. As barbering was one of James Sr.'s many skills, he often threatened to give Jim a buzz cut if he didn't keep his hair trimmed. Jim's sister Jake bailed him out many times by helping to style his hair in a way that kept it from flowing past his neck.

Apart from the theater, Jim was not much into the high school social scene of clubs and organizations. He could see what he later called "the juvenility of it." Of course, Jim was not always the poster child for maturity. One role almost any well-known comedian can put on his or her resume is class clown. It was no different with Jim. "If a teacher sets you up," he said once remembering high school, "you got to punch it." Once, Jim even posed as a student teacher at another school. No telling what the topic of discussion was that day.

Along with cutting up in class, Jim often skipped school with friends, frequenting nearby coffeehouses. He kept his buddies

HIGH SCHOOL YEARS

entertained by imitating movie stars and quoting poetry from Dylan Thomas in a Welsh accent. Because of his affinity for Dylan Thomas and the music of Bob Dylan, some of his friends referred to him as "Dylan."

One of the few extracurricular activities Jim was involved with outside of acting was a part-time job. He and some buddies worked at a discount department store called Mr. Wiggs. Jake remembers Jim pointing out three swing sets to her that he had assembled for display outside the store. They were full-sized with horses, swings and slides. Jake was impressed. Still, no matter what kind of potential Jim might have shown in other abilities, it was obvious what his passion was.

Acting was consuming Jim in so many ways, and it soon became a refuge as he began to encounter what would become a lifelong battle with depression. He started experiencing what he referred to as "the stares" – or dark moods – that sometimes lasted for weeks. He found that the more he immersed himself in his craft, the less inclined he was to becoming despondent. Ford had seen signs of his mental struggles at Children's Theatre when he could be way up or way down. During one week of rehearsals Jim told her that even though he had not been sleeping he still wasn't tired.

During this time, Jim's mother's psychological issues also became much more severe. When Jim was younger and the family lived in the close confines of the Bluegrass Park housing project, Louise seemed to benefit from a more social atmosphere. Her condition slowly worsened after the family moved to two different homes in the suburbs. In the mid-1960s her condition became so serious that she was admitted to a mental hospital more than once and eventually given electroshock therapy. With all that his mother was going through and two of his sisters now having moved out, Jim didn't have the same support system at home that he had known when he was younger. In high school, Thelma Beeler and the theater were becoming more important than ever to his emotional survival.

But as far as acting was concerned, Jim was not only surviving but excelling, receiving awards and accolades that made up for the ones that would never come from athletics or academics. At one awards ceremony, Beeler accompanied him downtown to one of the fanciest hotels in Lexington, where Jim received an award from The Pilot Club - a civic service organization for executive and professional women. Jim's sisters had thrown together an outfit for him at the last minute as he had given them little notice. He wore a pale-gold linen sport coat, dark-brown dress pants, a cream-colored shirt and a gold tie borrowed from his father's tie rack. Jake even shined his shoes. After the event, Beeler made a point of calling the house to thank his sisters for helping Jim look so good. She told them how proud she was of him. A photograph from the event shows a picture of the two: Beeler in a lovely dress and Jim in his gold jacket holding a large silver bowl.

Jim was also making Lafayette High School proud in other ways. At the state drama festival, he won the Best High School Actor in the State award two years in a row. The second year he won the honor, Jim enjoyed surprising his mother with his trophy after first fooling her that he had come up short.

(Author's note: During research for this book, I discovered that Jim repeated his senior year at Lafayette. My family and I had previously thought the reason so many people told us through the years they went to high school with Jim was because Lafayette was so large back then. But learning Jim spent four years there, not three, explains why he was so well known among his classmates.

The graduating classes of 1967 and 1968 both like to claim him as theirs.)

In Jim's second year as a senior, he kept in touch with an actor-friend from Lafayette: Clay Watkins had graduated two years earlier and had begun a journey toward an acting career. When Jim had received honorable mention his junior year at the State Drama Festival, it was Watkins who had won the top honor. Watkins did not go to college after graduating from high school in 1966. He chose instead to work in the Barnum and Bailey circus for a short stint before returning to Lexington and enrolling for a short time as a drama major at UK. He was eventually accepted into the American Academy of Dramatic Arts in New York City.

In the fall of 1967, Watkins was back in Lexington attending UK and hanging out with Jim. The two spent hours talking about their dreams. Watkins remembers how they would break into The Carriage House late at night, turn on the furnace, and pass the time talking about their future acting plans. When the two weren't discussing acting, they were cruising around town in Watkins' gold convertible Corvette. Watkins took Jim to parties at the home of a college friend named Joe Liles. Liles was pre-law and not involved in acting. Liles had also joined the ROTC and had attended basic training in Fort Benning, Ga. He had grown up in Muhlenberg County, Ky. Located in the far western part of the state, it is a major coal-producing region. Liles' father was an independent coal-mine operator.

One of the first times they all hung out was when they grabbed a bite at a burger joint. Liles remembers, "It turned out that after he ordered, Jim had no money to pay for his food, and Clay didn't have enough to cover him. I paid for Jim's food. He never really said anything, just quietly hung out and listened." Despite the unspectacular introduction, Liles and Jim became friends. Liles made a good impression on Jim's father, and he was invited to join the Varney Parkers on a few jobs. Over time, Jim came to value Liles' opinion. In some ways, Liles eventually became the older brother Jim never had. This enabled Liles to get through to Jim in ways others could not.

CHAPTER EIGHT

LEAVING LEXINGTON

Despite Jim's success in acting, his father was unconvinced he could make a living at it. He told Jim that no one would be coming to Lexington looking for an actor to star on Broadway or in a Hollywood movie. Liles remembers Big Jim exclaiming, "Bo will go to Hollywood when Hollywood comes to Turfland Mall." (Jim's parents began referring to Jim as Bo when he entered his teenage years; Turfland Mall was one of Jim's haunts.)

Jim knew his father had a point. Yet he also knew Big Jim was not fully aware of his growing commitment to making acting his career. When Jim's parents showed hesitancy about his plans to forego college and move away to pursue acting, he cleverly used many of his father's same words to justify leaving Lexington. Oldest sister Jo Gail admitted years later to the Lexington Herald-Leader that she and her sisters tried to warn Jim about show business. "You should prepare yourself for reality," Jo Gail said, "because it's a million-to-one shot that you'll ever make a living."

As Jim's final year at Lafayette came to an end, Watkins, still studying drama at UK, learned of a big audition at the Southern Theatre Conference in Atlanta for many of the repertory theaters in the region. Jim was immediately interested and soon tried to convince his parents of the potential of the new opportunity. Jim explained to them how actors worked their way up through stock companies to get to Broadway. He told them it would be like a summer vacation, and he would be fed and paid. He said that he was hoping to get into the Barter Theatre in Virginia but would probably accept whatever he was offered. He knew of Barter's excellent reputation from people like Mary Warner Ford, who had been there years before working alongside talented actors such as Ned Beatty.

Out of the 370 actors who auditioned at the conference, six were chosen, Jim and Watkins among them. Jim chose Barter from the seven theaters who wanted him. Jim believed that he needed to drop out of school immediately to start his training. His decision was made a little easier since his sub-par grades made it difficult for him to graduate. Jim's decision to leave school must have been bittersweet for Thelma Beeler. She had pushed him to succeed in the classroom, yet it was her commitment to his growth as an actor that had made the most impact.

When the school newspaper interviewed him about his acceptance to Barter, Jim said, "An actor is born at heart, but his talent must be developed." Although he had been showered with awards and honors in his high school career, he knew he had much more to learn.

Jim's mother was angry and disappointed with his decision to drop out. She and the rest of the family tried unsuccessfully to convince him to finish school. Surprisingly, though, Jim's father didn't share in his mother's anger. He had made a similarly unpopular decision as a young man when he joined the Army, and he empathized with his son who was now attempting to chart his own course. But Jim's father did make Jim promise to get his GED when he returned home.

The Barter Theatre, located in Abingdon, Va., earned its name during the lean times of the Great Depression, when many people could not afford tickets. Founder Robert Porterfield made it possible for patrons to exchange food for admission. This arrangement, which has been referred to as "trading ham for Hamlet," allowed the theater to stay afloat and eventually grow into one of the most respected acting institutions in the nation. Today it is still one of the last year-round professional resident repertory theaters in the country. When Jim arrived in the spring of 1968, Porterfield was still director.

"The Company" was the roster of Equity actors who played the leading roles in Barter's main stage productions. Jim and his fellow apprentices played small roles and did the bulk of the grunt work of set building, props, etc. Performances were held in The Playhouse, an old building that had been converted into a roughly 100-seat venue. Apprentices would also perform children's theater there in the afternoon and sometimes in the morning. In addition, at night, Equity actors would also do experimental (read: adult-language) plays there. So there were essentially three companies in operation.

Jim regularly sent letters home, such as this one, describing life at Barter:

Dear Mom,

I'm sorry I haven't written more, but they keep me on so much LSD that I don't know who I am in the afternoon. That's a line from a play I'm in right now. It's called "The Impossible Years." I play an Olympic swimmer named Andy McClaine. It's really a funny play. Alan King played the lead on Broadway.

You asked if I'm dating. Yes I am. At night, my roommate and I have some of the girls in the company come to our room with their record player, and pretty soon the people around us hear the music and the whole company shows up for the party. The company threw me a surprise birthday party complete with presents.

I'm sending you a schedule telling the plays I'm in and the dates they're playing so you can see them if you wish. Give my love to Daddy and Jake. (And keep sending $.)

Love,
Bo

Along with acting, Jim and his fellow classmates learned set design, lighting, makeup and costumes. On one occasion, Jim was sent to pick up lumber in a truck that the theater owned. As he glanced over at the glove compartment, he noticed that someone had scratched onto it, "Gregory Peck drove this truck." Jim was already aware that the acclaimed actor had studied at Barter, and he was excited that the truck provided a link to greatness.

Actor-writer Walter Williamson attended Barter with Jim. In addition to writing five nonfiction books and five works of fiction, Williamson has appeared in such movies the Adam Sandler comedies "Mr. Deeds" (2002) and "The Longest Yard" (2005). He also appeared in "The Omega Code" (1999) and did classical theater for over 30 years. Jim made an impression on Williamson from the start. Here is Williamson's recollection of his time with him:

"I do vividly remember that first night we all arrived in May or June. I was in the same suite with Jim but not in the same room. (There were) two rooms with two guys each, one bath in between. We were, of course, eying each other to see who the competition was. There was a big, old red Irish Setter named, I think, Riley, who had the run of the place. If your door was open he would wander in and drink out of your toilet and bark at you if it needed flushing. ...

"I had played Arthur in 'Camelot' at college a year or two before, and somehow either Jim or I had quoted the end of Act I while we were all unpacking. I had already heard Jim doing some of his funny voices earlier, and I was surprised that he knew that piece. He started doing a mock Richard Burton voice, and we ended up playing 'Can you top this?' with quotes from Shakespeare. What I hadn't anticipated was that this guy with the goofy voices could also produce such beautiful vocal sounds and such sensitive interpretations of classical work.

"'Dick Whittington (and His Cat)' was a kid's show, cast with just us apprentices. We played it in The Playhouse and toured it to half a dozen locations around the area. I was playing the sultan, and I think Jim was playing the captain of the ship Dick was traveling on. We took the show to Grundy, Va. Grundy was so narrow; you couldn't turn a car around on the main street. You had to go outside of town, turn around and go back through. We set up in the school building to do the show for a summer school for kids who had failed first and second grade. When we were loading up after the performance, there was a kid wearing bib overalls and no shirt, towhead, barefoot, standing by watching us moving the set pieces out. Jim and I and a couple of others stopped to sign his program. He said, 'Gorsh! I never seed a live fim-strip afore.' We joked and giggled about that encounter on the way back to Abingdon. But I got the feeling Jim saw something deeper in that exchange, as I did, even as he did a perfect imitation of the little fellow.

"My estimate of Jim then - and now - was that at his core he was an artist. He wore a costume of wild, foolish, goofy, antic jokes and simpleton stories. But that was, it seemed to me, just to hide and protect the tender purity of his real ambition buried deep inside. I got a glimpse of that being that first night. Then I watched over the course of the summer as he used his low humor to communicate with the world because, perhaps, he didn't want to risk tainting that artistic core. His wit seemed to be an easy way to address the world. But it was fed by the heat of that guarded art inside."

Williamson also spoke of his memories of performing with Jim in a 1993 Los Angeles Times article: "I have never in my life seen anyone more exciting doing serious classical theater – the focus, the concentration, the diction, everything. Onstage he was one of the most exciting performers I'd ever seen."

By the fall of 1968, Jim felt the time was right to take a shot at Broadway. He had been keeping in touch with Watkins, who was living in New York with his girlfriend while attending the American Academy of Dramatic Arts. Watkins let Jim stay at his apartment during his time there and recalls an inscription on Jim's footlocker that read "Broadway or Bust." Once Jim arrived, Watkins helped him find work doing technical and janitorial duties for Joseph Papp's "Shakespeare in the Park" at the Delacorte Theatre in Central Park. Watkins was working there as well. Jim tried out for a few plays outside his day job but didn't land any roles. He later referred to the auditioning experience as "mostly cattle calls and frustration."

Still, Jim had learned a great deal about stage acting from his time at Barter and in New York despite the fact he did not become an instant Broadway sensation. He returned to Lexington later that fall with a much better idea of what possibilities awaited him if he continued his current path as a stage actor. Jim wasted no time in keeping his acting skills sharp by returning to the Studio Players community theater and performing in several of their productions.

Back home, Jim was able to catch up with friends and family, including his cousin Ed McChord. The two shared a similar sense of humor and had their fair share of adventures. Ed, like Jim's father, was a prankster. One of Jim's favorite spots was a big, eerie-looking Osage orange tree standing next to the Carriage House, where Jim was performing with the Studio Players. One night, Jim and Ed were hanging out by the tree smoking cigarettes when Jim started in on a spooky tale. Jim didn't know that Ed had purchased a smoke bomb at a convenience store they had visited earlier. Ed quietly lit it and threw it into a hole in the tree ... and then proceeded to act terrified when the tree began to smoke. When Jim saw the tree exhaling the thick white cloud as if releasing an evil spirit, he sprung away like a cat and took off running. It took Ed a couple of blocks to catch up.

That winter, Ed helped Jim get a job as a lifeguard, of all things: It was ludicrous because Jim had still not learned to swim. The job was at the Continental Inn Motel's indoor pool, where Ed was also lifeguarding. Now Jim could pay for his double dates with Ed. Unfortunately, one of them almost ended in tragedy.

Just a few weeks after Christmas, Ed and Jim were taking their dates to a bar called the Terrace Room at Eastland Bowling Lanes in Lexington. Ed was driving his 1967 Austin-Healey Sprite, a two-seater with a small storage space in the back. Ed's date was nestled in that spot while Jim's date sat on his lap.

They were traveling down Eastland Parkway around 9 p.m. The car came upon an ice patch, popped the curb and bounced off a tension cable, which flipped the car upside-down. Ed landed with his torso halfway out of the car and was able, despite the severity of the situation, to crawl out with little struggle. For Jim and the two girls, still inside, it was more difficult to find a clear way out. The smell of leaking gasoline only made things more terrifying. Jim's date unknowingly used his chest to push off with her feet. She was wearing high heels. Jim later said he thought he could feel his collarbone separate. Jim finally managed to squeeze through a narrow opening, but with so much adrenaline pumping he didn't feel his ear nearly ripping off as it scraped across the pavement. The girls, being smaller, were able to slide out more easily.

The night watchman at the nearby Cockrell's Auto Body let the four inside the building to clean up until the ambulance arrived. Jim walked into the restroom and sat down on the toilet, fully clothed, using it as a chair. He didn't say much until Ed walked in to check on him and then he exclaimed (half-serious), "You've killed me, Eddie!"

In the minutes that followed, it was determined that the wreck was a result of someone hosing down a nearby parking lot. The runoff had frozen on the street. Even a police officer responding to the accident fell victim to the ice patch. He had hardly taken a step out of his cruiser before he slipped and fell.

An ambulance arrived, and with the help of the police cruiser everyone was taken to the University of Kentucky Hospital. After Ed was checked out, he walked over to the room where Jim's ear was being stitched up. The room was not hard to find. All he had to do was follow the sounds of Shakespeare being recited. Ed found a doctor (with an unlit Cuban cigar hanging from his mouth) stitching up Jim's ear while Jim bellowed out lines from Shakespeare. Jim told Ed that the sound of his voice helped drown out the sounds of being stitched up.

When describing what caused the wreck to his parents, Jim mentioned a fictitious bunch of brothers he and Ed often blamed for their exploits. "Those Buzzard boys shot our tires out," he explained to his mother. Luckily for everyone, it was something they had lived to joke about.

Despite X-rays and doctors' examinations, no break was ever found in Jim's collarbone. He was told that after the swelling went down, the injury would take care of itself. Unfortunately, his collarbone never looked the same. The right side tilted upward, forming a small lump. He became quite self-conscious about it and rarely wore open-necked shirts or anything else that exposed the area. It became yet another aspect of his physical appearance with which he was uncomfortable.

But whatever consequence Jim felt his looks would have on his acting career, they didn't seem to affect his love life in the least. By the summer of 1969, he was dating an actress friend named Julieanne Beasley (Author's note: Today she is Julieanne Pogue). They had been in the same circle of friends for a while; Jim had even dated her sister for a short time. Beasley had first met Jim when she had starred in "Niccolo and Nicolette" with him at Lexington Children's Theatre. She'd had a crush on him even then. Her father was an Army major (one of the original Green Berets), and her family had moved from Lexington to Okinawa and then to the Philippines for a good portion of her childhood. Her family returned to Lexington in June 1963, and she soon found herself acting with Jim once again.

Beasley had immense respect for Jim's ability as a stage actor while being equally impressed with the homespun characters he portrayed when entertaining friends. Today she says many of the hillbilly incarnations he was doing when they dated were "a breath away" from what would eventually become Ernest.

The two young actors bonded on many levels. Beyond a shared love of the stage, there was an intellectual connection and a fascination with exploring many of the spiritual elements of the world. Today Pogue (nee Beasley) remembers Jim having a great sense of the profound elements of life and the universe. Beyond a mutual physical attraction (Beasley would go on to be crowned Miss Lexington in 1971 and was a Miss Kentucky runner-up that same year), Jim was one of the most charming people she had ever met.

That summer the two found stage work at the Jenny Wiley Summer Theatre in Prestonsburg. They both starred in productions of "Carnival" and "Bye, Bye Birdie." The director of "Birdie," Jim Hazlett, has fond memories of Jim. Referring to him as a "wonderful clown," Hazlett says that it was hard to tell sometimes when Jim was being serious. Offstage, Jim would constantly entertain with impressions and routines about such things as his grandmother's Ford Mustang Cobra GT. Although Jim's focus was sometimes lacking, his ability to endear himself to others made it difficult to dislike him. Perhaps one thing affecting his focus was the constant temptation to pursue new opportunities.

Jim broke his contract with Jenny Wiley during "Birdie" to audition for a play in New York. He read for the role of Rocky in Sal Mineo's "Fortune and Men's Eyes," which follows the story of a young man named Smitty who is sent to prison for six months for a first-time drug offense. An unflinching picture of the brutal nature of prison life unfolds as Smitty is sexually assaulted by more powerful inmates.

Without a car, Jim still relied on friends and family to get around. Jim's cousin Ed McChord, who had just gotten married, drove his new wife and Jim to New York so Jim could audition. Unfortunately, Jim didn't get the part. Neither did Sylvester Stallone, Jim recounted years later. But Stallone's many talents would soon become evident in "Rocky," the compelling film about the hard-luck boxer who makes good. (Stallone was nominated for two Oscars in screenwriting and acting, and the film won Best Picture.)

LEAVING LEXINGTON

During Jim's short trip to New York, he decided to ask Beasley to marry him when he returned to Kentucky. For engagement gifts, he bought her a pearl ring and a garnet necklace, as well as two items that reflected his mystical side: an athame (a ceremonial dagger used in Wiccan rituals) and a crystal ball. Garnet had special meaning for Beasley. It was the stone used in the engagement rings of her mother and grandmother. Beasley accepted Jim's proposal. Their engagement lasted about a year and a half.

During their time together, Beasley was aware of Jim's drinking and how he often had an ornate flask of one kind or another in his pocket. She looks back today, having worked as a psychotherapist, and believes Jim might have been clinically depressed. Melancholic is a word she uses to describe him during their time together. But despite his drinking and depression, it was the long periods away from each other that doomed the relationship. Jim's commitment to acting required him to be on the road constantly. This made it nearly impossible to keep up the relationship, and the two mutually agreed to end the engagement, remaining good friends. (Today Beasley, in addition to being a licensed psychotherapist specializing in trauma and attachment issues, is a theatrical director/choreographer/actor/designer/singer and a book narrator for Audible.com and elsewhere. Her projects include acting as stage director for the University of Kentucky opera and director of educational theater for Los Angeles schools out of L.A.'s Stella Adler Studio).

Meanwhile, Jim found time to keep his promise to his father and earn his GED before starring in fall productions at the Studio Players in Lexington, including a pair of one-act plays written by English playwright Peter Shaffer. "The White Liars" and "Black Comedy" are commonly presented as a double-bill.

THE IMPORTANCE OF BEING ERNEST:
THE LIFE OF ACTOR JIM VARNEY

In the dark comedy "The White Liars," Jim played Tom, a lead singer in a rock band who visits a fortune teller with his manager at an English seaside resort. The manager attempts to bribe the fortune teller to use her abilities to put an end to the growing relationship between his girlfriend and Tom. In the farce "Black Comedy," Jim played Brindsley Miller, an unsuccessful sculptor who decides to steal his (apartment) neighbor's antiques to impress the visiting father of his fiancée and a wealthy art collector. Mayhem erupts when a blown fuse causes the lights to go out just as the neighbor returns, followed by a surprise visit from Brindsley's ex-mistress.

Jim received rave reviews from local critics for the double-bill. "Varney is the hit of the evening, and the contrast in his handling of the two roles is remarkable," wrote Mary Agnes Barnes of the Lexington Herald-Leader. She added, "Varney steals the show ("Black Comedy") – and both works and suffers in doing it. He does so many pratfalls that I expect he'll be black-and-blue by the time the show ends its run." Another local critic, Richard Schwein, was equally impressed. In his review of Jim's performance in "The White Liars" Schwein wrote, "He works easily with his put-on, working-class accent and 'true' middle-class London accent. His characterization of Tom is beyond reproach."

In the summer of 1970, Jim signed a contract to perform at the Pioneer Playhouse in nearby Danville, Ky. At the time, the playhouse was designated as the State Theatre of Kentucky. There he starred in "Boeing-Boeing," playing an American journalist named Bernard who enjoys the playboy life while stationed in Paris, France. He manages to successfully juggle three flight-attendant girlfriends who all work separate transatlantic routes. His world becomes complicated when Boeing planes are upgraded, bringing faster flights that increase the women's stopover times in Paris, causing them to overlap.

In Billy Edd Wheeler's musical comedy "Fire on the Mountain" Jim played a misogynist moonshiner named Uncle Jessie. The plot revolves around the arrival of a Yankee missionary social worker named Prissy into an Appalachian community. She opens a Bible school and is soon at odds with Jessie's nephew and his girlfriend over their living arrangement. Pioneer Playhouse's late founder, Eben Henson, was impressed with Jim's talent. Although actors such as Lee Majors and John Travolta also graced the stage of Pioneer Playhouse in their formative years, Henson once said that Jim was perhaps "the most unusual actor" ever to perform there. He also said that Jim packed houses night after night during the two-week run of "Mountain."

Henson was also involved in taking "Mountain" to a venue in Tennessee, with Jim reprising his role of Uncle Jessie. At the Third Masque Dinner Theatre in Chattanooga, Jim impressed audiences and earned praise from critics such as Robert Cooper of the Chattanooga Times who wrote, "Jim Varney as Uncle Jessie is the outstanding member of this excellent cast. Playing the part of a woman-hating moonshiner, the unfolding of his change of heart is something to see. He is truly a fine actor and presents the hillbilly character in a hilariously believable manner." Jim remained in Chattanooga through the fall and winter of 1970, performing in plays such as "Guys and Dolls," "Champagne Complex" and "A Funny Thing Happened on the Way to the Forum."

One of Jim's many haunts after returning home to Lexington was the green room of the University of Kentucky's Guignol Theatre. The green room served as the unofficial hangout for theater students, and although Jim never actually attended U.K., he enjoyed catching up with students who were old friends from high school and his neighborhood. It was there Jim met Charles Edward Pogue through Beasley. Pogue remembers Jim as a "vagabond

THE IMPORTANCE OF BEING ERNEST:
THE LIFE OF ACTOR JIM VARNEY

strolling player" who showed up for two or three weeks at a time and held court as he talked about his travels and entertained with his crazy cast of characters. The students were enthralled to be in the presence of a "working actor." (Today, Pogue is a noted screenwriter whose credits include "The Fly" – 1986; "Psycho III" – 1986; and "Dragonheart" – 1996).

Jim once accompanied Pogue and Beasley to their modern British drama class, where Harold Pinter's "The Homecoming" was being discussed. (Author's note: Pogue and Beasley are now married.) Jim had just finished touring with a company that had performed the play. He ended up leading the whole class in a discussion and performing scenes that included parts in addition to his own.

Pogue says everyone had "Varney stories" along with himself during this time. Pogue actually wrote a term paper in a folklore class that consisted of many of these tales of Jim's exploits. He received an "A" and wishes today he had followed his professor's advice to make a copy before handing it in. Being the final paper of the semester, it was not returned.

Although trips to U.K.'s green room no doubt boosted Jim's ego, actors on the big screen seemed to convince him that his appearance would limit his potential. The movie "Wuthering Heights" was released in theaters around this time. Jim's sister Jake was working with a girl who had seen the movie and noticed how much the actor playing Heathcliff resembled Jim. Jake took Jim to see it without mentioning what her friend had said. Jake said Jim was spellbound when he saw Timothy Dalton and acknowledged the resemblance. Maybe that helped Jim to one day see himself on the big screen. Or maybe it did the opposite, showing him a more polished version of himself that he would never be, like a brother who had gotten the better mix of genes.

In February 1972, a new opportunity arose for Jim, one that would further his acting career. He joined Fantastick Productions. Headquartered in Kingsport, Tenn., it was the state's only professional touring company at that time. The actors would meet in Kingsport to rehearse before heading out to perform in elementary and high schools throughout the state. They usually performed well-known children's stories such as "Rumpelstiltskin" and "Snow White." For the older children, the company performed more mature dramas presented in modern versions, such as "Antigone."

For many of the children attending, it was their first experience of a live show with professional actors. With two shows a day, the company was able to perform in front of thousands of kids by the end of the tour. Just as the live TV airing of "Peter Pan" had captured Jim's imagination as a 6-year-old, his participation in Fantastick Productions' work helped pass on the excitement of live theater to a new generation.

As the tour wound down, Jim and some of his fellow actors heard news of a theme park opening in Nashville called Opryland, started by the founders of the Grand Ole Opry, the famous country-music venue. The park was set to open in the summer of 1972, and the call was out for all types of talent to perform in their large outdoor shows. They wanted to offer more than entertainment based on a country-music theme. According to research and multiple interviews I did for this book, it wasn't long before Jim and a fellow actor from Fantastick, Melissa Ferrell, were performing at the new attraction. Although Jim didn't know it yet, this chapter of his life was leading him straight to Ernest.

In one of the Opryland folk shows, Jim played the part of an old man even though he was all of 23. Jim once said that just about every skill he had listed on his resume was used when performing at Opryland. Along with acting, Jim got a chance to sing and even played the dulcimer.

Yet despite the growing success, Jim was still self-conscious about his appearance. He thought he couldn't advance his career without changing it. He felt his nose was too large, his mouth too wide. There was little he thought could be done about his mouth, but he believed that with a more refined nose his face would look more symmetrical and handsome.

In August 1972, Jim finally made the decision to undergo a procedure to change his nose. The surgery was called a septorhinoplasty. It is a combination of rhinoplasty and septoplasty surgeries. Rhinoplasty is the cosmetic portion and septoplasty the corrective procedure that fixes the deviated septum. It took place at Central Baptist Hospital in Lexington. Jim's sister Jake was working at the hospital at the time as an X-ray technician and knew many of the staff involved in his surgery. She remembers one of the medical students finding it interesting to see the profession of "actor" written on her brother's chart.

Jim recuperated at his parents' house. He looked as if he had been beaten up. His eyes were black, and purple streaks ran across his swollen cheeks. A large bandage covered his nose and was taped to each side of his face, while his hair stuck out of the bandages in all directions.

One day, sister Jo Gail stopped by to visit and brought along her daughter, Shannon, who was almost 3. As soon as Shannon walked into the house, she was taken aback by Jim's bandaged face and clammed up. Knowing Shannon had been getting in trouble for climbing on kitchen counters at her home, Jim and his mother decided they would have fun with her. He asked Shannon, "I guess you're wondering what happened to me, huh? Well, I was climbing on Mama's counters in the kitchen and fell. She had been telling me to keep off of them but I didn't listen." He said this with a straight face while Jo Gail and his mother went along. "That's right," Jim's mother added, "Now I don't know if he will ever look like himself again." Needless to say, that broke Shannon of climbing for a while.

When it was time for Jim's bandages to come off, he was given a metal nose-protector to wear. He still had swelling in his face and around his eyes, which had turned a yellowish green. Because of the thickness of the skin on his nose he had been told he would need a follow-up surgery later on. But he seemed pleased with the results, which had given his nose a more "Roman" look. He was hopeful the second surgery would improve it even more.

CHAPTER NINE

FINDING GLORY WITH CHERRY

Although Jim longed to grace the stage of a major Broadway production, he still had to make a living in the meantime. In Tennessee Jim continued to find one opportunity after another. Perhaps it was fitting that an advertising agency based in Nashville ultimately provided Jim the opportunity of a lifetime, one that would lead to Tennessee becoming his permanent home. According to Joe Liles, in the fall of 1972, Melissa Ferrell got auditions for herself and Jim through a new talent agency in Nashville called TML (Talent and Model Land). A woman named Betty Clark ran it, and Clark sent the two out for commercials. Jim soon caught the eye of advertising men Thom Ferrell (no relation to Melissa) and John Cherry.

An ad agency named McDonald, Carden, Cherry and Ferrell was holding auditions for several female actors for a commercial for Purity Dairies. In the spot, a drill sergeant named Sergeant Glory demonstrated how to open the new plastic milk jug that Purity was now using. The character addressed two needs of the client: advertising the product and educating the customer about its new packaging.

As the camera pulled back, it was revealed that Sergeant Glory was not speaking to soldiers but to a group of female shoppers.

THE IMPORTANCE OF BEING ERNEST:
THE LIFE OF ACTOR JIM VARNEY

(According to Thom Ferrell, Melissa was attempting to land one of the female roles.) Thom Ferrell remembers his first encounter with Jim:

"Melissa said she was with someone I should take a look at. He had been doing theater in Lexington and wanted to work in Nashville. I saw his face and thought it was interesting. At first I didn't consider him for the part of Sergeant Glory, but he impressed me on how he could change characters in a second. I gave him some of the Sergeant Glory lines, and he was great. I spent more time with him explaining that I had made arrangements with the Marines for some mannerism training, and the hair and the earring would obviously have to go. The best I remember is that he snapped to attention, saluted and replied, 'Yes, sir!'"

The first Sergeant Glory commercial was a success, and soon the character was using his Army clout in subsequent commercials to motivate everyone from dairy workers to actual cows into producing a superior product.

Just as Jim's famous Ernest character would years later, Sergeant Glory inserted humor into a product where few saw advertising potential. Years later when being interviewed, Jim talked about the character and how the dairy industry had never before had a wow factor when it came to marketing. He jokingly claimed, "In the dairy business you either like milk or you don't. There's no superior cow." Organic farmers these days would probably beg to differ.

In addition to Sergeant Glory, Jim began performing in other TV ads for the agency using characters from his vast arsenal. Jim played everything from a Hungarian ringmaster to a sleazy car salesman who smoked a cigar and wore a pencil-thin mustache. It was the car-salesman commercials where John Cherry first experimented with filming Jim using a wide-angle lens. The way in which it amplified Jim's facial features worked well for the tone Cherry wanted. The wide-angle lens would become the standard when Ernest came along.

Taking advantage of Jim's ability to imitate famous people, Cherry also used Jim in radio ads imitating such celebrities as John Wayne.

During the time Jim was working with Cherry, he remained vigilant in his quest to make it on Broadway. He decided to return to New York in the summer of 1973. Watkins was still living there, and Jim hoped that he could help him find new opportunities. Just to have a good friend close by made the big city less lonely. According to Liles, Watkins was "quite the moral support" for Jim for many years.

Jim's dreams were big, but his bank account was not. Jim lived in a rundown apartment in Spanish Harlem. He was a starving artist. Liles came to see Jim in September 1973. Liles was living in Boston and doing well, working in PR, as well as training salesmen for a casket company. When Liles saw Jim's apartment and the malnourishment beginning to show on his frame, he took Jim out to buy groceries. As Liles remembers, "Jim was grabbing up boxes of oatmeal, bags of potatoes, jars of peanut butter, and it just went on."

The following Saturday Liles met up with Jim at Watkins' apartment. The three decided that Jim should try out some of his stand-up material at a popular new comedy club in the city: Rick Newman's Catch A Rising Star. It was open-mic night. During the cab ride over, they threw out lines and bits for Jim to consider. After they arrived, Jim was able to grab one the last spots. Even though his material was far from polished, Jim received a warm reception. That was enough for him to want to return. With the encouragement of other rising young comics like Freddie Prinze,

Jim's performances grew stronger. He also performed at another comedy club in the city called Pip's. It looked like stand-up was a better gateway for advancing his career than Broadway.

Still, he wanted to act, so much so that Jim returned to Lexington to save up more money and work on new routines for an eventual stab at Los Angeles. He thought maybe television or movies might hold opportunities. After seeing comedian Jimmie Walker land a starring role on the TV hit "Good Times" and watching Prinze rise to fame on "Chico and the Man," Jim hoped that playing the big clubs in Los Angeles would bring him similar success. The area had become the place to be for aspiring comedians thanks to Johnny Carson relocating "The Tonight Show" to Burbank.

But soon after his return to Lexington, a new romance began to take precedence over his career. Jim moved into an apartment with a new girlfriend and started to retreat from entertaining and, to his family's dismay, life altogether. Coincidentally, Liles had also moved back to Lexington after leaving his job in Boston. Liles lived close by and stopped by to see Jim several times a week. They would talk about acting and kick around ideas for routines and characters. It was obvious to Liles that both Jim and his girlfriend were not good for each other. He remembers seeing plates full of cigarette butts and decaying food piled up around their bed.

Jim's family didn't see much of him during this time. Sister Jake remembers going to his apartment once after he had asked her for money. When she arrived, Jim met her out front (likely, Jake surmised, so she wouldn't see the inside of his place). Jim's father did little to intervene. He figured Jim's struggles would help him realize acting was no longer in the cards, and he would soon begin working toward a real profession. But Liles knew Jim had real talent, and he wasn't cut out for a regular job. Liles believed all Jim was lacking was confidence and motivation.

Liles' efforts to motivate Jim finally paid off one day when Jim asked him to be his manager. Liles, surprised, replied, "What does a manager do?" Jim paused and then said, "I don't know ... manage?" Liles figured that whatever a manager did, Jim needed one. Liles believed then, as he does today, that Jim was in desperate need of moral support. Jim trusted Liles as someone who had his best interests at heart and would not take advantage of him financially. Liles looked at Jim's career from a long-term perspective: He believed Jim had broad appeal – that he could play numerous roles, not just country characters. Meanwhile, Jim's family approved of Liles for many reasons including the fact that Liles never used drugs or drank to excess.

Over the next few months Liles let Jim come over to his apartment any time he wanted to call long-distance to Nashville. Liles, as well as Jim's family, hoped that if Jim could get something going he would leave his girlfriend behind. It wasn't long before Betty Clark found work for Jim, and he was heading to Nashville in his father's car. After a short stint recording radio ads, Jim returned to Lexington excited about how things had gone. Liles encouraged him to return to Nashville and agreed to join him and work on new material if Jim would commit himself to working hard. Jim agreed. He and his girlfriend eventually parted, and Jim began concentrating full-time on his career again. Jim moved to Nashville first in the early fall of 1974, and Liles followed six weeks later. The two found a place to share in the basement of Dottie's Massage Parlor on Eighth Avenue. Along with managing Jim, Liles also paid his living expenses for about two years. Liles recalls Clark saying, "Thank God he has someone to help him."

THE IMPORTANCE OF BEING ERNEST:
THE LIFE OF ACTOR JIM VARNEY

In no time Clark got both of them small roles playing Confederate soldiers in Johnny Cash's "Ridin' the Rails: The American Railroad Story." Liles actually had no acting ambitions of his own and took the role because Clark asked him to. The one-hour TV special followed Cash as he took viewers back to important moments in the history of the American railroad. Cash narrated and sang railroad-themed songs throughout the production.

The filming of Jim and Liles' scene took place at the House of Cash – Johnny Cash's recording studio, which also housed his publishing operation in Hendersonville, Tenn. In the scene, the two sit at a nighttime campfire in the company of fellow Confederate soldiers while Cash sings "The Night They Drove Old Dixie Down." At one point, the camera pans across the faces of the soldiers, pausing on Jim who stares off into the distance. The grim look on Jim's face seemed to echo Cash's subsequent line about how the starving soldiers were barely alive in the last days of the Civil War. Jim could probably relate after his time in New York.

During the taping of "Rails," Jim ran into his friend Jack Routh; the two had met years earlier. Routh was a singer-songwriter and husband of Carlene Carter, the singer and daughter of June Carter, who was by now Cash's wife. Routh was also friends with Loney Hutchins, who ran the House of Cash publishing operations. Jim and Liles became good friends with Routh, Hutchins and their wives.

In the late spring of 1975, Liles convinced Jim to go to a local club called the Exit/In for a showcase night and perform stand-up. Despite his success in New York, Jim was nervous. He confessed to Liles that he had bombed in Nashville once before, when he was in town for Sergeant Glory work. Jim had been staying at a motor inn where an outlaw country singer was performing. Jim and the singer were talking during a break, and Jim asked if he could go onstage and perform a few minutes of material. The crowd's response was not what he expected: not a single laugh or chuckle in the house. Liles worked to build Jim's confidence back up while helping him prepare new material. Liles even went so far as to promise Jim he would join him onstage to perform if Jim bombed again. Liles was glad he didn't have to go through with his promise. Jim became an immediate hit, enabling Liles to get him additional bookings.

From the beginning, Jim's stand-up act was built upon his strength of imitation. One of Jim's early influences was comedian Jonathan Winters, who also used family members and local people from his hometown of Springfield, Ohio, as the foundation of many characters. Two of Winters' most popular characters were Maude Frickert and Elwood P. Suggins. Maude Frickert was based on an aunt of Winters' who, despite being crippled and bedridden much of her life, had a funny way of expressing herself. Winters would wear a dress, no make-up, glasses and a wig with a bun when portraying Frickert. He described her as a "hip old lady" whose age and conservative appearance allowed him to talk about controversial subjects without offending his audience.

Elwood P. Suggins was a hillbilly; Winters said he was based on men who had come from Kentucky to work in the Springfield factories. In one popular routine called "The American Farmer," Winters portrayed Suggins as a farmer who was paid by the government not to plant crops. Although the money was good, Suggins struggled to define for people what he actually did as a farmer.

Jim took his similar gift of mimicry and turned it into hilarious depictions of colorful characters also based on people in and around his hometown. Jim's innate ability to imitate Southerners made his material all the more authentic and funny. Although his parents did not have strong Southern accents (a Kentucky accent is more Midwestern as compared to, say, West Virginia), they did use colloquial phrases, many of which were uniquely Southern. Jim grew up hearing his mother say "over yonder" and the always-colorful, "She doesn't know s——— from apple butter!"

Jim used various small towns in Kentucky and Tennessee as backdrops for his stories. Some of the most memorable were fictitious places such as the notorious Bulljack, Ky. Like Winters, Jim gave his characters peculiar names such as Clyde Spurlin and Bunny Jeanette. Bunny was a female beautician who competes in talent contests demonstrating her skill rolling hair with frozen orange-juice cans. Clyde was a confused old man who calls a welding company inquiring about how they might repair the steel plate in the back of his wife's head. There was even a dubious county coroner named George Asher who embalmed the living.

Of all of Jim's early characters, mountain man Loyd Roe is arguably the funniest. In Jim's act, Loyd often talked about his 8-year-old son named Mistake. He claimed the child weighed 250 pounds and was over six feet tall. Mistake didn't have toys like normal kids. During one routine, Loyd talked about the chainsaw that Mistake carried around in a shoulder holster.

Some of the characters Jim brought to life in these routines would eventually resurface in various incarnations in the many movies, commercials and TV shows in which Jim would star. Loyd became Ernest's uncle, "Lloyd Worrell," in the television special "Hey Vern, It's My Family Album." The character later made his uncredited big-screen debut as the snake handler in the movie "Ernest Saves Christmas."

Soon after Liles joined Jim in Nashville, he browsed the yellow pages in the phone book for talent agencies and found out that William Morris had recently opened an office in the city. Before he got a chance to follow up, a William Morris representative approached Liles after one of Jim's performances at The Exit/In.

The rep had heard about Jim from the club's owner and was interested in signing him. Jim was skeptical at first, but Liles assured him the man was legitimate.

After some discussion, Jim eventually signed with William Morris. The signing had no effect on the business relationship between Jim and Liles, who remained Jim's manager. The first thing the agency needed was a bio of Jim. Liles quickly wrote up a page and a half of information. Liles admits, "The 'spin' and the BS was a little heavy but it worked." Also attached to the bio was a list of Jim's talents:

Accents and Dialects

Arabic
Australian
Carpathian
Italian
Irish
Mexican
Puerto Rican
Russian
Turkish
Welsh
Scotch – Edinburgh, Glasgow
British – Cockney, Earls Court, Liverpool, Midlands, Yorkshire

Impressions

Richard Burton
Peter O'Toole
Humphrey Bogart

THE IMPORTANCE OF BEING ERNEST: THE LIFE OF ACTOR JIM VARNEY

Paul Lynde
John Wayne

Special Skills

Buckdancing
Hamboning
Eefing (an Appalachian type of vocal percussion similar to beatboxing)
Juggling
Knife throwing
Acrobatics
Fencing
Dulcimer
Coin-Dexterity Tricks
Tightrope Walking
Speed Bag
Eye Crossing – independent control of eyes

After signing with William Morris, Jim and Liles had the expectation of bookings on the college circuit and exposure to TV, commercial and film departments in New York and Los Angeles. A videotape of Jim's commercials was made and copies distributed throughout the agency. Unfortunately, they didn't generate any interest at the New York office. They found the humor too "rural" and couldn't see past the production values to Jim's acting. Still, he got more bookings in Nashville, and although he didn't know it yet, the signing would pay off when he eventually reached Los Angeles.

Nashville wasn't Los Angeles, but it still had a number of big stars, perhaps none bigger than the "Man in Black" himself, Johnny

Cash. He showed up one evening at the Exit/In with his daughter Roseanne to see singer Dan Fogelberg. Jim happened to be the opening act that night. Liles remembers a line of people extending down the side of the building to the street waiting to get in. Liles spotted Cash and his daughter, and decided to introduce himself as a friend of Cash's son-in-law Jack Routh. "I invited him to come into the club as our guest. He declined because he was uncomfortable cutting in front of so many people." Liles didn't give up, explaining that his offer was more of a favor to a friend's father-in-law than a gesture to a famous star. Amused, Cash agreed to follow him in. Liles' invitation paid off. As he recalls, "Cash was knocked out by Jim's act and told Jack (Routh) and Loney (Hutchins) how great he thought he was." (Although Jim and Liles had played extras in Cash's TV special about the American railroad, they had not gotten to know him personally.)

Routh and Hutchins continued to stay in touch with Liles and Jim. They had also seen one of Jim's performances at the Exit/In and were impressed. Even though Routh and Hutchins had nothing in common professionally with Jim and Liles, the four had mutual respect and a desire to see each other succeed. Around this time Routh had a single released that was produced by Chet Atkins. Jim and Liles would constantly call the radio stations and request it.

Jim continued his stand-up appearances at the Exit/In, including a particularly well-received act when opening for Dr. Hook (a country-flavored rock band also known as "Dr. Hook & the Medicine Show"). Liles remembers the impact it made at the time:

"When Jim opened for Dr. Hook and the Medicine Show, that was a big deal. They had been opening for the Rolling Stones on a long European tour, and Dr. Hook got the audience so worked up, that the Stones had no place left to take them. So... Dr. Hook took over the 'headlining' position, and the Stones started going on first. That was an amazing achievement for any band in 1975. Jim had gone over great that night. His confidence, timing, everything was spot-on. The audience had Bobby Bare, Jessi Colter, Shel Silverstein and a bunch of people from the real Nashville musician scene. John (Johnny Cash) had heard about that."

Routh and Hutchins updated Cash about Jim whenever they could. It wasn't long before they arranged to bring Cash to see Jim perform again at the Exit/In. This time didn't go as smoothly as before. In fact, it really didn't "go" at all. Jim was supposed to open for outlaw country music singer David Allan Coe, but it turned out that the singer's contract had a rider specifying no opening act. Jim couldn't perform. (He had never received a confirmation from William Morris that would have given him the information.) But Jim ended up giving an impromptu performance to Cash, Coe and a few of their friends outside the club at the end of the night. Liles remembers:

"After Coe's show, Cash, Loney, Jack, Coe and Jim were in the parking lot for a long time talking, laughing and cutting up. Jim was on. He was ripping off quips, one-liners and making jokes in character voices. Johnny was cracking up, as was Coe. Coe had on this outrageous outfit that looked like three cowboys and an Indian rolled into one. ... parts of the vest looked like someone had sprayed it with silver paint. He had feathers in his big, oversized hat and was generally like a mid-'70s peacock. After a while, when everything was flowing smoothly, Jim sort of slapped Coe on the arm and said, "You know, I got an outfit just like that. Did you get yours at Sears too?" It was a sort of an Ernest voice. It cracked up Coe, and Cash liked it also."

Liles was apologetic about the mix-up that prevented Jim from performing. Cash didn't seem to mind, especially after having a great time at the end of the evening. The icon was getting to know

Jim on a personal level. The friendship was really a result of the perseverance of Hutchins and Routh looking to help out Jim any way they could.

Jim was finding his groove with his stand-up and still earning money with advertising work. Thom Ferrell had left the McDonald, Carden, Cherry and Ferrell agency after five years to start Thom 2 Productions. Jim did some work with Ferrell's company in 1975 portraying a pirate character in several ads while continuing the Sergeant Glory work for John Cherry's agency, which had changed its name to Carden & Cherry in 1974.

Jim continued traveling throughout Kentucky and Tennessee performing stand-up and preparing for his move to Los Angeles. In addition to polishing material for his act, he was also refining his physical features for potential TV or film roles. In the summer of 1975, he had the follow-up surgery on his nose. Sections were loosened and reattached after trimming and shaping. It was starting to look good, and Jim was hopeful he'd now be a contender for leading-man roles. The difference in his appearance was noticeable as it reflected even more of the "Roman" look Jim had wanted all along. Unfortunately, Jim did not follow the doctor's orders to refrain from physical activity following the surgery and injured his nose during a frisky encounter with a girlfriend. At that point, nothing could be done to reverse the damage. After a few days, Jim accepted responsibility for what had happened and the possibility that he might forever be limited to character roles. At what point he began to be truly more comfortable with his looks is not known. Liles remembers a conversation with Jim around 1995 when Jim was 46, where Jim seemed to have come to like the way he looked. Jim made a comment about his face having an interesting character to it. Liles was happy to hear that Jim was pleased with his looks even at such a late stage in his life.

THE IMPORTANCE OF BEING ERNEST:
THE LIFE OF ACTOR JIM VARNEY

In October, Jim opened for the band Blood, Sweat and Tears at Morehead University, located east of Lexington. It was a tough crowd for Jim. A reporter from the Lexington Herald-Leader interviewed him following his act, and Jim told the writer he was preparing to take a shot at Los Angeles: "Sometimes you make it overnight, sometimes it takes a long time. It just depends on how bad you want it." It was obvious that at this point Jim wanted it.

Jim sent a letter home to his parents just before Thanksgiving. In it, he talked about how Routh and his wife were expecting their first child and how excited everyone was. He also mentioned a party at Cash's place in Bon Aqua, Tenn., where he was to have performed but that had been cancelled. The last bit of news he included concerned a Sergeant Glory film (a 10-minute movie to be shown during tours of the Purity dairy plant) that he had just completed that was to pay him close to $1,000.

CHAPTER TEN

STRIKING IT RICH IN CALIFORNIA

By February 1976, Jim was feeling the time was right for Los Angeles. Liles planned to go with him. Thanks to the perseverance of Routh and Hutchins, Cash had given them the phone number and address of his West Coast agent, Marty Klein. Cash had asked Klein to help Jim out.

A few weeks after they found an apartment and settled in, Liles read in the Hollywood Reporter that Cash was going to be in town to accept his star on the Hollywood Walk of Fame that day at noon.

As Liles recalls, "I woke Jim up, showed him the article and we both scrambled to make ourselves presentable. We got there as the ceremony was already underway. After Johnny uncovered his star and was kneeling beside it posing for photos, I pushed Jim in close where he could talk to John and be seen. Cash was really happy to see him, as Jim said something right off that made Cash laugh. He told us to go behind the VIP site and wait for him. He joined us a few minutes later and invited Jim to come over to the 'Merv Griffin Show' that night and hang out."

Jim's first opportunity to perform stand-up in Los Angeles was at the now legendary Comedy Store. Alongside future giants such as Robin Williams and David Letterman, Jim found a new audience for his material while gaining needed exposure. Liles remembers

Jim teaching Williams to speak in "bulls--- Russian" that he had learned from his cousin Ed McChord who had majored in Russian Language and Literature in college.

Club owner Mitzi Shore liked Jim's act and helped him get bookings on the strip. Jim was soon performing at The Improv in Hollywood, The Horn in Santa Monica and Laff Stop in Santa Ana. Jim appreciated the opportunities Shore gave him as well as the use of her black limo, which had a television in the back, a real luxury at the time. He and fellow comic Skip Stephenson sometimes traveled together while performing in the area. "He and I played those clubs for four days a week and a couple of hundred bucks," Jim recalled. Jim later talked of his experiences doing stand-up and the brutal nature of perfecting a routine. "You die alone there," he once said when describing the reality of bombing.

Along with helping Jim find work, Liles assisted him in maneuvering his old car around the enormously steep roads of the Hollywood Hills. They had nicknamed Jim's 1960 Dodge Dart Pioneer "The Shark" because of its front-end appearance, with a seemingly endless row of vertical lines in its massive grill. It reminded them of the shark from the movie "Jaws," released the previous summer. Without a parking brake or gear, they had to place a brick underneath one of the wheels to keep the car from rolling away. Despite some close calls, the car survived and even made a couple more trips back to Tennessee and Kentucky. Jim's dad was surprised it had ever made it out of Lexington.

Liles woke up one morning in late March to find a note on their apartment door. It was from Routh: He was in Nashville. He had gotten their address from Jim's mother, called around Los Angeles and found someone to drop a note by their apartment. (Remember this is before cell phones and e-mail.) As if Los Angeles wasn't competitive enough, Jim and Liles were initially operating without a telephone. But they scraped up enough money to place a long-distance call back to Routh. He told them about a summer TV series that Cash was planning. Cash apparently wanted Jim to be a part of it. They were invited to come up to San Francisco where Cash was performing and attend a meeting with Cash's wife, June Carter, and some of the show's producers, all at Cash's expense.

Liles and Jim flew up for a couple of days for an informal audition. It was Jim's first time meeting Carter, whose input for the show was as important as her husband's. Carter, of course, was a celebrity in her own right as a member of the famous singing Carter family. She was also known for her comedy onstage and during performances. Jim performed some of his routines so Carter could see just what Cash had been raving about. Still, Cash's recommendation was not a slam-dunk. Carter was actually interested in having one of the funnier members of The Oak Ridge Boys write comedy for the show.

Liles says that after the meeting they were expecting an offer. But months went by, and they heard nothing. Liles says, "I finally got William Morris in New York to look into it, and Joe Cates (executive producer) was not interested, based on other comedians John and June had suggested. William Morris twisted (Cates') arm, showed him videos of (Jim's) commercials and (Cates) agreed to hire him sight unseen. It was what Cash wanted, and the endorsement of William Morris closed it."

The show, "Johnny Cash & Friends," was a summer replacement series scheduled to run for four weeks. The variety-show wave that had gained popularity in the '60s was still going strong in the '70s. The wave included Johnny's original ABC show, "The Johnny Cash Show," which aired 1969-71. In this second go 'round for Cash, CBS was trying to ride the momentum. Tapings took place inside the Opryhouse back in Nashville in front of capacity crowds.

THE IMPORTANCE OF BEING ERNEST:
THE LIFE OF ACTOR JIM VARNEY

Jim got to share the stage not only with Cash and Carter, but with rising, young comedian Steve Martin. It was right before Martin hit it big on "Saturday Night Live." Liles remembers Martin and Jim getting along well, although he says Martin didn't respond to Jim's jokes at first. It wasn't until Martin and a group of people associated with the show saw Jim perform at the Exit/In that Martin witnessed more of Jim's arsenal of voices and characters. Liles recalls, "Martin was blown away when Cletus J. Hocker (a wino character of Jim's) broke into his impressions of Peter O'Toole, Richard Burton and, lastly, Dylan Thomas." Martin made a point of telling Jim how much he enjoyed the Dylan Thomas impression. It turned out that both he and Jim had grown up listening to the same Dylan Thomas record. Jim told Martin that he was the first person in a long time to recognize who the impression was about. From that point on, Martin had a newfound respect for Jim, and their friendship grew from there. When Jim and Liles came back to Los Angeles, Martin invited them to catch his performance at the Troubadour Club. They all enjoyed catching up after the set.

Things were finally moving for Jim. Before the Johnny Cash show even aired, Jim made his first national television appearance on "The Merv Griffin Show" in May 1976. Jim's new agent at William Morris handled the booking. Griffin was impressed with Jim and invited him back.

Even though the four-episode "Johnny Cash & Friends" was a short run, Jim received positive reviews. Marshall Fallwell Jr. wrote about the show for Photoplay magazine. In mentioning Jim's performance and the talk about the possibility of a TV show in the future featuring him, he wrote, "You will definitely be hearing from Jim Varney again."

Now that Jim was in California, he was catching up with old friends who had also moved there. One was comedian buddy

Freddie Prinze, who had been trying to get in touch with Jim ever since they had performed together in New York. Jim had not given him any contact information other than that he was from Kentucky. On at least one occasion when Prinze was doing a radio appearance in Chicago, he called out to Jim while on the air – figuring the signal might well reach Kentucky – to please get in touch if he could hear him. Unfortunately, Jim's reunion with Prinze was their last contact before Prinze's suicide in 1977.

Jim was soon making the rounds with his stand-up on a variety of TV shows. One was Dinah Shore's show. Johnny Carson bandleader Doc Severinsen was another guest scheduled to appear the same day. Severinsen went on before Jim and shared a personal story about his battle with alcohol. As Jim watched from backstage, he realized that he needed to make a drastic change to the material he had planned to use. He was prepared to do his Cletus J. Hocker routine, the wino who cooked with wine. Jim realized how insensitive he would appear, and with Joe Liles' help, quickly explained the problem to the producers. The producers understood and supported him, even though they knew the new material wasn't going to be as strong or polished. "I'll always have a special respect for him doing that at that moment," says Liles. Severinsen and his manager later learned what had happened and were appreciative of Jim's sensitivity.

On October 19, 1976, Jim got a chance to display his talent on what comedians considered the ultimate television venue, "The Tonight Show Starring Johnny Carson." One of the show's scouts had seen Jim perform at The Comedy Store. Although the Carson people wanted Jim on the show, they didn't think that he was strong enough to appear when Carson was hosting. They scheduled Jim to be on when actor McLean Stephenson, famous for the TV series "M*A*S*H," was guest-hosting. While it was a pivotal opportunity, it prevented Jim from the possibility of obtaining the ultimate validation for a comic at the time – Johnny waving him over for a quick chat after the act. Doing so would instantly put the performer on the radar of the most powerful network executives and Hollywood casting agents.

Actor Jack Palance was one of the guests scheduled to appear on Carson the night Jim was to perform. Jim had just finished getting his makeup done when Jack Palance walked into the room. Jim said to Liles in a cowboy drawl, "Joseph Perry, that's the man who shot Shane," referring to Palance's Oscar-nominated gunfighter role in the movie "Shane." The makeup people thought it was funny, but Palance was visibly upset. Perhaps he had grown tired of being so closely associated with that role. Or perhaps it was the fact that a relative unknown talent had assumed he could joke around so openly with an established actor before being properly introduced. Whatever the reason, an awkward hush filled the room. Palance did not speak to Jim or acknowledge him afterward. Jim apologized, telling Palance how much he had loved him in the movie, but the damage was done.

Robert Blake, then the popular star of the hit detective show "Baretta," was hanging out backstage and recognized Jim from Merv Griffin's show. Jim was shaken up after what had happened in the makeup room. Blake assured him everything would be fine, and when Jim's name was called to go on, Blake placed his hand on Jim's back, pushed him toward the stage and hollered, "Go get 'em!"

Jim's performance was well received but not spectacular enough to provide any real boost to his career. Because of this, he still took advantage of any television opportunity, wherever it happened to be. As he did with "Johnny Cash and Friends," Jim traveled to Tennessee in August 1976 to perform on two episodes of the short-lived "Music Hall America." Taped in Opryland, the syndicated one-hour variety show featured comedy and music acts with rotating guest hosts.

Jim was also continuing work on his Sergeant Glory character for Carden & Cherry. Around November 1976, the agency flew him to Florida to shoot a commercial for a dairy. Jim had a scary experience at his hotel. He returned to his room exhausted from work, plopped down on his bed and drifted right to sleep. Someone broke in and stole the Rolex right off his wrist. Then they cut the pocket open on the blue jeans he was wearing and took his wallet. Sister Jake remembers Jim showing his mother the shirt he had been wearing, which had also been cut with a knife. Needless to say, it's fortunate Jim didn't wake up during the robbery.

Despite the fact that Carden & Cherry had sold Sergeant Glory to a few clients along with Purity, the character had finally run its course. John Cherry later admitted that he was still too inexperienced at the time to successfully parlay the character's success into additional markets. One thing he did know for sure was that Jim had talent. He later recalled, "Jim had that something, even then."

On one of Jim's visits home to Lexington he reunited with an old flame, Jackie Drew. He had found out from his sisters that she had recently divorced and was raising twin sons. He had developed a crush on Jackie in high school, and they had acted alongside each other in school plays. Jackie was tall and slender with long brown hair. One reporter interviewing her and Jim in 1982 wrote that she could pass for a model. She and Jim began dating, and on June 15, 1977, Jim's 28th birthday, they married in California. (It was also around this time that Jackie changed the spelling of her first name to Jacqui – and sometimes used Jaqi.) Jim now had the added responsibility of supporting a family while looking for his next big break.

THE IMPORTANCE OF BEING ERNEST:
THE LIFE OF ACTOR JIM VARNEY

Fortunately, Jim continued to find TV work. In the fall of 1977, Jim's Virgil Simms character began a recurring role on the Martin Mull and Fred Willard mock talk show, "Fernwood 2 Night." Fernwood was a spin-off from the TV show "Mary Hartman, Mary Hartman" and was produced by Norman Lear ("All in the Family," "Sanford and Son," "One Day at a Time," etc.) and Alan Thicke. Mull played the humorously glib host Barth Gimble, the twin brother of Garth Gimble whom he had played on "Mary Hartman." Willard was his foolish sidekick, Jerry Hubbard.

The show had the production values of local programming seen across much of the country, with its small stage and minimal set. Many guests were quirky characters from Middle America who provided easy targets for the show's host. Virgil Simms was a perfect fit.

Liles recalls the Virgil Simms character being created by Jim a couple of years earlier in Nashville. Virgil was originally conceived as a mechanic who worked at a gas station in the South. An early bit consisted of Virgil performing an oil change in exchange for a hit of acid from the car's hippie owner. The strength of the bit rested on Jim's ability to describe some of the crazy things he did in the garage while hallucinating. "I believe I put some Austin-Healey brake shoes on a Cadillac," recalled the mechanic in one of Jim's stand-up routines at the Exit/In. Many of the same elements of the mechanic on acid were used in one of his early appearances on Fernwood.

The character's unconventional qualities expanded even more when the talented Fernwood writers provided their input. Virgil's appearance consisted of polyester leisure suits that ranged in color from canary yellow to lime green. His greased-up, slicked-back hair and white shoes complemented his Southern charm.

Virgil also entertained with stories about moonlighting as an instructor at a community college, teaching a variety of oddball courses. In one episode, Virgil describes a new course he is teaching that offers truck drivers helpful advice and cooking tips when on the road. He explains to Barth just how inspiring a love song is to a lonely truck driver. In a follow-up appearance, Jim sings a tune called "Redneck Heaven" and shows off his knee-slapping hambone skills while belting out lyrics that reference moon pies and RC Cola.

Virgil, who idolized motorcycle daredevil Evel Knievel, was known as the mobile-home daredevil. During one episode, in a twist on Knievel's famous jumps, Virgil explains to Barth Gimble how he jumped over a row of motorcycles while driving a "fully equipped" Winnebago.

The opportunity for Jim to use one of his own characters in an improv setting was a refreshing change. Playing off the talents of people like Mull and Willard gave Jim's performances that much more of an impact. He made four appearances as Virgil on "Fernwood" during its first year. He appeared in three more episodes the following season (by then, the show's name had changed to "America 2-Night," for its location had changed from fictitious Fernwood, Ohio, to real-life Alta Coma, Calif.).

Jim also landed a part on an NBC pilot called "Riding High." Based on the 1975 movie "Hearts of the West," starring Jeff Bridges, "Riding High" followed the exploits of a writer of western novels hoping to live out his cowboy dreams. Although the pilot had been written by the noted Larry Gelbart of "M*A*S*H," it was not picked up by the network.

Jim's agent at William Morris soon found Jim an opportunity on another pilot that did get picked up by ABC. "Operation Petticoat" was a comedy starring John Astin and Richard Gilliland and based on the 1959 Cary Grant movie of the same name. The show follows the continuing adventures of a pink submarine (the color a result of having to mix what little red-and-white primer was available during hasty repairs) during World War II and its oddball crew, which includes a small group of attractive female nurses. Jim plays Seaman Broom, also referred to as "Doom and Gloom" Broom because of his habit of delivering troubling news. Jim's Southern accent helped him give a convincing portrayal of the West Virginia crewman. Jim's parents watched faithfully and came to the unbiased conclusion that Jim was the best one on the show. During one episode, they watched Jim's character get dumped into the Pacific Ocean. Louise was concerned, knowing Jim's inability to swim. Coincidentally, Jim called while they were watching. Jim assured Louise that he had never been in harm's way. Someone had coached him through enough of the basics to keep him afloat.

In the summer of 1978, ABC decided the large cast of "Petticoat" was too big to allow the show to be as funny as they had intended. They hired new producers and fired every cast member except Jim, Richard Brestoff and Melinda Naud. The changes proved ineffective, and low ratings prevented the show from completing a second season.

Liles visited Jim on the set at one of the last filmings of "Petticoat" for an important talk. Liles told Jim that he wanted Jim to look around and remember when and where he was when he heard what Liles was about to say. Liles then told him that when the show was over Jim should be prepared for at least six months to a year before anything of substance would happen career-wise. Liles assured him that he would be working hard, but it was a matter of getting the "machine" back up and running, finding a worthy project or creating one. Jim said he understood.

One of the hottest shows on TV at the time was the comedy "Alice." Like "Petticoat," it had been adapted from a popular movie. The show centers on a waitress named Alice, a recently widowed mother from New Jersey who has moved to Phoenix, Ariz., with her son looking to advance her singing career. Much of the show takes place at Mel's Diner, where Alice works alongside outspoken, man-crazy Flo; naïve and anxious Vera; and grumpy owner/cook Mel. In the fall of 1978, during the show's third season, Jim landed a guest-starring role as Flo's boyfriend, Milo Skinner. The episode, "Better Never Than Late," culminates with Flo and Milo foiling a robbery at the diner after Milo pulls a gun on the robber. It wasn't exactly James Bond, but Jim still got the girl and saved the day.

Jim continued performing stand-up while increasing his exposure through TV appearances, including return spots on "The Merv Griffin Show." Liles remembers Jim's last appearance on Griffin in the summer of 1979:

"Jim did a stand-up bit and sang 'Terrible Tawanna,' a song Jacqui wrote. The joke was that it was from a musical about a great white hunter in Africa. On the panel, he entertained Merv and (British actor) Michael York with various voices, impressions and dialects. He did several different British dialects, identifying them by the city. York sat back quite impressed, shook his head, smiled and said, 'Uncanny!'"

Along with an appearance on actor and singer Susan Anton's short-lived "Presenting Susan Anton" show, Jim appeared on comedian Norm Crosby's "The Comedy Shop." Actress Zsa Zsa Gabor was a special guest on the night Jim performed. Crosby asked Gabor to introduce Jim. The "v" in Varney gave Gabor trouble because of her Hungarian accent, but Crosby repeated Jim's name to allow everyone to clearly understand they were about to see a rising new talent. During his routine, Jim portrayed Cletus J. Hocker, the wino who hosted a show called "Cooking with Wine." Its entire premise was based on the fact that Cletus did not *cook* with wine, just under the influence of it. To add to the absurdity, Cletus suggested unconventional items as cooking aids, such as using a wine bottle as a rolling pin. Liles recalls how the character came about:

"Cletus J. Hocker was born in the car, (driving) in the Mojave Desert one hot night when we were on our way back to Nashville (from Los Angeles) to do the Cash summer series. Jim was in the passenger seat and started talking like a drunk and knocking around some lines about this guy hanging out near a dumpster and what he had found there. Soon it turned into a routine where this wino had a cooking-with-wine show. I threw out the name Cletus J. Hocker because I had seen it in a store window near South Mill Street (in Lexington, Ky.). Anyway, this guy had a sign in the window advertising his watch-repair business, and that was his name. Jim … agreed it was funny… (and) started using it."

Jim also landed an appearance on actor and comedian Alan King's one-hour special: "Alan King's Third Annual Final Warning." It was King's third edition of tips on how to survive the '70s. Also on the show were TV stars such as Gavin MacLeod of "Love Boat" and Hal Linden of "Barney Miller." Yet despite the television exposure and the company he was in, success in landing a permanent role on a network series continued to elude Jim.

Even though Liles had clearly warned him of a potential slowdown, Jim had a hard time dealing with it. He started drinking more, buying half-pints of whiskey that he referred to as "sipping whiskey." He was depressed, and the booze made his behavior obnoxious at times. As understanding as Liles was, he was tiring of Jim's conduct while still doing everything he could to advance his career.

Liles decided to create a show for Jim that could be pitched to the networks. Called "Jim Varney's Family Album," it was a

30-minute variety show that revolved around many of Jim's comedic characters. It was to be reminiscent of Sid Caesar and Imogene Coca's "Your Show of Shows," and the work of comedians like Monty Python and Ernie Kovacs. Liles went to Neiman Marcus and purchased a fancy leather-bound album with gold lettering and filled it with pictures of established characters of Jim's such as Virgil Simms and Cletus J. Hocker, among others. The proposal said: "The show will be devoid of: Named Guests, Known Songs, Lavish Sets, Beautiful Costumes, Breathtaking Dance Numbers and Other Redeeming Social Values. Each show will contain only original material and songs, unless they can be stolen from public domain. Nothing on the show should be construed as art." The entire thing was Liles' project, from concept to writing. It got attention at William Morris because it resembled a mini-pilot. It gave them something to show producers and network executives in order to get a dialogue started.

Meanwhile, in the summer of 1979 Liles was able to get Jim onto a comedy special airing on Showtime. Jim traveled to Houston to participate in "The Big Laff Off" at a new club called Rockefeller's. "Laff Off" was a stand-up comedy contest that pitted Jim against other talented young comics such as Ollie Joe Prater and Argus Hamilton. In describing Jim's act, Gregory Curtis of Texas Monthly called it, "an accomplished but slightly wearisome series of stories in a Kentucky hillbilly accent." Jim managed a second-place finish that included a cash prize. At the time, he needed the money just as much as the exposure.

On June 14, 1979, Jim began a two-week engagement opening for Mel Tillis at the Nugget outside Reno. Comedian Lonnie Shorr had recommended Jim to Tillis after working with Jim previously and being impressed with his act. Liles accompanied Jim and Jacqui while staying in touch with William Morris on the progress of the variety-show project. Jim's act was getting a warm reception, and he was hitting it off with Tillis. Then Liles received word from William Morris that a Fox TV executive was interested in "Family Album" and wanted to see Jim perform in a showcase – a small production that exposes actors to talent agents, producers and directors. Liles informed Jim of the good news and helped him prepare for the showcase, scheduled to take place when they returned to Los Angeles.

A week or two before the showcase, Jim and Jacqui went to a party one Sunday night. The next day they excitedly told Liles about an interesting couple they had met; they were looking forward to seeing them again soon. No names were mentioned, just that the couple had been "down to earth."

When Jim finally performed the showcase for the Fox TV executive, he was surprised to see that the executive was the husband of the couple he and Jacqui had met weeks before. Although Liles had told Jim the executive's full name repeatedly when discussing the show's status, Jim hadn't put it together when he had met him at the party.

The Fox executive passed on the show. It's unclear how the sequence of events may have played a part, whether the executive was offended that Jim didn't know who he was from the start or the like. The episode was the beginning of the end for Liles and Jim's business relationship. The mix-up, although minor in the scheme of things, encapsulated the difficulty Liles had been experiencing for some time in working with Jim. Jim seemed to be more interested in waiting for the next big thing to come along than putting forth the sustained effort required to make something concrete happen.

During the time Jim was in Reno opening for Mel Tillis, he and Jacqui had been invited out to visit Tillis' home in Nashville.

They decided to take him up on the offer and planned to go onto Lexington afterward to visit family and friends. Liles stayed in Los Angeles. While Jim and Jacqui were in Lexington, Liles received a call from Jim early one morning. Jim told Liles that he and Jacqui had been talking it over and decided that they should take over managing Jim's career. A couple of times in the past, usually on weekends when there was nothing to do but get in a stew or a funk, Jim had said to Liles that he wanted to fire him, drop William Morris and move back to Nashville. Liles had always managed to quietly "talk him off the ledge." This time, something clicked in Liles' head. He realized this was an opportunity for both of them to move on. When Jim paused to let his words sink in, which was usually the time where Liles started trying to talk him back into the relationship, Liles said instead that maybe that was a good idea, that Jim had a world-class agency behind him, he was now a familiar name in town and maybe they could do a better job of putting things together. Jim was a little taken aback. Liles said that he would give Jim all the information he needed to help make the transition as smooth as possible. Liles even assured Jim that he would be around to answer any questions or give advice.

The more Liles talked, the more he felt a burden being lifted from him. And Liles wouldn't have to worry about being blamed if Jim failed because it was Jim who was dumping him. After a surprised Jim let it all soak in, he agreed and they left it there. Liles knew that Jim did not expect it to end that way even though he had initiated it. Liles confessed, "Once we broke off the business relationship, I was on an adrenaline high for two days. I was just glad and relieved to be out of that situation." Liles always wished Jim well and helped him with situations over the years, but his assistance was limited to simple requests that never required extended involvement. Shortly after they parted, Jim's parents called

Liles to let him know they did not have any hard feelings. That meant a great deal to Liles after growing so close to the family over the years.

Not much happened for Jim for several months. He continued to do stand-up, playing in clubs as far down the coast as San Diego. It allowed him to make enough money to get by for a while. The year before, Jim had told Liles that he would "always be grateful" for Liles pushing him to do stand-up and helping him develop an act. It was something that he could always fall back on, he had told him.

Jim's next opportunity culminated in what has become one of the most famous TV failures of that era: the curiously titled "Pink Lady" show (aka "Pink Lady and Jeff"). Pink Lady was not an actual lady but a female Japanese singing duo consisting of Mie Nemoto and Kei Masuda, both 21. The attractive young pair had become a singing sensation in Japan. As they toured the world, their popularity grew. NBC president Fred Silverman noticed their success and decided to sign them to co-host a primetime variety show with stand-up comedian Jeff Altman in 1980.

Little did Silverman and the producers know that the songs the girls sang in English were memorized phonetically. The truth was that they could barely hold a conversation in English, which made learning comedic timing impossible. Jim later joked about the difficulties of creating comedy with an interpreter. Even though the girls struggled with the language barrier, Jim was impressed with their work ethic. He said they never complained about their workload despite having to keep up their concert appearances across the Pacific. He said their makeup was always perfect, and they never even seemed to break a sweat.

According to head writer Mark Evanier, when Jim was being cast, there was initial hesitation about Jim's looks by some people involved. But producer Marty Krofft insisted on Jim as the additional male sketch player. The struggling show suffered from numerous guest stars dropping out at the last minute (due to the show's increasingly low ratings) and resulting script changes. But on at least one occasion, that helped Jim. In one sketch, Buddy Ebsen was supposed to play Abe Lincoln. Jim filled in and was convincing as Lincoln being honored at a comedy roast.

Despite featuring popular guest stars and high-profile musical acts, the show's premise and the dying variety-show format proved too much to overcome. The show was cancelled before the sixth episode aired. Jim was out of work once again.

CHAPTER ELEVEN

BECOMING VERN'S FAVORITE NEIGHBOR

In July 1980, the Screen Actor's Guild (SAG) and the American Federation of Radio and Television Artists (AFTRA) began a strike in Hollywood when negotiations broke down over profits from the home-video market, including pay-TV and videocassette productions. All movie and primetime TV dramatic productions soon came to a halt. This was especially bad for Jim as he had already been without steady work for months. "There we were ... me, my wife and two sons living in Hollywood without work," Jim recalled in an interview a few years later. Running low on money and not knowing when the strike might end, Jim decided they should return home to Lexington. He had just over $1,000 to get his family and their belongings back to Kentucky.

Through the years Jim would repeatedly tell reporters that the strike was the reason he had left California. Liles always thought it was a convenient excuse. Despite the success Jim had experienced in California, Liles believes Jim never really felt like he fit in. Liles recalls the day they drove into town from Tennessee on Highway 405 from San Diego and seeing the Los Angeles skyline appear and stretch endlessly across the landscape. Liles observed a noticeable change in Jim's demeanor, going from happy to subdued, that lasted his entire stay on the West Coast.

The truth was that Jim had burned a few bridges – including some at William Morris - and the word around The Comedy Store was that he had stopped growing as an artist. It seemed that Mary Warner Ford's words might be coming true: Jim had the talent but not the discipline. It also didn't help that California was so far away from Kentucky, and all those miles made his homesickness that much worse.

With no real paying acting work available after moving back to Kentucky, Jim settled for a job driving a truck transporting crane parts for a company working for moving firm Vincent-Fister. Jake's husband, Jim McIntyre, got him the job. Jim never could have imagined when walking out onto the stage of "The Tonight Show" that he would be back in Kentucky four years later completely out of show business. After a month of driving a few loads to Cincinnati from Lexington, Jim decided the work was not for him. He managed to find other odd jobs such as laying tile. He did what he had to in order to provide for his family. He, Jacqui and the boys lived for a short while in an A-frame in Nonesuch, Ky. They eventually moved in with Jacqui's grandmother in Lexington. This was not how Jim, now 31, had envisioned his life at this stage.

Away from performing, Jim grew deeply depressed. Even though he had never "hit it big" in Los Angeles, he had still put together quite a resume. Now he was back home in Kentucky, seemingly starting from scratch and struggling to make ends meet. Beginning at the age of 8, his life had been consumed with acting. His journey had taken him far beyond the regional-theater circuit and nightclubs to which many people had assumed his career would be confined. In California he had appeared on the three major networks and had rubbed elbows with many of the biggest stars in the business. To return home with no future prospects was devastating.

Liles had always thought that when Jim moved back home from California he would eventually find work again in Nashville. What he could not have predicted was that Jim would find an acting role there that would bestow upon him more success – at least commercially – than he might have ever found in Los Angeles.

In Bowling Green, Ky., country singer Ronnie Milsap had recently purchased a theme park named Beech Bend. In addition to Milsap's name recognition, the park desperately needed a boost to help it compete with places like Opryland in nearby Nashville that had larger, more modern rides and far more attractive grounds. Along with changes planned for the park itself, a new ad campaign was in the works to highlight the park's affordable activities. John Cherry and Thom Ferrell, who was working with the Carden & Cherry agency as a consultant, began working with Beech Bend developing TV commercials. "We developed Ernest coming back from Beech Bend in one day. It was a creative session that lasted until the wee hours of the morning," recalled Cherry in a 1980 article in The Tennessean newspaper.

During my interview with Thom Ferrell, he discussed in greater detail the advertising approach that led to the birth of Ernest:

"I had been producing commercials for Opryland as well as for Six Flags. Buster (John Cherry) and Jerry Carden called me over to discuss their new account, Beech Bend. I said I would go up and scout for shooting possibilities and report my findings as to what they could do for a TV commercial. After seeing the park, I told Buster and Jerry showing the park would be a mistake at this time due to its condition (the log flume ride had algae in it). I suggested using a spokesman in some way until the improvements had been made by the new owner (Ronnie Milsap).

"Buster and I then got together over a bunch of beers and decided on an obnoxious neighbor telling about the park. Hence, Ernest was patterned after the warehouse employee who worked for Buster's dad's electrical supply company. ... we both knew (he) was a pain in the ass. The neighbor (Vern) was patterned after my State Farm insurance man (Vernon), who would be less likely to want to be annoyed by Ernest."

Perhaps there was synchronicity at work. The inspiration for Vern was a man who worked for State Farm. That company's popular tagline was and is "Like a Good Neighbor." Ernest would become the ultimate annoying neighbor.

After getting the premise down for the Beech Bend ads, all that remained was finding an actor to play Ernest. According to Ferrell, Jim was the first and only person considered. With Jim out of acting and living back in Kentucky, the timing could not have been better. Although Jim had no idea what the character would eventually mean to him and the culture at large, he was excited about the opportunity for paying work as an actor. Soon Jim was driving down to Nashville.

Because of the limited budget, the Vernon character would essentially be played by the cameraman, with the TV audience experiencing Ernest through Vernon's point of view. In the years that followed, Ernest came to refer to Vernon as just plain Vern.

Since Beech Bend could not offer the same caliber of rides as Opryland, Ernest humorously highlighted the fact that a family could spend a lot less money and still have a great time. Ernest also promoted such events as the J. R. look-alike contest (inspired by the star of the hit TV show at the time, "Dallas") and an appearance by the Dallas Cowboys cheerleaders. John Cherry used his own Nashville residence to shoot the commercials after being less than impressed with the scruffy appearance of the park.

The commercials ran for five weeks and were extremely popular, even winning awards. Although business picked up for a while, the park couldn't live up to Ernest's hype and closed shortly after the commercials aired. Since Ernest had been tailored specifically for Beech Bend, he was shelved for over a year, as the agency wasn't quite sure how to pitch the character to other clients.

Ernest seemed destined for the same fate as Sergeant Glory until a company that had previously used the Glory character became interested in Carden & Cherry's newest Jim Varney creation. Purity Dairies of Nashville liked the way Ernest appealed to children in the Beech Bend ads and thought he was a perfect fit for selling their milk and ice-cream products. In the latter part of 1981, Purity signed onto the Ernest campaign, and Jim's face was soon stretched across billboards and TV screens in Nashville. In Raleigh, N.C., Pine State Dairies also signed up.

Meanwhile, Jim was still trying to land a role in a TV series. In April 1982, he was cast in a pilot for NBC called, "The Show Must Go On." The hour-long show was hosted by actor E.G. Marshall and focused on the behind-the-scenes trials and tribulations of a stage show. In the end, it became yet another entry in the growing list of failed TV pilots on Jim's resume. Fortunately, Jim soon had all the work he could handle shooting commercials and making public appearances for Ernest's growing list of dairy clients.

With the money Ernest was beginning to bring in, Jim was finally able to afford his first house. In the summer of 1982, Jacqui and the boys moved from Lexington with Jim to their new home just north of Nashville in White House, Tenn. Ernest was now a full-time job, and the family had to adjust.

After Purity and Pine State, around three dozen dairies in the South and Midwest soon bought into Ernest's selling power. At this point, Ernest was becoming a hot commodity. The character and his brand of humor had tapped into a seldom-touched market of rural America, one especially rare for television advertising. Yet by far that wasn't the only place where Ernest was gaining fans. There seemed to be something about Ernest's slapstick humor that appealed to people from all walks of life. Carden & Cherry continued to win advertising awards for Ernest while pitching the character to businesses outside the dairy segment. Before long, Ernest was in 80 markets throughout the country.

In addition to Cherry and his team of writers, many others at the agency were involved in the huge task of handling the Ernest machine. Jerry Carden, John Cherry's partner in the company, oversaw the agency's account executives. John Cherry once joked, "Jerry's got the real creative part, dealing with the clients." One of the people who also dealt with his fair share of clients was Roy Lightner, vice president of marketing. If anyone could take on the enormous task of selling Ernest it was Lightner. He had spent most of his career working for N.W. Ayer & Son, the oldest advertising agency in the country. From Boston to New York, he had worked with big companies such as Goodyear, DuPont, Chrysler and Texaco. He retired in 1980 and moved to Nashville. After a short stint directing a television-ministry campaign, Lightner found himself in advertising once again. In early 1982, at the age of 60, Lightner joined Carden & Cherry and was soon logging thousands of miles a year, as he became an integral part of spreading Ernest across the country.

Lightner credits his success to clean living. Instead of hanging out in bars when he was out of town selling Ernest, he used his downtime to study up on prospective clients. He still lived by the slogan of N.W. Ayer and Son: "Keeping everlastingly at it brings success." His work ethic and boundless enthusiasm for Ernest proved a successful combination.

Although Lightner and Jim technically never worked "together," Jim helped Lightner's efforts by being accommodating to the new clients that Roy brought to the commercial shoots. Jim and Lightner got along well, and Jim enjoyed poking fun at Lightner's "buttoned up" demeanor: One time he gave Lightner an earring as a gift. To Jim's surprise, Lightner put it on. A picture of Lightner sporting the earring hung on the fridge door in the kitchen at Carden & Cherry for years.

Jim continued to pursue other acting opportunities, hoping to capitalize on his recent success. One was teaming up with Ferrell's production company to star in a 20-minute trailer promo called "Dillard and The Devil's Music." It was a project that Ferrell and Cherry had put together with a TV movie in mind. Jim played the part of an old wino, Dillard P. Simpson, who had been recruited by an angel in a battle between good and evil, where music was used to lure lost souls. Dillard was made to perform his duties while living a genie-like existence inside an old beer can. After a struggling young musician comes across the can on a street, he soon meets Dillard, who offers him assistance. Unfortunately, nothing ever came of the project.

In the fall of 1982, Jim landed his first TV series since the failed "Pink Lady." He was cast as a regular in the half-hour country music variety series "Tom T. Hall's Pop! Goes the Country" in Nashville. Country music singer-songwriter Hall had recently taken over as host from noted country DJ Ralph Emery (a change reflected in the show's title, which had previously just been "Pop! Goes the Country"). The show's tapings had moved from the Opry

THE IMPORTANCE OF BEING ERNEST: THE LIFE OF ACTOR JIM VARNEY

House to Opryland USA's Gaslight Theatre, and the set was made over with a nightclub feel. The main character Jim portrayed was a "totally cool" California hipster named Bobby Burbank. Bobby, like Ernest, believed he was much cooler than he actually was and usually found himself the butt of the joke. In addition, Jim was able to introduce some of his stand-up characters to a new audience, such as his sassy southern beauty queen, Bunny Jeanette. He wore bright-blue eye make-up, thick red lipstick and a big blonde curly wig when portraying Bunny as a cocktail waitress. In just a few years since the actor's strike, Jim's career was back on track. While not following the path he had originally dreamed of, he was finding consistent work as an actor and making enough money to provide for his family. Jim's aspirations of becoming a touted character actor once again felt within reach.

But before the 26 taped episodes of "Pop Goes the Country" featuring Jim could air, legal issues had to be worked out. Jim had recently filed suit against his new agent, Aubrey Mayhew, who had been representing him since January 1981. Jim wanted to void his contract on the grounds of non-performance. He claimed that Mayhew had not lived up to many of the promises he had originally made. Liles says Jim told him that Mayhew wanted Jim to perform stand-up wherever he happened to locate a gig, no matter where it was. That was not the type of career-boosting work Jim had envisioned when signing with Mayhew, who had started Little Darlin' records in the '60s and had launched the career of country singer Johnny Paycheck and other artists.

Mayhew countersued, arguing that Jim "refused or neglected to come to Nashville (from Lexington) for the purpose of recording and preparing him for his career." In addition, Mayhew wanted 50 percent of Jim's income from his commercial and TV appearances, and included Purity, Carden & Cherry, and Show Biz (the company that distributed "Tom T's Pop! Goes the Country Club") in his cross-complaint. Both sides eventually settled with Jim being ordered to pay Mayhew back the $2,000 that Mayhew had loaned him at the beginning of their association. Betty Clark, whose Nashville talent agency had worked with Jim the previous ten years, soon took over as Jim's manager.

Meanwhile, Jim continued to do stand-up at clubs in and around Nashville. His wife, Jacqui, helped write many of the routines and sometimes joined him onstage. At the famous Bluebird Café, the two performed what Jacqui joked was "kind of a Benny Hillbilly show." One of their acts was a parody on the life and times of Mr. and Mrs. Marlin Perkins. Marlin Perkins was host of the long-running TV show "Mutual of Omaha's Wild Kingdom."

The next opportunity for acting came in 1983 when Jim was offered a role on a new TV show for NBC called "The Rousters." Jim's character, Evan Earp, and his brother, Wyatt Earp III (played by Chad Everett of the beloved TV series "Medical Center"), were great-grandsons of Wyatt Earp, the famous gunfighter of the American West. In the show, Wyatt works as a bouncer for a traveling carnival while his gun-toting mother attempts to keep the family's violent legacy alive by finding work as a bounty hunter. "The Rousters" was one of many shows from the late, legendary TV producer Stephen J. Cannell, whose long list of hits included "The Rockford Files," "Baretta," "The Greatest American Hero" and later, "The A-Team" and "21 Jump Street." According to Jo Swerling Jr., executive producer of "The Rousters," "When Cannell wrote the pilot, he wrote the role of Evan for Varney after seeing his tapes." With a cast that included other noted actors such as Mimi Rogers and Hoyt Axton, hopes were high that it could be another Cannell hit.

The "Rousters" pilot was taped in April, and in May NBC added it to their fall schedule. Jim was surprised and excited when he heard the news. He planned a temporary move to Los Angeles over the summer with Jacqui and the boys; he wanted them close by while he worked. Jim had come to love his stepsons as if they were his own flesh and blood.

During the show's short run, it was pre-empted twice and shifted to different nights, which took a toll on ratings. Even though Jim thought it was a quality show, it didn't make it past the first season.

The demands of filming an hour-long TV show were immense. It was the most grueling work schedule Jim had ever experienced professionally. Jacqui and the boys had ended up remaining at home in Tennessee during his time shooting. The long stretches away from family proved too great a strain on the marriage, and Jacqui asked for a divorce. Jim was devastated, having thought so many of his struggles were behind him.

Yet he barely had time to dwell on the divorce or his cancelled show, as the Ernest clients kept growing. The character was becoming a household name. Jim had actually been flying back and forth from Los Angeles to Nashville during the shooting of "The Rousters" to keep the Ernest commercials going.

Back in Jim's hometown, everyone was reading about his latest successes in the Lexington Herald-Leader. Reporters from the paper interviewed him many times. In one piece, Jim spoke of his newfound stardom and gave insight into what drove him as an actor. He said, "I never really wanted to be a star, though ... I think that term is badly overused. I just always wanted to act and entertain people." Jim also discussed his long-held desire of doing serious acting, perhaps even playing a villain. Jim's mother was interviewed for one story and remarked, "He looks so funny as Ernest that it's kind of strange to think that he used to do Shakespeare."

Lexington was also enjoying its first glimpse of Jim as Ernest, as his Convenient Food Mart commercials began playing in the area. Les Bosse, advertising director for Convenient's parent company, Conna Corp of Louisville, said then, "It's possibly the best advertising campaign we've ever had." Like so many clients of Carden & Cherry, Conna Corp. received countless letters asking who Ernest was and how many more commercials were set to air.

In March 1984, the Kentucky State Senate passed a resolution honoring Jim. His father accompanied him to Frankfort where senators gave him a standing ovation. The Woodford Sun, a nearby newspaper, covered the event and printed a photo of Jim and his father meeting with Governor Martha Layne Collins. Jim's father carried a copy of that newspaper photo folded up in his billfold until the day he died. To have such an honor bestowed on his son obviously made him proud and perhaps served as validation of the type of man he had always hoped Jim would become.

Jim's celebrity status was gaining him invitations to a variety of social functions, including prominent ones in his home state. Beginning in the 1950s, Hamburg Place, the noted horse farm, was the site of the famous Derby Eve party thrown every year by owner-socialite Anita Madden and her husband. The star-studded parties were always exhibitions of Southern opulence and then some. Many had themes such as "Rapture of the Deep" and "Ultimate Odyssey," which featured males and females dressed as Greek gods. In May 1984, Jim was a celebrity guest at the event, held on the same grounds where he had once parked cars for his father and where his grandfather had once worked as a horseman and gardener.

Although Jim was understandably popular in Lexington and Nashville, other states were just as crazy over him. In truth, Ernest was going viral, appealing to the country's blue-collar workers, people with Southern roots and anyone else who appreciated Ernest's kooky, down-home style. A Tulsa, Okla., TV station where Ernest commercials aired for Braum's groceries had to go to special lengths to deal with the flood of phone calls about Ernest. The station actually ran a special message on the screen early each morning to inform viewers of the times the commercials would air. Customers at a Braum's market in Choctaw, Okla., which had served as a shooting location for an Ernest commercial, would act out scenes from the commercial filmed there. It involved Ernest taking cottage cheese from the dairy case and dancing with it while approaching the checkout counter.

In another much-loved commercial, Ernest climbs to the top of Vern's ladder. Pushy Ernest interrupts Vern, who is on the roof, to tell him about the latest product he needs to buy. Vern doesn't respond but just kicks out the ladder, sending Ernest falling backward into the yard. Many of Ernest's intrusions left Jim with bumps, bruises, even burns. Another popular commercial shows Ernest interrupting Vern's outdoor cookout by hovering over his grill and giving him his (usual) unwarranted advice. Vern – again, always a man of few words – doesn't bother to tell Ernest about the grill being hot and gets the last laugh when Ernest leans on it and is scorched.

As the interest in Ernest continued to take on a life of its own, a TV special centering on the character and his back story seemed fitting. The result: a one-hour syndicated TV special called "Hey Vern, It's My Family Album." Originally referred to in some news articles as "The Ernest 'n' Vern Comedy Special," the show was filmed in Nashville during the spring of 1984. Consisting of six sketches, each introduced by Ernest, the special highlighted some of his peculiar family members. One member it didn't feature was Edna, a woman Ernest occasionally mentioned in the commercials.

BECOMING VERN'S FAVORITE NEIGHBOR

She, like Vern, was always offscreen. Viewers were led to assume that she was likely his wife. (Author's note: Apart from having "Family Album" in their titles, there is virtually no similarity between this special and the variety show Joe Liles pitched in the late 1970s. And, unless Jim mentioned it to them, I believe it is doubtful any of the Ernest writers knew of its existence.)

In each sketch of the show, Jim portrays humorous characters outside of Ernest. Many people thought some of them were funnier than Ernest. One is Lloyd Worrell, adapted from his stand-up character Loyd Roe. Along with a second "l" added to his first name, Lloyd's last name has been changed and the character reinvented as Ernest's great-uncle. Ernest claims, as Jim did in his stand-up routine, that Lloyd is the meanest man in the world. In the special, the distinction is even stated on Lloyd's dilapidated mailbox, which reads "Lloyd Worrell, MMW." "<u>Meanest</u> Man in the World" is written just below it.

In the show, Jim plays the part of Lloyd in full costume and makeup. His clothing is ragged, resembling that worn by Jed Clampett, TV's hillbilly billionaire. In this version, with missing teeth and a hunched-over stance, Lloyd is more downtrodden than his stand-up character but still mean as a snake.

In the skit, Lloyd has a wife named Ruth along with a son, Mistake. They live in a rural ramshackle house surrounded by a yard littered with scrap. The family is so poor they actually pretend to eat. Lloyd sits at a table, and Ruth brings him an empty plate. He takes his knife and fork and begins to cut into his imaginary steak after telling his wife he had been looking forward to eating lobster. Even when escaping into the momentary comfort of an imaginary world, poor ol' Lloyd still ends up deprived.

Charlie Chaplin had explored the idea of starvation-induced lunacy nearly 60 years earlier in the silent film "The Gold Rush."

THE IMPORTANCE OF BEING ERNEST:
THE LIFE OF ACTOR JIM VARNEY

In it, Chaplin's gold-prospector character becomes so hungry that he resorts to boiling his right shoe on the stove. After sitting down at the table to eat his leather entrée, he has to fight off fellow prospector Big Jim for what they both think is the most appetizing part.

Meanwhile, after getting his fill of make-believe steak, Lloyd's foul mood returns. His son, Mistake, becomes the focus of Lloyd's physical and verbal assaults. A full-grown man much larger than Jim portrays 8-year-old Mistake. Being far too big a boy for Lloyd to administer corporal punishment, Lloyd concludes that the best way to keep his son under control is to "work on him Psych-ah-logikly." (One has to question, though, just how effective anyone who pretends to eat will be using psychology to influence someone else.)

After Mistake's initial hesitation, Lloyd convinces him that it's time for bed. Once Mistake is tucked in, Lloyd proceeds to read him a bedtime story from the Yellow Pages. Referring to it as "The big book," Lloyd quotes entries as if it were the Bible.

He goes on to read to Mistake a supposedly prophetic bedtime story about the boy's life that concludes with Mistake falling off the edge of the world and mashing his finger. Mistake gets the last laugh when he grabs a toy – a boulder-sized rock – from behind his bed and hurls it at Lloyd, smashing his father into the wall.

The show aired in the 80 or so markets across the country where Ernest ads were already popular. The Ernest clients in those markets benefited from the added exposure of their star salesman. Although the special was clearly a vehicle promoting Ernest, it also resembled something of a demo reel of characters that Jim hoped might catch the eye of a TV or movie producer.

In Nashville, Ernest's home base, a special premiere was held at the Tennessee State Fairgrounds. Fans were treated to "fancy" appetizers such as crème-filled Pattycakes and Goo Goo Clusters served with milk and orange juice. Jim, dressed as Ernest, arrived, fittingly, on a Nashville metro bus.

Ernest was now moving into so many markets, it was inevitable that the story of the character's success would reach the national scene. In 1984, two of the three major networks shined a spotlight on the advertising phenomenon. Dan Rather and the CBS Evening News covered the Ernest craze and did a follow-up story the following year. In the second piece were commercial clips, behind-the-scenes footage, interview segments with Jim and John Cherry, and a look at the variety of Ernest merchandise Jim's popularity had spawned. One of the funniest moments was a clip of Ernest making an appearance at a Clemson football game when a male police officer rushed onto the field to kiss him on the cheek. The last commercial shown in the CBS story must have really gotten to Rather, who was watching the pre-recorded segment from his desk. Vern's hands are seen opening a heart-shaped box of chocolates only to find Ernest's face protruding out of the center. Ernest, alternating between looking at the camera and looking at his right toward some of the chocolates, says, "Be mine, Vern! Hand me that caramel!" As Rather returned on-camera, his eyes were watering and he confessed, laughing; "We lose it sometimes ... we're losing it now."

On ABC's "Good Morning America," Jim enjoyed the rare opportunity to participate in a nationally aired live studio interview. Appearing as himself, dressed in a sweater with a dress-shirt collar exposed, Jim sat across from host Joan Lunden. Much of Jim's warmth and charm came across, and he actually appeared slightly shy and somewhat reserved, as many comedians do when they're not in character. But it may have had as much to do with Lunden's movie-star looks as it did with Jim appearing live in front of a national audience.

THE IMPORTANCE OF BEING ERNEST:
THE LIFE OF ACTOR JIM VARNEY

In March 1985, Ernest finally landed on the third major network when Tom Brokaw covered the Ernest craze on the "NBC Nightly News." The introduction to the segment showed Jim in full Shakespeare attire, reciting lines on an empty stage. That was followed with the story of Ernest's rise to fame and continued popularity. The segment concluded by returning to Jim reciting Shakespeare. In what may be one of the funniest screen moments of Jim's career, he turned to the camera after delivering a line from Hamlet and said, "Know what I mean Vern?" It was all Brokaw could do to keep a straight face as he said good night to viewers.

CHAPTER TWELVE

THE SECRET OF ERNEST'S SUCCESS

Jim always told interviewers that Charlie Chaplin was his biggest influence when it came to Ernest. Jim said once, "Physical comedy is a comedy that works in any language, and Chaplin knew that. His success was based on the fact that he never opened his mouth to get a laugh. I think people like physical comedy, which is why cartoons are so successful." Another time Jim said, "I try to make (Ernest) clownish and I don't want him too low-key, and he's physically funny."

Although they were eras apart, the two shared common traits. Both actors used their expressive faces to draw an audience in and evoke sympathy despite their mischievous ways. While Jim worked in the era of sound, like Chaplin he still used his face to give expressions like "Eeeeewwww" a cartoonish look.

And like Chaplin, Jim was at his funniest when he didn't speak (or barely did). In a courtroom scene of the movie "Ernest Goes to Jail," Ernest, serving as a juror, tries to be as quiet as possible while dealing with a pen that explodes in his mouth. His attempts to use a piece of paper to soak up the ink only make things worse. He becomes so frantic about hiding the mess that he resorts to eating the ink-soaked paper. In another commercial, Ernest inspects a bag of potato chips as he feels all around, turning it on its side, looking more and more desperate as he examines it. At the very end, he realizes there are no chips left and cries, "All gone!" before smashing the empty bag into his face. Ernest is literally left holding the bag. John Cherry admitted later that Jim had come up with much of the bit on the spot, leaving the crew cracking up.

Even Chaplin's relationship with Mack Sennett mirrored the one between Jim and John Cherry. Sennett, like Cherry, allowed his star to have quite a bit of creative input.

Before Chaplin came along, Sennett's Keystone Film Company had introduced the world to the Keystone Cops, whose comic influence has been enormous. Movies like "Police Academy" and "Smokey and the Bandit" have carried on the Keystone formula through the years. Even the popular TV series "Dukes of Hazzard" features bumbling cops getting big laughs. The more arrogant the lawman, the more enjoyable for the audience to see him stumble. The same type of routine played out time and again in the Ernest commercials, where Ernest always pays a price for being so obnoxious to neighbor Vern.

Sennett's rival, Hal Roach, brought Laurel and Hardy to the big screen. Roach's slapstick masterpieces also shaped much of Jim's appreciation of comedy in his formative years. Jim often mentioned both Sennett and Roach when discussing his influences.

Jim never felt playing the fool was beneath him. He took satisfaction in the fact that many actors would not be fearless enough to be so outrageous or look so silly. Any actor the least bit obsessed with his or her looks would not want to see themselves close up in a wide-angle lens. He also thought he was excelling in a type of acting that was more difficult than many assumed. In a 1987 television interview with WKBW out of Buffalo, N.Y., Jim said, "You can do a dramatic scene 14 different ways. If you don't tell a joke the right way, if the punch line's timing is off, it's not funny."

THE SECRET OF ERNEST'S SUCCESS

Because the character of the fool had been so significant in many of Shakespeare's plays, Jim had a sense of pride carrying on the tradition ... even if his fool was hawking ice cream on TV.

Jim often mentioned his Shakespeare background when discussing the discipline it instilled in his acting. It assisted him in memorizing the multiple scripts he was responsible for in a single shooting day. Ernest writer Glenn Petach said once, "Jim could look at a script for 10 minutes and have it memorized entirely." Another Ernest writer, Coke Sams, was equally amazed. He remembered, "It could be WWKD, WWJR, and then WWM – he would switch call letters. He could focus so completely that he allowed a level of production none of us had ever seen before or since, actually." Jim told the Daily Oklahoman in 1987, "I can learn scripts faster than anybody alive." The skill proved valuable since cue cards were nearly impossible to use with Jim so close to the camera lens. Jim's gift for memorization gave him the ability to use his focus on finding ways to make every commercial funnier.

Jim once offered a simplified explanation of the process of an Ernest commercial. It revealed how his brain had become hardwired to the formula. "We've got just 30 seconds to do the pitch, set up the punch line and then punch it. Actually it takes 28.8 seconds. By now, I have a 30-second timer in my head."

John Cherry was always complimentary of Jim's portrayal of Ernest. Even before the success of any of the Ernest movies, he told an advertising magazine, "One of the reasons Jim is so good is because he gives you 100 percent." He would even compare Jim to Chaplin by describing the way Jim used his facial expressions to draw in an audience. No matter how much praise was showered upon Cherry for his role in the character's incarnation and success, he always said, "If there wasn't a Jim Varney there wouldn't be an Ernest at all."

THE IMPORTANCE OF BEING ERNEST: THE LIFE OF ACTOR JIM VARNEY

Although Chaplin provided Jim with much of his slapstick inspiration, some fans thought the Ernest T. Bass character from "The Andy Griffith Show" had provided the blueprint. Those fans may have been residents of North Carolina, home to both the fictional Mayberry and one of Ernest's first clients, Pine State Dairies. Although both characters share the same name and reflect hillbilly stereotypes, Ernest T. Bass was definitely not the inspiration. As discussed earlier, Ernest was based on a man who had worked with Cherry's father "… the most obnoxious person" Cherry had ever met.

Jim easily adapted to the persona of the overbearing, know-it-all good ol' boy. Perhaps there was no better description of Ernest's resume than one made by Jim to a newspaper in 1985: "He's an inventor. He cross-breeds small appliances and power tools." As far as Ernest's last name was concerned, Cherry said he got it from a former State Treasurer of Tennessee. Cherry always thought that when someone said "Worrell" it sounded like they had marbles in their mouth.

Due to the limited budget in the beginning, it was decided that cameraman Jim May, reacting to Jim's movements with a hand-held camera, would, in essence, play Vern. Writer Coke Sams recalled, "It was cheaper to throw a camera on some guy's shoulder, and it made the commercials more active." The arrangement became permanent as it was evident the camera movements also added a more intimate feel, while the wide-angle lens magnified Jim's contorted facial expressions.

Jim May occasionally received assistance, combined with dazzling special effects. Cherry sometimes served as Vern's voice, and writer Sams did everything from making mini pancakes rain down on Ernest's head to kicking the ladder away from the roof in one of their most popular bits.

THE SECRET OF ERNEST'S SUCCESS

From the beginning, Cherry's Nashville home served as command central. From piling film crews into bedrooms to utilizing sections of the roof where Jim could be pushed off a ladder, Cherry regularly sacrificed his residence to provide a low-cost, local-looking shoot.

The small production scale helped the film crew crank out multiple commercials a day. Cherry would have multiple sets prepared so the crew could immediately go to the next commercial. The whole thing was so efficient that filming 16 commercials a day became the norm.

Because of the physicality in so much of Ernest's performances, injuries were always a danger. In one instance, Jim could have very well lost an eye. The commercial shows Ernest popping in on Vern while Vern plays darts. Ernest stands directly in front of Vern, who would not mind using Ernest's nose for a bull's eye. After a few lines during the filming, Jim and Sams got out of sync, and Sams threw a dart that whizzed within inches of Jim's face. The crew in the room fell silent.

But Jim never backed away from doing everything he could to make each stunt as realistic as possible. The small sickly kid who never lived up to the athletic expectations of his father was actually so successful at physical comedy *because* of his athleticism. Coke Sams once said, "With all of the physical comedy, he was just ripped. He was one of those guys who was incredibly strong for his weight and size." In the ever-popular window-slam bit, the small block that protected Jim's fingers sometimes prevented the window from landing without the right amount of force. Jim occasionally removed the block and endured the pain for the sake of comedy. Luckily, he never suffered a major injury beyond a chipped tooth and occasional bumps and bruises.

THE IMPORTANCE OF BEING ERNEST:
THE LIFE OF ACTOR JIM VARNEY

The Ernest commercials never graduated to fancy sets or expensive effects. As Cherry once said, "You're buying entertainment ... not beautiful product shots." The focus was always Jim's performance. Beyond Jim's magic and Cherry's direction, it was the writers who provided the funny scripts and imaginative ideas that ended up winning countless awards. Cherry, one of the writers himself, was surrounded by an equally talented team for years: Coke Sams, Dan Butler, Glenn Petach, Steve Leasure and the late Gil Templeton. After displaying their talent for commercials, they went on to write for the Ernest character as he moved into TV and movies. They proved that writers in Nashville could pen more than country songs.

Much of the success of these projects was due to the collaboration between Cherry and Studio Productions (which later became Ruckus Film). Studio was founded in 1979 by Coke Sams, Jim May and Mary Matthews. Sams took over some of the writing duties while May focused on cinematography. Their long tenure with Ernest made them an instrumental part of the character's success.

Yet ultimately, it was the relationship between Jim and John Cherry that was key to Ernest's success. According to Sams, "Cherry would ask you to do anything, and Jim would try to do anything." Sams believes that they were lucky to run into each other because each man was so essential to the other's success.

Cherry was aware that a commercial would sometimes read funnier than what happened during filming. Other times the opposite happened: A small change could make an average script work much better. He wouldn't try and push what was thought to be a funny premise if it just wasn't working.

In addition, Cherry invited collaboration on the set – not only Jim and the writers but anyone willing to speak up. Jim said once,

THE SECRET OF ERNEST'S SUCCESS

"Everybody on the crew, even a grip, feels free to contribute to the commercials. Anybody can come up with the payoff line."

The brainstorming got Ernest into some of the most ridiculous situations imaginable, from carving a turkey with a chainsaw to hanging upside-down in a chimney dressed as Santa Claus. Jim said that there was even a "dumb scale" they had established from these sessions. One commercial known as "Bobbing for water," where Ernest dunks his face into a large tub, was once at the top of the list.

As popular as Ernest was becoming, Cherry was aware that the commercials remained far from a "love at first sight" experience for numerous television viewers. In Ernest's early years, Purity Dairies dealt with upset viewers after commercials aired showing Ernest taking a milk bath. Some customers threatened to boycott their products. One man who called complained, "A repulsive-looking man in a tub of milk is anything but appetizing." Fortunately, Purity kept the ads going, and viewers soon warmed to Ernest's antics. Similar scenarios played out many times over the years. Cherry continually assured clients that many of the same people who initially complained would later become some of Ernest's biggest fans, and businesses would see sales climb. In the end, TV stations and clients almost always ended up getting calls from the public asking when the commercials would air again.

Even though some viewers would never be won over by Ernest, a growing client list proved that the numbers were in Ernest's favor. Cherry admitted of his creation, "Some people love him; some people hate him. Fortunately, more people love him."

Cherry and Jim were asked repeatedly in interviews what their theories were for Ernest's immense popularity and staying power. Cherry took the subject seriously. One aspect that Cherry mentioned in explaining why such an obnoxious character connected with people was the fact that he was vulnerable. This allowed Ernest, despite his obnoxiousness, to generate enough empathy to win over audiences. In the end, everyone could laugh and perhaps identify with him in some way. Jim always thought that Ernest was just like someone everybody probably knew, be it friend, family member, co-worker or neighbor.

In a 2009 appearance on "Inside the Actors Studio," actor/comedian Ricky Gervais discussed some of these very same qualities as they related to comedy. Gervais said, "The most important thing in comedy is empathy." He then continued, "Laurel and Hardy got it right 100 years ago, and it hasn't been improved upon."

Laurel and Hardy had been two of Jim's favorite comedians as a child. And Jim's expressive face and ability to connect with viewers helped bring about his own brand of empathy and, in one memorable Christmas commercial, a good amount of sympathy. The commercial, "Love Thy Neighbor," aired in two parts within days of each other. The first showed Ernest being excluded from a Christmas party, with Vern shutting the front door in Ernest's face. Many viewers called Carden & Cherry outraged that they would do something like that to poor ol' Ernest during the holidays. They had no idea that the upcoming second part showed Ernest nailing Vern in the face with a snowball while yelling, "Happy New Year Vernon!" It was the upset reaction from viewers to Ernest being shut out that seemed to convince Cherry that Ernest was a sympathetic enough character to someday carry a feature-length film.

Cherry also said once, "If you can find something that will entertain while it sells, you have a winner." Ernest clients loved the fact that the commercials were not only original and funny but created a strong, positive product identification. Cream o'Weber dairies once gave a viewer survey to test how well its Ernest commercials were connecting with viewers. They found that 96 percent remembered the character, and 91 percent remembered the product. Whatever the premise of the commercial and no matter how outrageous Ernest's actions, the product was always foremost in the spot.

Other elements were at work in the Ernest commercials that benefited the client. Carden & Cherry capitalized on the local feel of each commercial by continuing to shoot most of them at Cherry's home, a comfortable setting that became familiar to the viewer over time. Yet although the commercials had a neighborhood feel, the location was unidentifiable. Since most of the products Ernest pushed were local or regional, it was easy for people living as far away as California to believe the commercials were being filmed around the corner with a local actor and crew. Many viewers came to believe that Jim was local to whatever area in which the commercials were airing. When Carden & Cherry caught on to this phenomenon, they kept quiet about Jim's true hometown during his personal appearances at client locations.

Ernest's unpretentious nature also gave viewers a certain level of comfort in whatever he was pushing on Vern. As annoying as Ernest could be, he had an underlying honesty and sincerity. Viewers trusted his message even if his actions were clumsy and intrusive. California car dealership owner John L. Sullivan, who used Ernest for years, once said, "He's just a good old down-home individual you can believe. He isn't a suede-shoe operator selling you a bill of goods." That was exactly the message Cherry hoped his clients and their customers were getting when they watched Ernest. John Cherry once said, "One of the best salesmen I ever knew told me that the better part of what you were selling was security. You weren't selling the product, you were selling security." He said the salesman brought a teddy bear along with him when meeting with clients to illustrate that message. No matter how funny viewers thought Ernest to be, they never thought he was clever enough to pull one over on them. Cherry would laugh about the fact that Ernest could make almost anyone believe, "I may be at the bottom of the heap, but I'm above that guy."

Both the anecdotal evidence and the financial data reaffirmed that Ernest was good for business. Cliff Cummings saw how Ernest helped sales after using the campaign at Tysons Toyota dealership in Tysons Corner, Va. He teamed up with Carden & Cherry again after taking over his own dealership in Fairfax, Va. Cummings once described how customers would say, "I want to buy my car because of Ernest." He further explained how his truck sales dramatically increased at the same time his car sales kept a steady pace. This was during a time when many other local dealerships were suffering. He realized that the advertising had to be responsible for much of his success. Meanwhile, in Indianapolis a chain of ice-cream parlors reported that banana-split sales skyrocketed the week after advertising with Ernest. They sold almost 11,000 banana splits. They normally averaged 100 a week (plus, the campaign ran in winter!). And according to Roy Lightner, senior marketing vice president at Carden & Cherry, Trauth Dairy in Newport, Ky., saw a 10-percent increase in sales every year they used Ernest. Lightner laughed about the time the president of Trauth showed him a new addition to their plant, proclaiming, "This is what Ernest built."

When Ernest first became popular through his success with the dairies, Carden & Cherry never thought he would gain traction in markets beyond the Southeast, save for the Midwest, and that was a maybe. They were wrong. Ernest's humor proved to have no limits. Tom Sparks, an executive at Carden & Cherry joked, "People up North love him; maybe because they think they're laughing at us." The agency was also surprised when a

THE SECRET OF ERNEST'S SUCCESS

Hawaiian bank became interested in using the campaign. In addition to the bank airing the ads in Hawaii, it also had Ernest's voice dubbed in Japanese to enable them to run their commercials in Guam. Jim loved to joke about how much he enjoyed watching himself speak Japanese.

Ernest had come a long way after an unspectacular start with a failing amusement park and a year on the shelf. But once the character got rolling, there wasn't anything he couldn't sell. From buttermilk to natural gas, Ernest was an "expert" on a variety of things he thought that Vern should be buying. One industry, however, proved a tougher sell at first: the TV news business. Ernest set out to conquer new territory.

A news station's professionalism, or gravitas, was and is at the core of its appeal to viewers. Stations worried that using Ernest alongside television anchors to advertise the evening news could cause viewers to question the station's integrity. Even if newscasters retained their professional demeanor in the ads, their mere association with such a goofy character could raise questions about their journalistic abilities. Despite any initial concerns, many stations decided to sign Ernest to promote their newscasts.

As the Ernest news promos began to debut in various markets, some newspapers responded as if their entire communities were being insulted. In one Cleveland newspaper article, the reporter was relentless in asking the sales manager of Cleveland's Channel 61 news station what was behind his decision to bring in the Ernest campaign. Perhaps as an attempt to appease the reporter, the sales manager confessed, "Ernest is more of a gimmick. He's not something you go with for a four- or five-year plan."

THE IMPORTANCE OF BEING ERNEST:
THE LIFE OF ACTOR JIM VARNEY

In New Mexico, two competing news stations around Albuquerque wrestled with whether to go with Ernest. The one that chose to do so also placed Ernest's huge grin on dozens of billboards. The general manager of the competing station explained why he had passed: "It might go over in the Carolinas ... but not here."

In the spring of 1986, a TV management workshop was held at the National Association of Broadcasters convention in Dallas. One of the speakers was a promotion specialist who worked for CBS. During his speech, he criticized stations that had used the Ernest campaigns.

Obviously, many in the TV news business still held onto the long-standing belief that a clown could sell cheeseburgers and fries but not the primetime news at 5. But the results were in the numbers: Numerous news stations saw their ratings surge after running the Ernest campaigns. The success of the ads forced many companies in a variety of industries to rethink their dated, man-in-three-piece suit approach. If a company was willing to take a risk and absorb some initial criticism, Ernest soon had them seeing dollar signs.

Carden & Cherry realized they had hit the lottery with Ernest and were reaping the benefits of a 20-year payout compared to a one-time cash option. They repeatedly refused lucrative offers for a national campaign to avoid a quick burnout of the character. Their strategy of continued small-market saturation would be nearly impossible today with the reach of the Internet. Another advantage they had was the limited number of TV channels. Said Coke Sams, "When the commercials started gathering steam in most places, it was right before cable exploded. It was back when most any town had ABC, NBC, CBS and public television – and that was about it. So it was a big deal

THE SECRET OF ERNEST'S SUCCESS

to have local spots on the local news, local morning show, or whatever local programming. Of all the markets, basically we were selling to three channels."

Carden & Cherry resisted other potential short-term payoffs to ensure ongoing success. John Cherry wouldn't reveal Vern's face on camera. Jim did once say, however, that he wanted to play the role of Vern if there was ever a decision to show him.

Yet despite Ernest's success, there was always a concern that a large-scale Ernest ad campaign for a big client could suffer the same fate as the Wendy's "Where's the Beef?" commercials. The famous commercial showed three granny types standing at a fast-food counter inspecting a hamburger. The humor in the contrast between the giant bun and the tiny hamburger is soon eclipsed by Clara Peller's character asking, "Where's the beef?" in her deep raspy voice. Jim, who was always complimentary of his peers, told reporters Peller's timing was perfect, and she had a "cute and innocent way of delivering it." Although funny and successful, the Wendy's campaign was over after a couple of years. One big advantage Ernest may have had was that his taglines "Hey Vern" and "KnowhutImean?" were more general. "Where's the beef?" was more of a punch line than a tagline, making it less adaptable for creating new ads.

The success of Ernest, Peller, auto mogul Joe Isuzu and the fast-talking John Moschitta from the FedEx ads, demonstrated how audiences were growing increasingly fond of a more comedic approach to TV marketing. Commercials played during the Super Bowl today consist almost entirely of humorous concepts and characters, but that wasn't always the case in the 1970s.

In realizing what a hot commodity they possessed, Carden & Cherry became astute in understanding what worked, and they did not hesitate to turn down clients they thought might set Ernest up for failure. They would not accept a client offer if the budget or creative freedom was lacking. They also insisted on retaining creative control. Cherry did not want to tinker with a formula that had such a track record. He would simply explain to the client, "It works. I don't know how, but it works."

The arrangement Carden & Cherry set up allowed the client to select from a large number of adaptable scripts that had been successful. Cherry remained conservative when it came to altering anything in Ernest's delivery. Ernest's now-trademarked catchphrases "Hey Vern" and "KnowhutImean" had become almost as popular as the character himself. Jim was soon being referred to as the "Hey Vern" guy almost as much as Ernest. As far as Ernest's appearance, only minor modifications by a client were permitted. The cap and vest became to Ernest what the leather jacket was to Fonzie on the TV sitcom "Happy Days." Just as Fonzie wore his jacket at inappropriate times for comedic effect – like when he went water skiing in the infamous shark-jumping episode – Ernest wore his cap and vest everywhere, from the shower to the swimming pool. Keeping the cap and vest on in the craziest of settings obviously added to the humor, but it also clearly identified a character who was becoming an extremely powerful brand. Cherry was really advertising two products at once.

Throughout the entire life of the Ernest campaigns, the identifiable images of the character remained the khaki baseball cap and denim vest. While blue jeans and a gray T-shirt usually rounded out the outfit, the cap and vest rarely moved. Said Jim, "We dressed Ernest in the gray T-shirt and blue-jean vest like he'd gone to Kmart and bought out the 'Blue Light Special.'" He said that the

THE SECRET OF ERNEST'S SUCCESS

plain khaki baseball cap could sometimes be hard to find, but he usually could rely on JCPenney to keep him in stock.

Product merchandising began at the request of clients. Companies were eager to find additional ways to capitalize on the positive association that Ernest had with their products. Soon, Carden & Cherry was able to sell quite a bit of merchandise by featuring Ernest without any client affiliation, selling merchandise solely on the power of Ernest's celebrity. Fans showed their adulation by snapping up greeting cards, bumper stickers, T-shirts and pins. Just as Carden & Cherry was careful about how Ernest was presented onscreen, the agency also made sure that any merchandise it licensed fit into the agency's kid-friendly approach. Now, Ernest truly was a commodity.

Jim's ability to connect with his fans through his commercials was eclipsed only by the thrill he gave them through his many public appearances. Braum's Dairy, nationwide but based in Oklahoma, brought him in for tours twice a year, including visits to stores in cities like Tulsa and Oklahoma City, as well as in another big market: Dallas. On a Dallas visit, news of his appearance created a backup so big on Interstate 635, Jim's driver had to maneuver onto the shoulder to get Jim there on time. One weekend in Columbia, S.C., he drew an estimated 5,000 people to a car dealership. Jim often stayed past the scheduled time to sign autographs.

Perhaps no appearance demonstrated Jim's commitment to Ernest over his own ego more than a 1985 Christmas parade in Raleigh, N.C., for Pine State Dairies. He rode along the extremely long parade route dressed as Ernest while sitting atop a fake cow. His accessibility to fans added to the personal connection and local feel that the commercials conveyed.

THE IMPORTANCE OF BEING ERNEST: THE LIFE OF ACTOR JIM VARNEY

"BIG JIM" – JAMES VARNEY SR. WHILE STATIONED IN HAWAII IN THE 1930S. IT WAS A WORLD AWAY FROM THE APPALACHIAN COAL MINES OF HIS YOUTH. (PHOTO COURTESY OF THE VARNEY FAMILY COLLECTION.)

JIM HAD THIS PICTURE OF HIS FATHER – AS A BOXER IN HIS PRIME – HANGING IN HIS HOME IN WHITE HOUSE, TENN. (PHOTO COURTESY OF THE VARNEY FAMILY COLLECTION.)

THE SECRET OF ERNEST'S SUCCESS

The acting in Jim's blood likely came from his mother, Louise, shown here in 1935. Louise acted in church plays as a teenager in Lexington, Ky. (Photo courtesy of the Varney Family Collection.)

Jim's mother, shown here in 1945, struggled with depression throughout her life, as did Jim himself. (Photo courtesy of the Varney Family Collection.)

THE IMPORTANCE OF BEING ERNEST:
THE LIFE OF ACTOR JIM VARNEY

Jim (far right), his mother and sisters at the post office in Varney, W. Va., in 1952. It was the only trip the entire family ever took together. Jim always took pride in his mountain roots. (Photo courtesy of the Varney Family Collection.)

Jim at about 5 years old. Although he never developed into the athlete his father had hoped for, Big Jim was always proud of his son. (Photo courtesy of the Varney Family Collection.)

THE SECRET OF ERNEST'S SUCCESS

JIM AND HIS OLDEST SISTER, JO GAIL, WHO BECAME A SECOND MOTHER TO HIM. (PHOTO COURTESY OF THE VARNEY FAMILY COLLECTION.)

JIM WEARING MICKEY MOUSE EARS IN 1956. LITTLE DID JIM KNOW THAT DECADES LATER HE WOULD SIGN A MOVIE DEAL WITH DISNEY. (PHOTO COURTESY OF THE VARNEY FAMILY COLLECTION.)

THE IMPORTANCE OF BEING ERNEST:
THE LIFE OF ACTOR JIM VARNEY

Jim as the prince in "Sleeping Beauty" with Meg (nee Ulmer) Moye at the Lexington Children's Theatre in the early 1960s. "In the final performance he surprised me by giving me a real kiss in the wake-up scene," says Moye today. "It was scandalous on the set, but it was so Jim." (Photo courtesy of Meg Moye.)

The Varney Parkers: A 15-year-old Jim and his father during a job parking cars for an event. Big Jim created the side business to help support his family. (Photo courtesy of the Varney Family Collection.)

THE SECRET OF ERNEST'S SUCCESS

JIM DOING HIS BEST JAMES BOND IN HIS BACKYARD. AS A TEENAGER, JIM LOVED SEAN CONNERY'S CHARACTER SO MUCH, HE BOUGHT A ROLEX FOR $125 (AS CLOSE AS HE COULD COME TO BOND'S ROLEX) AND HAD "007" ENGRAVED ON THE BACK. (PHOTO COURTESY OF THE VARNEY FAMILY COLLECTION.)

JIM POSING WITH ONE OF TWO BEST HIGH SCHOOL ACTOR IN THE STATE TROPHIES HE WON AS A TEENAGER IN KENTUCKY. (PHOTO COURTESY OF THE VARNEY FAMILY COLLECTION.)

THE IMPORTANCE OF BEING ERNEST: THE LIFE OF ACTOR JIM VARNEY

Jim performing stand-up in 1975 at Nashville's Exit/In. Johnny Cash showed up one night at the club and was "knocked out" by Jim's act. The two eventually became friends. (Copyright 2011, Marshall Fallwell Jr. All rights reserved.)

THE SECRET OF ERNEST'S SUCCESS

Jim during a photo shoot in 1976, shortly after he arrived in Los Angeles to try and make it as an actor and comedian. (Photo courtesy of Joe Liles.)

In Los Angeles, Jim started out at the Comedy Store, alongside future greats like Robin Williams and David Letterman. (Photo courtesy of Joe Liles.)

THE IMPORTANCE OF BEING ERNEST:
THE LIFE OF ACTOR JIM VARNEY

A PUBLICITY SHOT OF JIM AS A YOUNG MAN ECHOED HIS LOVE OF COWBOYS, STARTING WITH THE TV CHARACTERS HE WATCHED AS A CHILD: HOPALONG CASSIDY AND THE LONE RANGER. (PHOTO COURTESY OF JOE LILES.)

JIM IN THE EARLY 1980S, RIGHT AROUND THE TIME ERNEST WAS STARTING TO BECOME A HOUSEHOLD NAME. ERNEST'S SLAPSTICK HUMOR APPEALED TO PEOPLE FROM ALL WALKS OF LIFE. (PHOTO COURTESY OF THE VARNEY FAMILY COLLECTION.)

THE SECRET OF ERNEST'S SUCCESS

JIM GAVE NEPHEW JUSTIN A LESSON ON A WATCH DURING CHRISTMAS EVE 1983. JIM'S LIFELONG FASCINATION WITH ANTIQUE WATCHES (AND KNIVES AND SWORDS) BEGAN AS A CHILD. AS AN ADULT, JIM BESTOWED COUNTLESS FRIENDS AND FAMILY MEMBERS WITH WATCHES AS GIFTS. (PHOTO COURTESY OF THE VARNEY FAMILY COLLECTION.)

JIM AND VIDEOGRAPHER ROB NEUHAUSER OF CLEVELAND'S WCLQ TV-61 IN 1985. THROUGHOUT THE ENTIRE LIFE OF THE ERNEST CAMPAIGNS, THE IDENTIFIABLE IMAGES OF THE CHARACTER REMAINED THE KHAKI BASEBALL CAP AND DENIM VEST. (PHOTO COURTESY OF ROB NEUHAUSER.)

THE IMPORTANCE OF BEING ERNEST: THE LIFE OF ACTOR JIM VARNEY

Jim as Bubba, an Ernest-type character designed to appeal to young people on Jackie Bushman's "Buckmasters" hunting show on the Nashville Network. In the 1990s, Bubba garnered a large following. (Photo courtesy of Buckmasters, LLC.)

As bumbling hunter Bubba, Jim taught safety to young hunters in a series of hugely popular educational videos in the 1990s. (Photo courtesy of Buckmasters, LLC.)

THE SECRET OF ERNEST'S SUCCESS

JIM AND JACKIE BUSHMAN WERE FAST FRIENDS. WHEN BUSHMAN ARRIVED AT THE 1993 PREMIERE FOR "THE BEVERLY HILLBILLIES," JIM TOLD THE PRESS THAT "THE BUCKMASTER" WAS HIS "HUNTING CONSULTANT." (PHOTO COURTESY OF BUCKMASTERS, LLC.)

CHAPTER THIRTEEN

GLOOM BEAMS, HEARTBREAK AND A LITTLE LUCK

As busy as Jim stayed portraying Ernest, he enjoyed revealing other sides of his personality to the public. He was still living just outside of Nashville, and with his love of music it was no surprise that Jim made fast friends with country-music stars around the city. That led to his appearance in Hank Williams Jr.'s music video, "All My Rowdy Friends Are Coming Over Tonight." Despite the video being jam-packed with country music legends, Jim was featured in two different scenes. In one, he rides a bull. In another, he relaxes with two girls in a hot tub. The video won "Video of the Year" at the Academy of Country Music Awards in 1984. The song became even more popular years later when ABC and then ESPN used it (re-written and titled "All My Rowdy Friends Are Here on Monday Night") for their intro to Monday Night Football from 1989 until 2011.

Meanwhile, the "Family Album" hourlong special was such a success that a full-length feature film was written to feature Jim in a new comedic role. The movie was titled "Dr. Otto and the Riddle of the Gloom Beam." It was written by Coke Sams and John Cherry with Jim and Ernest writers Daniel Butler, Glenn Petach and Steve Leasure contributing additional dialogue. It was filmed in the Nashville area in about three weeks during the latter part of 1984. The entire production took only five months with a budget of just under $1 million.

The movie's plot is as offbeat as the title. Mad scientist Dr. Otto creates a magnetic ray capable of erasing credit cards and computer tapes across the globe. Dr. Otto speaks with a German accent and often unleashes an evil laugh during the execution of his dastardly deeds. The doctor's appearance is indescribably weird. His costume resembles a pair of football shoulder pads decorated like a tacky Christmas tree, with twinkling lights and all. One scene reveals the white socks and black dress shoes that complement the look. The most outlandish aspect of his appearance is the human hand (belonging to Ernest writer Glenn Petach) that rests atop Otto's head like a hat. Like an animal tail, the movements of the hand seem to reflect his moods.

Dr. Otto's nemesis is Lance Sterling, an all-American type who has been a thorn in Otto's side since a grade-school science fair. Jim portrays a variety of characters, which would become a hallmark of every feature Cherry directed him in. There is the tough-talking Aussie Rudd Hardtact, Laughin' Jack the pirate, the rich snob Guy Dandy and the dour Auntie Nelda. All are different identities Dr. Otto embodies to keep Lance Sterling off his trail.

The movie's humor can best be described as Monty Python in its style. Jim and the Ernest writers were fans of British humor. Jim also enjoyed specific English comedians such as Rowan Atkinson and Tracy Ullman. A separate movie title was actually created for European fans to appeal more to their presumed offbeat sense of humor. That title, "Never Get Poop on Your Shoes," was a reference to a line Dr. Otto uses to describe the ability of the film's hero, Lance Sterling, to go through life virtually unscathed. Jim had a movie poster with the alternate "Poop" title hanging on one of the walls in his kitchen (of all places) for years.

One of the interviews Jim gave in busy 1984 was to Arch Campbell at WRC-TV during a promotional tour in Washington, D.C. Campbell mentioned how Clara Peller from the Wendy's "Where's The Beef?" ads was already becoming passé and asked Jim why his commercials were still going strong. Appearing as Ernest, Jim mentioned that Clara had made only a few commercials compared to the nearly 900 that he had made. At the end of the interview, Jim was asked what advice he had for Vern. Jim looked right into the camera and replied, "Walk slow, and drink a lot of water." When the cameras returned to the studio following the segment, Campbell roared with laughter before telling his fellow anchors how much he had enjoyed talking to Jim. He said that Jim was a "very nice guy," and added, a touch surprised, "very shy too."

Jim closed out the year on the road. This time he was in Houston with some of his country-music friends. He co-hosted "Willie Nelson's New Year's Eve Party" on HBO, the first concert special the network ever aired, with Kris Kristofferson and Johnny Cash. Appearing as himself and dressed in a tuxedo, the appearance gave the public a glimpse of what Jim was really like in person. But he did manage to fit in a Johnny Cash impression and could not resist mixing in a bit of Ernest before the night was over.

At 35, just as Jim was moving beyond the devastation of his divorce, he was faced with a huge setback. He lost his father, his biggest hero. Jim's career was about to be launched into the stratosphere. But he would be without the one person whose approval and opinion he valued most.

On January 11, 1985, Jim's father suffered a heart attack in his sleep. An ambulance rushed him and wife, Louise, to the hospital where Jim's sisters soon arrived. After only 30 minutes, the doctor walked into the waiting room to inform the family that James Sr. had died. The death was a shock to Jim and his sisters. They were used to their mother being sick, but they always saw their father as invincible. But after his death, when looking at a picture of their parents taken months earlier, it was evident how sick their father looked. They were surprised that none of them had noticed. The family eventually discovered that James Sr. had suffered from symptoms he thought were bouts of indigestion. But they must have been signs of serious heart trouble. Instead of going to the doctor, he had treated the episodes with over-the-counter medication.

During much of his father's visitation at the funeral home, Jim retreated to the downstairs refreshment area. It was obvious to his sisters and other family members that Jim was deeply affected by their father's passing. They knew Jim had been drinking and were concerned about how he was going to handle the unexpected loss.

After his father's death, Jim's workload became even greater. But it was salve to his grief. Jim was scheduled for a two-week run performing stand-up at Maxim's in Las Vegas beginning in mid-February. Working as his straight man was comedian-friend Mike Price. It took Jim a few performances to shake off the rust, but he was soon selling out, forcing the hotel to move him to one of their larger venues.

Las Vegas residents were familiar with Ernest thanks to commercials Jim had made for their local Channel 8 News. Although the act included an impressive array of memorable characters, a fair amount of Ernest was included. Jim spent the spring of 1985 continuing his public appearances as Ernest, even throwing out the first pitch at a Cleveland Indians baseball game. The busy commercial shooting schedule continued as post-production finished up on Dr. Otto, set for a summer release.

GLOOM BEAMS, HEARTBREAK AND A LITTLE LUCK

It was no surprise that when promotions started rolling out for "Dr. Otto," Ernest was front and center. John Cherry attempted to capitalize on the popularity of the Ernest character while reinforcing to the public that this was the same man portraying the bizarre-looking Dr. Otto. In TV spots and posters promoting the movie, Ernest took up nearly the entire ad.

"Otto" was released independently in the Southern and Midwestern states where Ernest was already popular. Cherry planned to seek nationwide distribution if ticket sales reflected real demand for additional screens. Unfortunately, sales were disappointing. If a crowd was interested in seeing Jim in a non-Ernest role, Dr. Otto wasn't it.

Reviews were mostly negative, and fans rushing to theaters hoping to see Jim as Ernest – or a character close to him – were disappointed. Even Lexington Herald-Leader writer Don Edwards, a friend and fan of Jim's, couldn't hide his poor opinion of the film. But in his review Edwards managed to praise Jim's talent while seeming to offer professional advice: "Hollywood is missing a bet on Varney. But you can do only so much from Nashville." Little did Edwards know that Disney was working on an Ernest movie deal that would prove that filmmaking in Nashville could compete with Hollywood. Of course, Edwards was probably imagining Jim in roles other than Ernest.

Jim was hoping that, like "Family Album,""Dr. Otto" would demonstrate more of his range. He said at the time, "After four years, I'm too identified with Ernest. The movie is one way to break that." Hollywood, being a business, may have focused more on the poor reception of Jim in a non-Ernest role than any potential he may have shown portraying different characters in the movie.

Looking back at the failure of "Dr. Otto," Cherry once admitted, "Jim and I just wanted to do it, and we had our heads handed to us." He did take some consolation in the fact that they still had videocassette rentals to help recoup some of their investment. The growing segment of the industry would prove profitable for Carden & Cherry when future Ernest films became strong rentals.

As great as the Ernest success was for Jim, he was mindful of preventing it from overtaking the acting career he desired. By filming "Family Album" and "Dr. Otto," along with pushing his own name in Vegas, he was trying to show he wasn't a one-trick pony. The balancing act would prove more difficult as more lucrative offers came Ernest's way.

The Indianapolis area had become familiar with Ernest after seeing his commercials for such businesses as Roberts Dairy. Russ Dellen, a car dealer in the area, decided he wanted in on the Ernest phenomenon. The only problem was that Roberts Dairy had exclusive rights in that market. Luckily for Dellen, he was a buddy of Pete Roberts, who owned the dairy. Before long, Roy Lightner was able to convince Roberts' Board of Directors to allow Dellen to use Ernest. He explained to them that Ernest ads for Dellen could only reinforce the tie that Roberts had with the character. After all, the two companies were not even in the same industry. Roberts' board had no problem with it, and Ernest was soon starring in commercials for Dellen's dealerships.

The relationship proved fortuitous. In May 1985, the annual Indy 500 Festival was held. Like every year, thousands of people descended on Indianapolis to attend the festival events leading up to the Indianapolis 500 Race. The theme of the festival was "The Wonderful World of Disney," with cartoon icon Mickey Mouse serving as grand marshal of the celebrity car parade around the famed track. Dellen had asked Carden & Cherry if Ernest could make an appearance at the parade on behalf of his business. They obliged.

GLOOM BEAMS, HEARTBREAK AND A LITTLE LUCK

During the parade, Mickey Mouse received predictable applause as he waved to the throngs of cheering onlookers. Jim, dressed as Ernest, followed shortly behind riding atop a red convertible. As people began to recognize the blue-jean vest and khaki cap, they cheered wildly, far more than for Mickey. Ernest's huge reception was not lost on Disney's new CEO, Michael Eisner, and new studio head Jeffrey Katzenberg, both of whom were in the crowd. Eisner later recalled the experience: "I was at the Indianapolis 500 … and there was a parade … 500,000 people were there. The governor went by and: applause. Mickey Mouse went by: more applause. All of a sudden, Jim Varney went by (as Ernest), and 500,000 people went berserk. So I said, 'We ought to do something about that.'"

Eisner quickly arranged a meeting with Cherry, who gave him a crash course on Ernest. Although Ernest had been a phenomenon for a few years, the West Coast and the Northeast were, for the most part, clueless. Disney was about to help change all that. A movie deal was eventually reached where Disney agreed to pick the films up for distribution.

Perhaps it was fate that Jim would someday work for Disney. One of the first images of Jim as a child captured by his cousins' video camera was of him smiling big for the camera and wearing a Mickey Mouse Club cap.

As Ernest was preparing to break into movies, the commercials remained a red-hot commodity. By June 1985, around 60 companies had signed up to use Ernest in nearly 100 markets. Now, along with the greeting cards and bumper stickers, there a fan club and even a book entitled "Ernest P. Worrell Book of Knowledge." Jim explained, "It's not a big book. We're not talking 'War and Peace,' we're talking more like a pamphlet."

At a time when Jim was enjoying more professional success than ever, he was dealing with more sad family news. After being diagnosed with breast cancer in 1982, oldest sister Jo Gail received a radical mastectomy and endured chemotherapy and radiation until 1983. Her cancer then went into remission, with the family praying it would not return. But a year later, Jo Gail found a node in her neck, and the news was bad. Her cancer had returned, and she would have to have more chemo.

In the fall of 1985, a fashion show cancer benefit titled "Southern Gentlemen in Style," was held at the Kentucky governor's mansion. It was a project of the University of Kentucky's Phi Beta Psi sorority. Jo Gail's battle with the disease made the event all the more personal for Jim as he served as master of ceremonies.

Despite her treatments and the family's support, Jo's cancer eventually spread to her lungs and brain. On March 1, 1986, at 46, she lost her brave battle with the disease. The day she died was cold and snowy, similar to the day Jim's father had passed on the year before. Jim cancelled his appearances for two months. Losing two family members so close together was difficult for Jim and his entire family. Still dealing with the loss of his father, Jim leaned on his other two sisters for support. He began to call more often, usually late at night, to talk for hours about whatever was on his mind. Topics included current events, history, the newest jokes he had heard and his latest jewelry acquisitions. He and Jake would debate such matters as the longstanding argument over whether Shakespeare had written all of his works. He talked to Sandy about his dreams. One he referred to as "The Actor's Dream," where he would be standing onstage and could not remember his lines. With the increasing demands of his growing fame, he needed his family's support more than ever.

Although Ernest was still shying away from national campaigns, he was setting his sights on a large market that Jim called, "the home of the forty-five second minute," that is, New York City.

GLOOM BEAMS, HEARTBREAK AND A LITTLE LUCK

After signing with Coca-Cola, his first international client, Ernest was set to conquer the Big Apple. The writers thought up a pitch that mocked New York's highbrow attitude toward the rest of the country, especially when it came to rednecks like Ernest. The commercial opens with Ernest rummaging through Vern's wine cellar, tossing dusty wine bottles over his shoulder that he believes to be old and stale. Ernest then attempts to show Vern a supposedly tastier choice as he pours Sprite into a wine glass from a two-liter plastic bottle. He takes a sip and begins describing the flavor as if he were a wine connoisseur promoting a fine merlot. The whole wine-cellar theme seemed fitting for the New York campaign and also built upon Vern's personality from his earliest incarnation. From the beginning, John Cherry saw Vern as a tea-sipper type in the mold of snobbish characters such as Major Winchester from TV's "M*A*S*H."

The American Bed Co. was the second client in the New York market to advertise with Ernest. At that time, mattress companies suffered from the same problem Carden & Cherry's dairy clients used to have when it came to advertising. Mattresses, like milk, never had that wow factor. But as the founder of The American Bed Co. put it, "Jim made them 'rememberable.'"

Cherry didn't seem too worried about Ernest's Northeast appeal when asked if the character was sophisticated enough for New York. Cherry was well aware of how the media questioned the character's appeal beyond the South. He joked once, "Ernest has a lot of fans in Washington, D.C. that claim to be sophisticated."

From Time Magazine to "CNN Headline News," Ernest's arrival on the New York scene had everyone taking notice. CNN filmed Jim, dressed as Ernest, waving to passers-by as he stood outside Manhattan's St. Moritz hotel. Many tourists recognized him, and one lady remarked, "He has the biggest smile from Texas." It was always interesting to see how the local feel of the commercials led people to believe Ernest was from their hometown. How funny it was that a Kentucky actor was making a Texan feel at home in New York City.

Of all the interviews Jim granted during the years following his fame as Ernest, the most noteworthy may have been for the University of Kentucky's student newspaper, "The Kentucky Kernel" in May 1986. The story was memorable not so much for its content but for the photo.

While being interviewed, Jim was cleaning one of his handguns and talking about his interest in them. One of the photos that accompanied the story was of him holding the gun. What added to the dark mood was the look on Jim's face, which came off as sinister when he was actually deep in thought. Throw in the fact that his familiar khaki baseball cap was not there to cover his thick curly hair, and the picture resembled more of a "Most Wanted" poster than a newspaper article.

Another person quoted in the Kernel article was a girlfriend, Lianne Mize (now Russell), who had actually arranged the interview, as she was a friend of the reporter's sister. Mize had met Jim in 1984 through a mutual friend, shortly after his divorce with Jacqui. The tall, dark-haired beauty in her mid-20s lived just outside of Lexington. The relationship became serious, and Jim gave her an antique pearl ring that initiated what she referred to years later as their "quasi-engagement." Today, Russell (nee Mize) remembers how deeply affected Jim was by his father's passing and how important family was to him.

Despite a bad break-up in May 1986, Mize remained friends with Jim for the rest of his life. Her memories of Jim include many of the same themes as other girlfriends, those where lessons on knives and watches were required. She remembers Jim smoking the Meerschaum pipes that he enjoyed collecting. These smoking pipes, made with a soft white mineral called Meerschaum, have been carved for centuries by skilled craftsmen into intricate designs such as faces, animals and a variety of motifs. One of her favorite memories relates to Jim's love of King Arthur. He was a fan of the book "The Mists of Avalon," a retelling of the King Arthur legend. As a result of the book, Jim became interested in the alder tree and its supposed mystical powers. One year, Mize gave Jim 100 Alder saplings as a birthday gift, and he planted them in the shape of a giant "J" on his property in White House, Tenn. The trees, like his antique knives and jewelry, provided Jim a physical link to centuries past, where he often dreamed of having lived.

Jim's love of history led him to visit England many times. From Shakespeare's cottage to Stonehenge, Jim enjoyed seeing historical places that he had only read about growing up. He even made a visit to the Varney ancestral home in Buckinghamshire, England, known as Claydon House. His imagination must have run wild as he walked the halls and grounds of his ancestors.

Through the years, Jim had many conversations with his sister Jake about the connection he felt to England and his belief that he had experienced past lives. He believed he had been an actor in many different generations going all the way back to the time of King Arthur. He had not necessarily been a famous actor, he thought, but had experienced both extreme poverty and great wealth. He told Jake that he felt a strong sense of déjà vu during his trips to England.

From King Arthur to Thomas Becket (Archbishop of Canterbury), life in medieval times fascinated Jim. A castle located just outside Lexington in Versailles, Ky., had been built in the late 1960s as a gift from an adoring husband to his wife. The surreal contrast of the imposing structure and its massive turrets against busy Highway U.S. 60 (which the castle borders) has been turning drivers' heads ever since it was built. During a visit to sister Sandy's house in the mid-'80s, Jim casually mentioned the possibility of perhaps owning the castle someday. He joked about wanting to host a Victorian era tea party on the front lawn while politely waving to cars driving by. The family laughed at the visual, knowing it would not be at all unlikely that he would follow through.

Nashville continued to provide Jim many opportunities to stay busy when he wasn't falling off ladders or mashing his fingers in windows. In April of 1986, just months after being a guest star on "Hee Haw," he emceed a recording session of the 90-piece Nashville Symphony. Country-music stars such as Chet Atkins and Hank Williams Jr. played along with the symphony while recording classic country songs at the Tennessee Performing Arts Center. A few weeks later, Jim showed up in Washington, D.C., at a place where no one would ever have believed Ernest would be invited.

Larry Speakes, the White House Press Secretary at the time, decided to play a prank on the press corps. He informed them that the new deputy assistant to the president for economic policy was going to speak. The reporters got a surprise when Jim walked out dressed as Ernest, acting as the advisor. Along with Ernest, Jim portrayed a few more of his favorite characters, including mean ol' Lloyd. He brought along hats to help him transition into each character.

CHAPTER FOURTEEN

ERNEST IN THE MOVIES

In the summer of 1986, Ernest fans around the country rejoiced when it was announced that a movie called "Ernest Goes to Camp" would be released the following spring. Nashville residents were soon reading in the local newspapers about Disney representatives scouting the area for locations.

That fall, the "Camp" movie crew descended on the small town of Dickson, Tenn., to start shooting at the Montgomery Bell State Park, which would serve as Kamp Kikakee in the movie. The crew consisted of many of the same people who had filmed the Ernest commercials, in addition to others recruited from the area.

Jim brought his mother down from Lexington to visit the set. She was impressed with the whole production and enjoyed meeting and getting her picture taken with Iron Eyes Cody, the actor famous for playing Native Americans (although he was actually of Italian descent).

Many of the boys playing campers were acting for the first time. Most were local kids who enjoyed the opportunity to work with someone they had grown up watching on TV commercials. They soon grew comfortable enough with Jim to have a little fun with him on the set.

THE IMPORTANCE OF BEING ERNEST:
THE LIFE OF ACTOR JIM VARNEY

There were around 26 Ernest outfits in wardrobe, enough to endure the many pratfalls in the script. Early one morning, a bunch of the boys decided to dress up in the costumes and surprise Jim as he walked up the road to the set. Jim admitted that he had to question if he was really awake when he saw the few dozen smiling mini-Ernests.

The plot of "Camp" involves Ernest working as maintenance man at a summer camp. His dream to be a camp counselor is soon answered when the camp director assigns him to look after a group of juvenile delinquents sent from a youth detention center. As one of the few adults who treats the juveniles with respect, Ernest is eventually able to win them over. When an evil mining company manipulates the owner of the camp property to sign away the land, Ernest and the boys team up to help. By constructing clever weapons, including parachuting snapping turtles, they successfully destroy the company's equipment and save the camp.

One major decision John Cherry had to confront with the film was the way in which Vern's character would be portrayed. The commercials were always seen through Vern's point of view, but that shooting style would not be practical for the big screen. This meant that the only way to include Vern would be to reveal him on the other side of the camera. But showing Vern (even partially) after so long could blow the perception of him that Ernest's fans had built up through the years. Ultimately it was decided not to show Vern, but Ernest did manage to bring his name up on occasion. In a campfire scene, for example, Ernest mentions his friend "Vernon" when recalling a version of the classic "hook killer" story mentioned in another summer camp movie, the Bill Murray hit "Meatballs."

Even though Vern didn't make it into the movie, audiences were sure to recognize well-known faces that John Cherry cast opposite Jim. John Vernon, who portrayed Dean Wormer in "Animal

House," played a merciless construction boss, and Gailard Sartain signed on as camp chef Jake. Sartain, a consistently underrated actor, had excelled in comedic and dramatic roles. From Francis Ford Coppola's film "The Outsiders" to the popular TV Series "The Dukes of Hazzard" and "Hee Haw," Sartain displayed enormous range. In "Camp," Sartain's knack for comedy is on full display. His character spends much of the time in the camp's kitchen perfecting a dish he dubbed "Eggs Erroneous." The sight of the foamy green concoction leads one to believe that its ingredients are more "erroneous" than "egg." Every time he thinks of a new way to improve the recipe, his eyes dart back and forth like pinballs. Despite sharing little screen time with Jim, Sartain perfectly conveys the brand of humor that John Cherry was looking for in the film.

The writers retained many of the physical elements that were strongly identified with Ernest's appeal. Whether he was falling out of a school bus, smashing his face into a lunch tray, getting body-slammed by a vending machine, attacked by his homemade outdoor grill or beaten up by ex-NFL great Lyle Alzado, Jim endured more than his fair share of stunts. Alzado was expertly cast as a construction worker with a bad disposition. Jim filmed his entire fight scene with Alzado without the assistance of a stuntman to ensure the close-ups would look authentic. Jim was holding up fine until Alzado, not realizing Jim was right behind him, swung his arm back and smashed Jim right in the nose. Jim later revealed, "The loud crack you hear on the soundtrack wasn't added later." Jim was luckier than many of the quarterbacks Alzado had faced in his football career, as he was – miraculously – able to walk away uninjured after the encounter.

Although no one considered Ernest anything approaching a complex character, the movie did allow writers an opportunity to give Ernest more substance than had been portrayed in the commercials. In a scene where Ernest is feeling down in the dumps, he sings a song to himself called, "Gee I'm Glad It's Raining." The lyrics revealed a more sensitive side of the character that rarely surfaced in the flurry of his constant foolishness. The song remains a favorite of many Ernest fans and is often used today in Internet tribute videos to Jim.

Being a Disney movie, "Ernest Goes to Camp" was aimed at the 8- to 14-year-old audience. Jim had previously spoken of Ernest's characteristics as being like that of an 8-year-old. It was true in many ways. Ernest and Vern's relationship resembled the one between comic-strip character Dennis the Menace and neighbor Mr. Wilson. Dennis, who was written to be around 8, was always wandering over to his neighbor's house uninvited. His intrusions, although well meaning, were often invasive and occasionally destructive. Ernest had the same childlike energy and curiosity, and while not as cute as Dennis, he endeared himself to an audience in the same way.

"Ernest Goes to Camp" not only allowed Jim to display his slapstick abilities on the big screen, he proved that the character could carry an entire movie. Earlier he wasn't so sure it could be done. He had actually told the Atlanta Journal-Constitution in October 1985 that he never would portray Ernest in a movie. "Could you watch two hours of Gomer Pyle?" he had said. Perhaps it was the partnership offer from a studio with a name like Disney and the lucrative terms that changed his mind. It was never a question of Jim's acting ability but more about how he could make the character work in a different medium. While Ernest had appeared in "Dr. Otto," it had been only a cameo.

Along with the writers, Cherry deserves much of the credit for taking the elements that made Ernest work in commercials and translating them successfully to the big screen with "Camp."

Directing a feature film for Disney was a big leap for Cherry, and he proved that he was up to the challenge. In a 2005 interview for The Tennessean, Cherry recalled the pressure. "It took five weeks to shoot," he said of the movie. "It terrified me, and it never ceased to terrify me."

Cherry's many talents complemented Jim's. He had studied at Florida's Ringling Arts School (now the Ringling College of Art and Design). His artistic skills included proficiency with painting in oil and watercolor. For "Camp" he created storyboards for Jim that demonstrated how Ernest's actions were to play out in a scene. Jim compared Cherry's artistic talents to those of director Terry Gilliam, a member of Monty Python and creator of their imaginative and often-surreal animation.

As Jim was preparing to take Ernest to movie screens, a video of one of his Las Vegas shows from the previous year was set to air on Nashville's community access channel. "Jim Varney: Live in Las Vegas" was supposed to be on multiple times to allow local fans to see another side of Jim.

After pressure on the station from Jim's manager, Betty Clark, the special never aired. She claimed that her concerns were related to the inferior quality of the tape itself and not over any material in the act. In a newspaper story concerning the cancelled airings in The Tennessean, Jim let his feelings be known. He said Clark's apprehension related more to Ernest's image and the overall relationships with clients such as Purity Dairies. He told the reporter that he had been doing Ernest for six years and was looking to grow. "It can be bad to stay in one character for too long," he added. Perhaps he summed up his frustration most accurately when responding to a statement made in the article by the channel's program director. The director said he didn't know who "owned" Jim Varney. Jim responded bluntly, "I'm beginning to wonder that myself."

As upset as Jim seemed during the whole episode, he had to realize that the local airing of a smalltime video (shot by a cameraman hired by Jim and comedian Mike Price) would hardly lead to being contacted by agents or studio executives for a starring role in the next Hollywood blockbuster. His frustration probably centered more on his intense desire for the public to see another side of him.

Yet as much as Jim wanted to expand, he still wasn't willing to give up Ernest to pursue other opportunities. It was hard to walk away from the fame and large paychecks. He had already played the part of the struggling actor-comedian in New York and Los Angeles. He was closing in on 40 and probably didn't feel like going through those challenges for a second round. He loved his comfortable existence living outside of Nashville, a city that continued to bring him more consistent work than anywhere else he had ever lived.

As demanding as the commercials and public appearances could be, Jim was well aware of how fortunate he was to play Ernest. "Where else can you get paid to chainsaw a turkey?" he asked a writer for Louisville's Courier-Journal. In a Nashville Banner article, which ran the day before "Camp" hit the theaters, Jim said, "I've always been afraid of that (typecasting) with this character. I'm taking a real gamble with this film. (but) ... it would be silly of me not to take advantage of the offer when it's made. ... (and) Broadway's not exactly beating my door down." It was obvious to Jim that playing Ernest in a Disney movie could take his identity with the character to a whole new level.

"Ernest Goes to Camp" was released on May 22, 1987. Jim thought with the late-spring release, kids could see it before heading off to summer camp. On the film's opening day, a Hollywood-esque red-carpet premiere was held in Nashville. Jim arrived in a tuxedo, sporting a black satin baseball cap. It was an ensemble that only someone like Ernest, or perhaps Randy Quaid's "Cousin Eddie" character from the National Lampoon Vacation movies, would find fashionable. Many media outlets, including Entertainment Tonight, showed up to interview Jim and John Cherry. It was the first time a movie had been made based entirely on a character who had originated in TV commercials.

Realizing that critics would likely not be kind, Disney decided not to hold advance screenings for the press. But they needn't have worried. In the South and Midwest, where many Ernest commercials had aired, ticket sales were high. With an estimated budget of $3 million and a resulting gross of $23 million, Disney was extremely happy with the results. The box-office take may have been a surprise, but the skewering from critics was not. Cherry took the poor reviews in stride. He had expected it. He said, "They're (critics) trying to find artistic value to something that's purely a commercial enterprise." Then he added, "It's like an art critic reviewing a baseball card." He said that he was not worried since kids buy more movie tickets than critics anyway. In 2009, Steve Martin spoke to the Associated Press about his own experiences with bad reviews. He mentioned the poor reviews American critics gave "The Jerk" when it was released. He said, "Comedy is not a critics' medium, it just isn't."

The bad reviews for "Camp" sometimes went beyond the typical one-star critique. One critic took his bashing so far as to say that Jim Varney was a "grotesque figure." It was almost as if critics were furious over having to endure the 90-minute movie in order to write the review. Funny enough, some radio ads promoting the movie had humorously claimed, "It may be the least-important

THE IMPORTANCE OF BEING ERNEST:
THE LIFE OF ACTOR JIM VARNEY

90 minutes of your life." At least the critics had been given fair warning.

Jim spent the week following the movie's release as a guest on "The New Hollywood Squares" game show. He was returning to California as a star. Most people move to Nashville to make it big in country music. Jim had managed to find a way to become a movie star in Music City.

While working on "Camp," Jim had been approached by popular country singer Roger Miller, who wrote the music and lyrics for the Broadway play "Big River," a musical version of the Huckleberry Finn story. Miller asked Jim if he would play the role of Huck's father, Pappy Finn. John Goodman initially starred in the part but bowed out after accepting a movie role. Jim reluctantly had to turn the part down because of obligations to "Camp." During the musical's successful run, Miller himself played Pappy for a short stretch.

The play premiered April 25, 1985, at the Eugene O'Neill Theatre in New York City. It became a runaway hit and a critical success, winning seven Tony awards including Best Musical, with Miller earning one for best score. (To this day, he is the only country artist to win a Tony Award.)

In a 1996 interview with a Montreal radio station, Jim said regretfully, "I thought I'd never turn down a role on Broadway." In the coming years, it seemed that the musical never ventured far from Jim's mind. In the 1990s Jim recorded a cover of Roger Miller's "River in the Rain" from the play. It was Miller's last major hit, climbing to No. 36 on the country chart in 1985. In November 1999, in one of Jim's final interviews, he spoke with Beverly Keel of the alternative weekly Nashville Scene about having one regret: "Looking back now, I'd like to have cut in and out of Ernest more." Later on, he was asked about "Big River" and replied, "I have no regrets, I just like to work." The contradiction seems to illustrate how difficult it was for Jim to come to terms with missed opportunities.

At this stage, Jim was also answering more and more questions about how the character's popularity might affect his future acting career. He admitted that the transition from commercials to movies had not gone as originally planned. He joked, "I've always gotten things backwards. I mean, I started out doing Shakespeare, and now I'm doing this." But his overall outlook seemed optimistic. He repeatedly stated that he didn't see Ernest as a roadblock and didn't believe he would need to give up the character in order to pursue further acting opportunities. It's almost as if he thought that the power of his optimism could create a self-fulfilling prophecy.

He often reminded reporters how Robin Williams, his former Comedy Store alum, had broken away from his zany Mork character to find serious movie roles. Jim may have been shortsighted when comparing himself to Williams, who had given up Mork years before being cast in serious roles, a few of which earned him Academy Award nominations.

Another actor Jim mentioned when discussing typecasting was Art Carney. Carney had played Jackie Gleason's best friend and neighbor, Ed Norton, on the legendary 1950s TV series "The Honeymooners." The character's trademark look was much like Ernest's, with his own style of vest, T-shirt and hat. Carney went on to win an Oscar at the age of 56 for his dramatic role in the movie "Harry and Tonto." Even though Carney's achievement came later in his career, it seemed to give Jim hope during the times when he wrestled with the long-term effects of playing Ernest. But as Jim would find out, Ernest would overshadow almost every other role he would ever play and be a major roadblock to many more he hoped to pursue.

THE IMPORTANCE OF BEING ERNEST: THE LIFE OF ACTOR JIM VARNEY

Around 1988, Jim and Betty Clark parted ways, and a friend of Jim's arranged a meeting with agent Phil Walden. Walden rose to prominence in the music industry starting in 1959 when he began managing Otis Redding. Two years after Redding's tragic death in 1967, Walden formed Capricorn Records with his brother Alan and record executive Frank Fenter. Along with the help of Atlantic Records executive Jerry Wexler, Capricorn helped launch the careers of The Allman Brothers and the Marshall Tucker Band, among others.

But in 1979 Capricorn's successful run came to an end, and Walden declared bankruptcy. He moved to Nashville from Macon, Ga., in 1984 and tried to work his way back into the music business with little success. Throughout that time, he battled drug and alcohol abuse, finally becoming sober on December 30, 1987. He was forever grateful to Jim for giving him the opportunity to manage him. He later said, "Jim Varney virtually saved my life."

Walden soon got Jim signed to the ICM Partners talent agency. He also introduced him to William "Hoot" Gibson, a friend and Nashville attorney who began representing Jim.

Even though Walden had mostly dealt with music groups and artists, he did have experience with actor/comedians from his days with Capricorn. Martin Mull, an actor Jim had previously worked with, recorded four comedy albums with Capricorn in the 1970s. It was Walden's background in the music industry that may have contributed to Jim's decision to sign with him. Jim was continuing to pursue recording opportunities.

But one of Jim's first ventures into music was more about pushing then-wife Jacqui's career than it was his own singing ambitions. With the help of Joe Liles, Jim had cut a demo tape in the summer of 1978 at the house of a musician and engineer who lived on Mulholland Drive in Southern California. Along with singing songs Jacqui wrote, he also recorded ones that his sister Jake had written during the time she had dated a musician. Jake had originally written "Born in a Boxcar" for Merle Haggard and hoped Jim would find a way to give it to him. Jake knew that when Haggard was born, his family had been living in an old boxcar they had converted into a home. Although inspired by Haggard, the lyrics about life on a railroad might be more fitting for a Johnny Cash tune:

One rainy night I met a man
A hobo just like me
He looked something like the picture of my dad
He died in my arms in a freight car out of Denver
I wrapped him in the only coat I had

When Jim sang country, his sound was deep and melodic but with a hint of roughness, reminiscent of Cash and Haggard. Later on, years of smoking would lend an even deeper, raspier edge. Yet on the song many of his fans are familiar with, "Gee I'm Glad It's Raining," from "Ernest Goes to Camp," Jim's voice is gentle and even lilting, on par with the childlike qualities of his character. In addition to the Appalachian dulcimer and harmonica, Jim also played a little guitar.

Shortly before Jim hired Walden, he told a number of reporters that he was working on a blues album with guitarist Grant Boatwright on Music Row in Nashville. Like so many of Jim's previous attempts at producing an album, nothing was ever released. He had even hoped to record a duet with music legend Neil Young, an old friend of Boatright's. But a collaboration on Young's song "The Ways of Love" never materialized. The song was eventually recorded but not as a duet (although Linda Ronstadt did sing background vocals). It was released on Young's 1989 album "Freedom."

THE IMPORTANCE OF BEING ERNEST:
THE LIFE OF ACTOR JIM VARNEY

Unlike his movie success, Jim's foray into music seemed to be one long string of disappointments. Only one album released during this time included Jim's participation, and although Jim's role was minimal he was ecstatic about the opportunity. He was asked to play his dulcimer on "Dixie Darlin" for the Carter Family album "Wildwood Flower." The album featured an updated ensemble of the family, consisting of sisters Helen, Anita, June and June's daughter Carlene.

In addition to managing Jim, Walden also briefly managed Billy Bob Thornton. Through Walden, Jim and Thornton began a lifelong friendship. Jim brought up Thornton's name from time to time when visiting his family back in Lexington. He talked often about a "brilliant" screenplay called "Sling Blade" that Thornton had written. Jim's family had a difficult time understanding what sounded so great about a story called "Sling Blade" written by some guy named Billy Bob. The family was pleasantly surprised years later when they saw what a compelling story it was. In the film, a simple-minded man is released from a mental hospital after murdering his mother and her lover as a child. He befriends a young boy and sacrifices everything to protect the boy and his mother from her violent boyfriend. Thornton would go on to win an Academy Award for Best Adapted Screenplay for the film. Jim had obviously known what he was talking about. (The film is an adaptation of a 1994 short film of Thornton's: "Some Folks Call It a Sling Blade.")

Even as Walden was enjoying the time he was spending as Jim's manager, he still longed to return to the music industry. In a roundabout way, Jim helped him do it. Walden traveled to Los Angeles many times in the late '80s and early '90s to meet with movie executives on Jim's behalf. On one trip, he met with music industry attorney Lee Phillips, who had represented Walden during the Capricorn days. These meetings eventually led to discussions with Warner Brothers about resurrecting Capricorn. An agreement was eventually reached, and in 1991, the Georgia rock band Widespread Panic released the first Capricorn album in more than 10 years. Years later, drummer Todd Nance of Widespread Panic gave credit to Jim when speaking of Capricorn. "Yeah, Jim Varney was the reason Capricorn was resurrected because he was so successful."

CHAPTER FIFTEEN

PLUVIO

Jim said you should always name the place where you live. He named his home in White House, Tenn., "Pluvio" after the Latin word pluvia, which means rain. For him, it was "The Place of Rain." The first few times Jim visited it when looking for a home to buy, rain was falling, so he thought the name fitting. He called it home for the rest of his life.

The house was not a movie star's mansion by any means. It was a brick ranch with a full basement, 2,600 square feet. He later added an outdoor deck and swimming pool. It was surrounded by about 10 acres with a creek running through. Deer, pheasant and wild turkeys roamed the grounds. Jim kept a small pear tree near the kitchen just for the deer, and he hung hummingbird feeders on the front porch. He cut most of the grass himself. He loved pruning trees and had studied a Japanese technique that gave them a flowing look. He would actually take it upon himself to prune the trees of family members when visiting. Sister Jake's neighbors were surprised one day to see Ernest in her front yard displaying his mastery with lopping shears.

Jim spent most of his waking hours in his living room. The shelves were filled with books, movies and various items he had purchased from specialty shops all over the country. The books ranged from watch guides to Shakespeare's plays. During a conversation, he could grab any book and within seconds find the page related to what was being discussed.

Studying the pictures hanging on the walls of Jim's home gave a glimpse into the many sides of his personality. In his study hung a large, framed picture of his father as a boxer in his prime, an imposing figure in his gloves and trunks. Many images of Charlie Chaplin hung around the home, including a full-length one of the beloved tramp in his living room.

One picture that looked ordinary at first glance displayed more of Jim's twisted side. It was a photograph of the DeLorean Motor Company's emblem and a car key resting on top of what looked like a folded-up white cloth. Upon closer inspection, the cloth was a small mound of fine white powder intended to resemble cocaine. It was an obvious reference to the 1982 cocaine-trafficking charge against the auto company's founder, John DeLorean. But perhaps the most interesting, or at least thought-provoking, framed piece in Jim's house was a square of white cloth with a phrase embroidered on it in green thread: "If you want the truth, follow the money."

In the kitchen, Jim not only ate but wrote music and constantly examined his beloved watches. On the door of the refrigerator were pictures of Jim's pets and family members, along with letters and artwork sent to him by young fans.

Scattered throughout the house were Jim's assorted knives, many of them pocketknives. During his life, he amassed more than 4,000 in his collection, which came to include everything from a solid copper pocketknife to a World War II German dagger. As with his watches, he respected the craftsmanship.

Coke Sams was one of many of Jim's friends who hung out at his house over the years. Jim loved to talk about history, especially if it concerned how guns and knives evolved. Sams remembers Jim talking at length about the development of civilization through the use of simple tools. Jim enjoyed tracing the history of knives, from skinning knives to hunting knives.

Jim's land was a constant source of entertainment for him. When he wasn't talking history, he was outside having fun with his toys. Sams spent numerous days with Jim shooting guns, bows and arrows, even a potato cannon. Jim had been told that Civil War soldiers were buried in a plot under a grove of trees on the property. Sams recalls Jim trying to recreate the scene where the soldiers had died. Jim imagined a soldier taking a drink from a certain spot by the creek and how someone hiding on the other side may have surprised him.

Jim occasionally told stories of Pluvio being haunted. Sometimes he talked about seeing vague, dark figures among the Civil War gravestones. Jim said one of the most memorable episodes occurred one morning when he looked out into the front yard and saw an old man using a garden hoe. Jim put down his coffee cup in preparation to go out and ask the man how he had gotten through the locked gate. By the time Jim looked back up, the man had disappeared. Whatever these experiences were, Jim couldn't explain them. He didn't consider them sinister; they only seemed to add to the mystique of the home and refuge he loved.

Jim had numerous pets that kept him company during the many years he lived at Pluvio (where much of the time he was single). One of his dogs was a Jack Russell named Bill (aka William, Will and "Honey Boy" Bill). Bill constantly wandered the property and often brought snakes to the door that he had killed. Jim talked about Bill and all his pets as if they were people, some with actual careers. He said Bill was popular with the ladies, but Jim eventually made an honest man out of him when he bought him a "little wife" named Sam (also a Jack Russell). Together they had a litter. Jim kept one and named him Boone. Jim talked about Boone being a movie star in his own right.

Another "movie star" pet Jim owned was a cat he named John Barrymore. The cat had interesting markings above his mouth that resembled the well-trimmed moustache of the famous stage actor. Other cats he owned included a black one named Night Life and two white ones named Tallulah and Maytag.

Two of the last dogs Jim owned were Karina, a rescued champion racing greyhound, and Maggie, a pit bull. He often bragged with parental pride about Karina's speed and her ability to do "zero to 60 in seven seconds." For Jim, his pets were his children.

CHAPTER SIXTEEN

HOBO STEW

Being a bachelor much of his life, Jim learned by necessity to cook for himself. Chili was one of his best dishes, as he seemed to prefer "one-pot" meals, which were often the easiest to prepare. One of his specialties was what he called "hobo soup" or "hobo stew." The steps were simple, he said. Just throw the contents of your refrigerator into one pot. He admitted that the only problem with the dish was the fact that you could never accurately recreate it.

Jim sometimes mentioned how his father had been a hobo of sorts for a bit. A family story went that in the summer of 1934, Big Jim and his brother-in-law Everett caught a train from Lexington and eventually made it down to Texas in a boxcar. What kind of work they were looking for is not known. A letter Jim wrote to his parents 50 years after the episode makes reference to the trip.

"Yesterday I did the United Way kickoff in Amarillo, Texas, and Pappy, it was held in the old Santa Fe train yard. Just think, it was the first time since the 1930s that a 'Jim Varney' was in the Amarillo yard, and I didn't have to whip even one railroad bull!"

Jim welcomed the chance to display his cooking skills when he made an appearance in 1987 on Florence Henderson's "Country Kitchen" cooking show on the Nashville Network. The dish he demonstrated was curry pepper steak. Part of the dish consisted of a mixture of water, onions and cornstarch for a gravy. Henderson and Jim shared a laugh with the studio audience when the ingredients failed to thicken and looked more like onion slices floating in milky water. Things did not go much better during the commercial break. Evidently, extra cornstarch was added, but it ended up being too much. When mentioning the dish after returning from commercial, Jim explained, "It's always best to use a little less than a half-pound of cornstarch for four people." He continued, "You have to *slice* the gravy when you do that."

When Jim and Henderson discussed their upbringings, Jim revealed that he had researched her biography and found that they had a Kentucky connection. Henderson had lived for a short time in Owensboro. Jim joked that he was a "Hill William" from Lexington. Again, this was the term he loved to use in describing a certain upper class of Southern hillbilly. A Hill William, for example, enjoyed the luxury of indoor plumbing.

Although the finished steak dish was never shown to the TV audience, Henderson did think enough of it to include it in her cookbook from the show: "A Little Cooking, a Little Talking and a Whole Lot of Fun."

Meanwhile, as thin as Jim stayed, you could never tell by looking at him how much he loved to eat. Nothing pleased him more than a plateful of Southern food and breakfasts of biscuits and gravy. Perhaps Jim's biggest weakness was candy, especially the homemade kind. Growing up, his mother always had a dessert prepared following supper. From her, he learned to make such favorites as chocolate fudge and cream candy. His sister Sandy remembers visiting the set of "Ernest Scared Stupid" and noticing a sign in Jim's dressing room warning people to stay away from Mr. Varney's candy bowl. Fortunately, he could gorge himself on all the sweets he wanted without gaining a pound.

Jim's father always said his son ate like a dog, meaning that he ate a lot when he was hungry but little else other times. Even journalists would note in their articles the way Jim attacked a plate of food during interviews. When visiting his family back home, Jim could easily put away a couple of plates of food and two or three desserts. When he had the time, he ate healthy, but the stretches on the road took a toll on his diet as he resorted to starches and sweets.

Unfortunately, candy wasn't Jim's only unhealthy habit. Reporters often wrote about how he chain-smoked. He laughed off one interviewer's comment by joking, "Naw, I'm not a chain smoker. They're real hard to light, and you have to carry that big torch." The truth was, very little time would pass between him putting out one cigarette and lighting up the next.

CHAPTER SEVENTEEN

HANDGUN WEDDING

Jane Hale, who went by Janie, was an attractive young brunette Jim met through a mutual friend at a pool party at his home around 1986. Janie was a travel agent in Nashville at the time and from Huntington, Ind. She actually had no idea who Ernest was when they met. As their conversation progressed, Jim told her he worked for a dairy company. In a sense it was true, since a good portion of the money from the dairy clients made its way into his pockets. She was thinking that maybe he drove a dairy truck. She found out the truth, and the jig was up. The two began dating and soon, she was handling many of his day-to-day business affairs as well as taking on the role of his biggest fan.

On June 11, 1988, Jim married Janie at his home in White House, Tenn. I was 15 at the time and videotaped the ceremony and much of the reception and other happenings that followed. It was a beautiful sunny Saturday afternoon, providing a picturesque setting as friends and family gathered in a ceremony on the back of the property. Among the many friends of Jim's in attendance were Jim and Jon Hager. Known as The Hager Twins, the identical twin brothers were a country-music-and-comedy duo who gained fame on "Hee Haw."

THE IMPORTANCE OF BEING ERNEST: THE LIFE OF ACTOR JIM VARNEY

A federal judge officiated. Jim's good friend Buck Finley served as best man. Janie's sister Sharon was matron of honor, Jim's niece Andrea maid of honor.

During the ceremony, the judge mentioned how unusual it was that he was performing a wedding ceremony because federal judges, unlike lower-court judges, didn't have that authority by law. (For this occasion, the General Assembly of Tennessee had to grant the authority.) The judge said, "The Founding Fathers, in their infinite wisdom, did not wish to make marriage a federal offense." He then added, to laughter, "Jim Varney getting married does rise to such a level."

As friends and family posed for pictures after the ceremony, the young daughter of one of the guests began to cry after being placed beside Jim. Jim looked at the photographer and said, "We're abusing this child." It was his kickoff line as he quickly turned into the MC of his own wedding.

At the reception, Jim couldn't resist making faces as guests took pictures of him and Janie holding the knife beside the cake. As Janie proceeded to slice into it, he yelled as if she was cutting into his flesh. Jim's mother couldn't help but laugh while futilely attempting to convey to Jim the seriousness of the occasion.

A small group remained at the house after the reception. Finley brought out two guitars and announced that he and Jim were going to play a couple of songs they had been working on. Both can best be classified as Southern rock. In the love song "Tonight We Own the Moon," Jim overpowered Finley's voice. And in the upbeat anthem "Time Waits for No One," Jim smacked his thigh and nearly sprang up from the couch as he reached for the notes.

Just when things were finally winding down, Jim decided to give everyone a demonstration on the "effectiveness" of his bulletproof vest. Everyone followed him outside. He placed the vest on the ground near the house, went back up to the deck, drew a handgun and fired into the vest. He then retrieved the vest and showed everyone where the bullet had hit, going into detail about the properties of Kevlar fiber. For guests hoping that the wedding would reflect Jim's personality, the event did not disappoint.

CHAPTER EIGHTEEN

SAVING CHRISTMAS

Jim and Janie had little time to relax as newlyweds. The morning after the wedding, the couple left for Los Angeles to attend the CBS Affiliates Dinner for Jim's upcoming children's show, "Hey Vern, It's Ernest," set to premiere in September. Carden & Cherry had declined previous offers to put Ernest in a TV show, but now that they had a successful movie under their belt, they had more confidence on how to make the character work beyond a 30-second commercial.

The Ernest TV series can best be described as a combination of many of the different Ernest projects that Jim and John Cherry had done up until then. It was a little bit of the Ernest commercials with a splash of Dr. Otto, combined with "Ernest Goes to Camp." Each episode had a clear theme, and the actors in each sketch touched on that theme in funny, imaginative ways. Cherry and the writers aimed for something beyond the usual cartoon fare. The show's humor included jokes and references that parents would also find humorous.

Along with the usual cast of Ernest writers, Jim's ex-wife, Jacqui (now going by her maiden name, Drew), wrote material that earned her a place in the opening credits.

THE IMPORTANCE OF BEING ERNEST:
THE LIFE OF ACTOR JIM VARNEY

The network originally wanted the show to be a cartoon with Jim voicing Ernest. If that had ever happened, so many of the expressive features of Jim's face would have been lost. The wide-angle lens already added so much of the cartoon element anyway. Animation wasn't necessary.

Gailard Sartain, no stranger to sketch comedy, joined Jim on the show and contributed many funny characters, including Lonnie Don, a dubious sound-effects expert who hosted a segment called "Lonnie Don's School of Hollywood Sound Effects." The running gag was that every sound he attempted to teach the viewers involved him placing the palm of his hand over his mouth and making a farting sound. Sartain's most memorable character was probably Chuck, half of a Laurel and Hardy-type duo. Chuck was the fast-talking, highly energetic half who bossed poor brother Bobby around. The rail-thin Bobby, played by Nashville librarian Bill Byrge, showed little emotion and rarely said a word as he followed Chuck's orders. Both actors had been cast in commercials for Carden & Cherry playing the same characters a few years earlier. The popular duo also ended up making big-screen appearances in "Ernest Saves Christmas" and "Ernest Goes to Jail."

One of the many imaginative non-human characters created for the Saturday show was a buck-toothed puppet named Dust Bunny. The bunny's ability to make Ernest sneeze was almost as impressive as the speed at which Dust Bunny's own sneezes propelled him in and out of the room. The puppet wore a miniature pair of Chuck Taylors and told jokes such as how he was the offspring of lint and a hairball. Probably the funniest and most ridiculous of Jim's characters was Baby Ernest. It was basically Ernest's head protruding through a cutout in a bassinet, connected to an infant-sized body. Things he overheard from his parents, such as his father telling his mother her door was ajar ("a jar") after entering the car, constantly amused Baby Ernest. At the end of every Baby Ernest segment he exclaimed, "Boy, grown-ups sure talk funny. Know what I mean?"

Spin Magazine was one of the many publications that gave the show a positive review. When a music magazine showers praise on a children's show, you know it is not typical Saturday-morning fare. As CBS children's programming director Judy Price claimed in the Dallas Morning News, "Weird does work for children if it's good weird."

The intention of Cherry, Jim and all the writers was to create a show that parents would want to watch *with* their kids. They were ahead of their time considering the eventual rise of movies like "Shrek." Tongue-in-cheek humor was the rule on "Hey Vern" rather than the exception.

Perhaps the show's 30-minute time frame and sketch format also enticed the writers into creating a Monty Python feel. After all, the team of Nashville writers, although extremely talented, did not have any experience writing for children's television. But their inexperience led to a refreshing perspective, allowing them to create something new and original. Jim thought too many cartoons with "kids blowing up robots" ran on Saturday mornings, and the landscape needed shaking up.

Although it was a busy time, Jim and Janie did manage to get away for a three-day vacation to nearby Gatlinburg, Tenn., located in the Smoky Mountains. Jim did his usual browsing of the knife and gun shops while gorging himself on the tourist mecca's famous fudge and saltwater taffy.

That same year, the next Ernest movie finally came together. A tropical-island movie concept that had been thrown around for months was ultimately scrapped in favor of a Christmas tale. Planned for a November release, "Ernest Saves Christmas," was the second feature film for the character. The budget was double that of "Camp," but at an estimated $6 million it was still low by Hollywood standards. The biggest problem Cherry encountered on the set turned out to be of the four-legged variety. The reindeer used in the movie were owned by Steve Martin's "Working Wildlife," a Los Angeles company specializing in animal actors. Right before their big scene, the reindeer shed their antlers. One remedy discussed was using some type of prosthetic. But after learning how tender reindeer heads are with their antlers gone, the idea was scrapped. No special effects like those we have today existed. All Cherry could do was wait patiently for the antlers to grow back. Unfortunately, the delay in production was expensive. Sounding like an angry Santa Claus, Cherry said to the Nashville Banner, "Reindeer antlers cost me a quarter-million dollars!" But filming the movie in the brand-new Disney-MGM studio in Orlando helped improve production values while keeping overall costs down.

As shooting was wrapping up on "Christmas," Jim flew out to Los Angeles for The Comedy Store's "Fifteen Year Reunion" show. Held at the Universal Amphitheatre, the event featured many of the biggest names to pass through the legendary club. Jim performed a short set alongside stars such as Richard Pryor, Robin Williams, David Letterman and Arsenio Hall. It had been a few years since Jim had performed stand-up, and reviews reflected on what might have been a little rust. The Dallas Morning News wrote, "An incognito and seemingly uncomfortable Jim Varney fired short bursts of one-liners."

As far as "Christmas," the plot involves Ernest working as a cab driver in Orlando, Fla. One of his customers happens to be the real-life Santa Claus, in town to turn over his duties to a new candidate, a local TV star who hosts a children's show. During the ride with Santa, a teenage female runaway calling herself Harmony

Starr jumps into the cab and is soon befriended by Ernest. When Ernest drops Santa off at his destination, Santa discovers that he has only play money on him. Ernest decides not to charge him and is subsequently fired. His boss kicks him to the curb along with a large red bag that Santa had accidentally left in Ernest's cab.

As Ernest and Harmony try to track down Santa, a funny subplot plays out where Chuck and Bobby (played by Gailard Sartain and Bill Byrge) are working as warehouse storage agents trying to make sense of a peculiar crate. Despite obvious clues in the paperwork that the crate is full of reindeer, it takes Chuck and Bobby finally seeing Santa's gravity-defying creatures standing upside-down on the warehouse ceiling (after escaping) to realize something is up.

Meanwhile, Ernest and Harmony stop by Vern's house to put up a Christmas tree. This is the only time Vern "appears" in an Ernest movie and, like the commercials, the audience never sees his face, only his point of view. Temptation soon gets the best of Harmony, and she takes off with Santa's bag only to return with it after her conscience prevails. She then helps Ernest and Santa find his successor, locate the reindeer and ultimately save Christmas.

During the week of the movie's release, Jim was asked why it had received a PG rating. "Unusual cruelty to reindeer," he replied. Cherry said later that he thought "Ernest Saves Christmas" was the best of the franchise. The box-office total of $28 million (the biggest return of any "Ernest" movie) showed that he wasn't the only one who felt that way. "Christmas" continues to have the most enduring success of all the Ernest films and has become a holiday classic.

Along with making Christmas memorable on the big screen, Jim never missed a visit home to Lexington to share the holiday with family. Holidays were the rare times they got to see him. Needless to say, he was the star attraction.

The Varney family gathered every Christmas Eve and celebrated, as countless families do, by stuffing their faces and exchanging gifts. Jim was usually the last to arrive, due to social commitments with friends in the area. He always showed up with plenty of presents and an appetite that rivaled a horse's.

He would hold court in the kitchen, entertaining family members for hours. The excitement he brought to every gathering was far more electric than the lights on the tree. He told stories, showed off his latest knife or watch purchase and imitated Johnny Cash. I remember the times he gave me lessons on topics ranging from the pagan aspects of Christmas to the correct usage of the bezel on my diver's watch that measured oxygen-tank levels.

Through the years, Jim's mother had established a standard pair of Christmas presents for her son: a silk scarf and a tin of homemade candy. Jim could easily identify the two gifts under the tree but would still attempt to inject suspense into the occasion. Holding what was obviously the scarf in one hand and the candy in the other he would say, "One of these is 2 pounds of candy, and the other is a silk scarf. I wonder which is which."

One year, when the Christmas party was at sister Sandy's house, her husband was having a difficult time getting the fire going. Jim walked over to the fireplace to help. After assessing the situation, he asked for a hair dryer. Everyone looked at him quizzically. Before they knew it, Jim had used the hair dryer to ignite the glowing embers and create a blazing fire. Santa Claus himself couldn't have been as cool.

In addition to the new children's TV show, Jim was having discussions with CBS about starring in a non-Ernest series. The prime-time detective show was set around an Inspector Clouseau-type character with a Southern spin. He said, "It's going to be a little Rockford (Files), a little Barnaby Jones and a little Barney Fife." Depending on the filming dates of the next Ernest movie, Jim hoped the show would be ready for the fall line-up. Unfortunately, like so many non-Ernest forays, nothing ever came of it.

The New Year's Eve special was the last work Jim did for CBS. The children's show was cancelled after the first season. Despite a letter-writing campaign from the Ernest Fan Club, the 13th and last episode of the season, which aired on December 24, 1988, turned out to be the show's finale. Although it had received critical acclaim, some of the humor may have been too sophisticated for the kids who tuned in. Cherry thought the show, referred to by some as a "poor man's Pee-wee's Playhouse," would have flourished in another time slot such as Sunday evening.

The disappointment over the cancellation became less painful after Jim was nominated for a Daytime Emmy Award for Outstanding Performer in a Children's Series. He received the ultimate late birthday present on June 20, 1989, when he won the award (he had turned 40 five days earlier). Just a year earlier he had been nominated for a Razzie Award for Worst New Star in "Ernest Goes to Camp." (The Razzies are the anti-Oscars).

CHAPTER NINETEEN

THE LINE BLURS BETWEEN JIM AND ERNEST

Jim understood that being recognized was just part of fame. Of course, most people identified him with Ernest, and many even referred to him as Ernest while asking him to recite catchphrases and sign autographs. For the most part, Jim liked the recognition and was patient with fans. The few times he got exasperated were when someone would ask him to re-enact an entire bit from a commercial. He once recalled his reply, "I'm sorry, but I don't have my window with me." Some people actually called him Vern instead of Ernest. It was surprising how many people recognized Jim so quickly in public. Most of the time he looked un-Ernest-like. Without the familiar baseball cap, his thick curly hair was revealed. He was usually wearing a silk shirt with the two top buttons undone and a fair amount of jewelry. His near-perfect posture complemented the fluidness of his movements, which were more like those of a dancer than a klutzy TV pitchman. It was similar to watching the contrast between Christopher Reeve's awkward Clark Kent and Superman.

But what was a minor annoyance is his personal life became a huge roadblock in his professional one. Jim said that he made a point to come onto talk shows and other TV appearances dressed as himself to prove "there's an actual me there." He hoped this would prevent him from becoming too identified with the character. It may have worked early on, but soon the line between Jim and Ernest became more and more blurred, and Jim seemed to give in to the fact that the industry and the public could not separate them.

At the 1986 Music City News Country Awards, as he had at the premiere of the first Ernest movie, Jim appeared in a tuxedo with an Ernest-themed black satin baseball cap. He was introduced as Ernest and began to act the part in a short scripted piece informing viewers about the details of the voting process. He wore the same formalwear when co-hosting CBS' "Happy New Year, America 1988" two years later. His co-hosts referred to him as "Jim" even though he repeatedly called himself Ernest and essentially played the character during most of the show.

In 1989, Jim participated in HBO's "Comic Relief," the hugely successful comedy benefit created in the late '80s and hosted by Robin Williams, Billy Crystal and Whoopi Goldberg. It raised millions of dollars for the homeless while showcasing many of the biggest names in comedy. But instead of Jim performing as himself, he participated in an eyebrow-raising sketch as Ernest.

A young woman dressed in lingerie, and her male lover, also dressed in women's lingerie and wearing a leather mask, were getting frisky in the bedroom. Jim, dressed as Ernest, lifts up the bedroom window from the outside, leans in and yells, "Hey Vern!" With his childlike mind, Ernest believes the two are horsing around in their Halloween outfits. Before the skit ends, Jim pulls out a Comic Relief T-shirt and begins hawking it as if he was on a TV commercial. Of course, the whole sketch wouldn't have been complete without his fingers being slammed in the falling window.

THE LINE BLURS BETWEEN JIM AND ERNEST

Jim was always willing to do anything for charity, but it's unknown if he was asked to appear as Ernest or if it was his decision. He went on to play Ernest throughout the entire benefit show. It's hard to imagine Robin Williams wanting to dress as Mork or Martin Short playing his Ed Grimley character during the entirety of their appearances on the special. Even at the close of the show, when all of the performers came out dressed in their Comic Relief T-shirts, Jim wore a vest over his with the familiar khaki baseball cap on his head. Whether he realized it or not, these appearances were cementing his association with Ernest.

Still, Jim kept trying to break out. His next movie provided him a non-Ernest role that was still within the realm of comedy. In September 1988, Jim spent a week in Atlanta filming scenes for the independent comedy, "Fast Food." In the movie, Jim plays restaurant owner Wrangler Bob. Sporting a white suit topped off with a white cowboy hat, he looks like a skinny version of Boss Hogg, the greedy commissioner from "Dukes of Hazzard." The plot centers around Wrangler Bob waging a personal war on a young woman and her wild college friends after she refuses to sell him the family gas station he has been eyeing for a new restaurant location. They become so irritated by his antics that they open their own restaurant to compete with him. The place proves to be a formidable competitor once employees unknowingly create a secret sauce that turns customers into sex maniacs.

The movie was released in April 1989 and fizzled out after poor reviews and sparse attendance. Film critic Richard Roeper said, "The script of 'Fast Food' is so devoid of imagination that it would have been more interesting to film the cast lunches." His comment referred to the colorful cast that included not only Jim, but recently retired adult-film star Traci Lords and actor Michael J. Pollard, among others. After moving so squarely into the kid genre with

THE IMPORTANCE OF BEING ERNEST:
THE LIFE OF ACTOR JIM VARNEY

the Disney movies and the children's show on CBS, it was interesting that Jim took a role in such an adult-themed movie. Disney could not have been thrilled. Since the movie made few waves at the box office, it stayed under the radar and caused no apparent conflict with his kid-friendly image.

One thing that made life less demanding for Jim during the fall and winter of 1988 was the fact that he wasn't shooting any Ernest commercials. He was negotiating a new contract with Carden & Cherry. Talks centered on the commercials Jim shot for the agency and had no bearing on the ongoing movie deal with Disney. Negotiations were slow. Nearly a full year went by without an Ernest commercial being made. By mid-1989, Jim eventually received a new three-year deal that was to take the Ernest character into Europe and Asia. Jim joked later about how he had remained calm throughout the ordeal, knowing that "Paul Newman can't do Ernest."

The break in shooting commercials did allow him more time for his family. His mother had been diagnosed with leukemia around 1987; now being widowed, she needed her family more than ever. Jim helped out around the house when he visited, including keeping Louise's kitchen knives razor-sharp. Although in his mind he was just making it easier for her to use them, her leukemia slowed the healing of any, even minor, cuts or scrapes. Luckily, the knives never caused her any problems. But whenever a friend or family member came by to prepare a meal and reached for a knife, Louise said, "Bo's been here, so be careful."

Meanwhile, although the Ernest team was disappointed by the cancelling of the children's show, more movies remained on the Disney contract. One idea under serious consideration was called "Ernest Spaced Out." The basic plot involved Ernest getting snatched by aliens and taken back to their planet. At some point that was put on hold, and later that summer it was announced that "Ernest Goes to Jail" would be the character's next adventure. Shooting was set to begin in Nashville in the fall of 1989. "Jail" finds poor Ernest going to the slammer in place of his doppleganger who just so happens to be an evil crime boss.

While Jim was still deciding where in his house to display his new Emmy award, he found out he was to receive another honor that would be almost as meaningful: induction into Lafayette High School's newly created Hall of Fame. It was the year of the high school's 50th anniversary, and the reunion council made the decision to induct 20 alumni. On July 15, a ceremony was held at the University of Kentucky's Commonwealth Stadium on a beautiful Saturday afternoon with a few thousand people in attendance. Other inductees included former Kentucky governor John Y. Brown and longtime NBC Sports commentator Tom Hammond.

Jim's popularity was continuing to grow nationwide. And Ernest's phrases were popping up in the unlikeliest places. One Tennessee Baptist church used Ernest humor when placing a message on its signboard. It read, "Hey Vern, only three more days of Bible school, Ya know what I mean?"

As busy as Jim was with movie and TV projects, he was still committed to promoting Ernest through countless public appearances. In August 1989, Jim and Ernest writer Dan Butler went on the state-fair circuit, beginning with an appearance at the Illinois State Fair in Springfield. Fans of Ernest, many dressed in caps and vests, showed up on the day called "Ernest Comes to the Fair." They delighted in watching Jim smash a whipped-cream pie into the face of a robot toting a water-machine gun. Later Jim served as grand marshal of the parade. Close to a million people attended, and countless fans came home with autographed photos of Ernest.

In the fall of 1989, shooting on "Ernest Goes to Jail" began. The Tennessee State Penitentiary was chosen for the exterior shots.

THE IMPORTANCE OF BEING ERNEST:
THE LIFE OF ACTOR JIM VARNEY

Much of the interior shots were filmed in an old Nashville warehouse. In addition to Ernest, Jim played Ernest's doppelganger, Felix Nash. This evil-twin plot gave Jim a chance to show audiences his ability to play a more serious role with a different look.

In the movie, Ernest is working as a custodian at a bank. After being summoned for jury duty, a crooked defense lawyer notices how much Ernest resembles crime boss Felix Nash. A plot is soon hatched: The jurors tour the prison that houses Felix, and a switch is made between the two. Ernest finds himself on Death Row, while Felix takes on his identity at the bank. When the electric chair malfunctions on the day of Felix's (Ernest's) scheduled execution, the resulting jolt Ernest receives gives him superhuman powers that enable him to finally bring Felix to justice.

Jim was familiar with the role of the villain from his younger years. He recalled once, "They always cast me as the villain or the bozo. It was one end or the other. I never got the romantic leads – I don't know why. With my good looks you'd think they would offer them to me all the time."

Jack Turner, one of Jim's castmates from his days at the Third Masque Theatre in Chattanooga in the '70s, remembers what turned out to be an amazingly accurate prediction of Jim's. As the two were talking about future roles, Jim told him, "I think I'll probably wind up as the jester or some kind of joker most of the time." But as much as Jim loved comedy, his longing for something more dramatic never seemed to fade. Jim was optimistic that the Felix Nash character might open up some eyes in Hollywood. He said during the time, "Maybe I'll be reading with Harry Dean Stanton and fighting over a villain role." (Like Jim, Central Kentucky native Stanton attended Lafayette High School.)

As Jim prepared for his dual-role, he found inspiration from Peter Sellers' Inspector Clouseau. He credited Sellers with keeping alive the practice of actors playing multiple roles. Jim hadn't had a chance to play a villain onscreen since the largely unknown Dr. Otto. In addition to playing Felix Nash in the movie, Jim also broke out the wig and makeup for a character called Auntie Nelda. She had actually first appeared in "Dr. Otto." Often complaining about a son named Hymie who never treats her right, Auntie Nelda is a dour old lady who speaks in a deep monotone. She uses a walker and wears a neck brace. The brace adds to the humor of Jim's portrayal, as he would squish his jaw into it causing his face to appear fleshier and more wrinkled. Ample padding gives Auntie Nelda a disproportionately wide figure to go along with her oversized breasts. Her dress, hat and pearl necklace make her look as if she is ready for church. Her sullen face includes heavy eye makeup and thick, bright-red lipstick. She peers down through glasses resting on the end of her long nose, looking as if she is studying – and more often than not, judging – whoever is on the other end.

As usual, Jim was performing some of the bigger stunts himself. For the flying sequences inside the bank, he wore a harness similar to the one Christopher Reeve wore in "Superman." He joked that it was "a real pain in the crotch." A souped-up floor polisher that could reach speeds of up to 20 mph was constructed for the action sequences. In one scene, where Ernest attempts to restrain the floor waxer, he utters a line that connected Jim right back to his childhood fantasies. As he is flying through the air he says, "Peter Pan, eat your heart out." Just as Ernest was flying high, so was Jim's career.

Since Jim had now become a big part of the Disney family, he began making appearances on their shows. In 1989, he appeared on the half-hour special "Walt Disney Celebrity Circus," promoting a new Disneyland ride called "Ernest Goes to Splash Mountain." Later, he appeared on the "New Mickey Mouse Club." The following year he showed up on the John Landis-directed "Disneyland's 35th Anniversary Special."

Even popular talk-show host David Letterman found a way to use Ernest's popularity. Letterman's writers had begun injecting Ernest into their popular Top Ten lists, always referring to him as the "Hey Vern" guy. Beginning in the late '80s, and even continuing a few years beyond Jim's death, they included him in no less than 12 lists over a 15-year span.

Letterman writer Bill Scheft shed some light on perhaps why in a piece Scheft wrote for Sports Illustrated in 2009. In describing David Letterman's affection for how star athlete Peyton Manning played the stooge in various TV commercials, he wrote, "To call someone a 'TV stooge' is the ultimate accolade from Dave. To be a stooge is to willingly participate with no ego, no concern for how it all looks."

In addition, one little-known fact is that a few of Letterman's memorable non-sequiturs uttered through the years are borrowed from a character named Elrod Napier in one of Jim's old routines. Jim had written the character late one night at a Shoney's restaurant in Lexington. Elrod is a chubby boy around 12 years old from the South. Instead of playing outside, he prefers to sit around and scratch his back while watching TV all day. On their move to California, Joe Liles contributed a piece of the routine that helped tie it all together. "Elrod, Elrod, help Momma water the lawn. Elrod honey... these buckets is heavy!" is a line Liles thought of in a Denny's restroom north of San Diego. When Liles returned to the table and told Jim the line, Jim started laughing so hard he spilled his coffee.

In Jim's act, lazy Elrod was always in front of the tube asking his mother the same annoying questions. "What time is it?" became Elrod's catchphrase, along with, "Are you cookin' beans?" and "Is

THE LINE BLURS BETWEEN JIM AND ERNEST

Zorro on?" (Author's note: Comedian Jeff Altman does a great imitation of Elrod when praising Jim's talent in the Special Features segment of the "Pink Lady and Jeff" DVD collection.) Elrod always got a great response when Jim performed the routine on the "Merv Griffin Show." With the respect Letterman seemed to have for Jim, it's curious that Jim never made an appearance on his show.

Some people say you haven't arrived until you a perfume is named after you, someone plays you in a movie or a doll is made in your likeness. When Jim came home to Lexington for Christmas in 1989, he brought along a box full of Ernest dolls. The 15-inch figure made by Kenner had a string that when pulled, spoke up to six different Ernest phrases. But the recordings played back too fast. If the string was given slight resistance, allowing it to retract more slowly, the voice began to sound much more like Jim. He once joked that kids must have been sticking pins in the dolls because he was having a lot of unexplained aches and pains.

In February 1990, the Atlanta Braves front office thought they could use Ernest to raise attendance, which had fallen to last in the league. Being in the South, where Ernest historically flourished, the move seemed like a no-brainer. A one-year contract was ironed out including TV and print ads, as well as promotional appearances at Atlanta-Fulton County Stadium.

An open house was arranged soon after the contract was finalized to allow fans to come to the stadium and meet Ernest in person. The only problem was that it was not Jim, just a life-size cardboard replica of Ernest. Parents toting excited kids were less than thrilled. The rocky start of the campaign was a sign of things to come.

The magical selling power of Ernest proved to be no match for a sports franchise piling up more losses than wins. For Braves fans who did not like Ernest, he added insult to injury. Two years later the Atlanta Journal Constitution wrote, "A lot of Atlantans associate Ernest P. Worrell with the Atlanta Braves' last-place finish in 1990. The article added, "Some even credit the 1991 surge to the World Series to Varney's departure from the club's TV commercials."

Undeterred, Carden & Cherry tried to work some Ernest magic for an NFL team a few years later. Jim shot a few commercials for the Kansas City Chiefs to promote ticket sales. Although the Chiefs experience went more smoothly, it was Ernest's last foray into advertising for professional sports.

In the early spring of 1990 Jim went on a 12-city promotional tour for "Ernest Goes to Jail." In what had become a routine, Jim made time to visit children's hospitals such as the Texas Scottish Rite Hospital for Crippled Children in Dallas. Jim visited thousands of sick children through the years as Ernest. If kids were well enough, sometimes he took them out for lunch. He jokingly claimed to have eaten more Happy Meals than any living adult. He was passionate about helping kids who needed his humor most.

CHAPTER TWENTY

"HEY VERN!"

In 1991 Jim and Janie ended their marriage after three years. In the "E! True Hollywood Story" about Jim, Janie said his work took a toll on their relationship. "He'd be going here, I'd be going there," she said. They did remain good friends, and she also stayed on as his assistant. During this time, another important relationship of Jim's ended. After a successful collaboration that lasted around four years, Jim and Phil Walden parted ways. Jim's attorney, Hoot Gibson, began handling Jim's management duties.

But Jim's career was still moving at full speed. In the late spring of 1991, filming began on the last Disney-backed Ernest picture, "Ernest Scared Stupid." In the movie, Ernest plays a sanitation worker who unknowingly releases a demonic troll from underneath a cursed old tree where his relative Phineas Worrell had buried it many years earlier. Before long, many other trolls begin invading his small town, turning innocent children into statues. It is soon up to Ernest to stop them. He receives help from neighborhood kids in searching for a way to eradicate the evil trolls. An eccentric old lady played by Eartha Kitt provides Ernest with some of the tools needed to stop the creatures.

Before deciding on the name for the spooky tale, many other titles were considered, among them "Ernest and the Trolls" and

THE IMPORTANCE OF BEING ERNEST:
THE LIFE OF ACTOR JIM VARNEY

"Ernest and the Curse," along with "Ernest Scared Stiff." With "Scared Stiff," some Disney executives became concerned that parents might not appreciate the unintended adult reference. "Ernest Scared Stupid" made the most sense. Jim joked, "It's the degree he'd be scared to. Scared into stupidity."

As was the case with the previous Ernest movies, "Scared Stupid" received mostly poor reviews. Gene Siskel and Roger Ebert both gave it a "thumbs down," and Ebert admitted that it was the first Ernest movie he had ever seen. He actually said he could imagine liking the movie if he was 8 but could not recommend it otherwise. That really wasn't such a bad review given the intended audience.

When Jim was doing interviews following the "Scared Stupid" premiere, he once again discussed with honesty his love-hate relationship with Ernest: "For several years this character has been extremely prohibitive to my (non-Ernest) career." Since 1987 he had made four Ernest movies, 13 episodes of an Ernest-themed TV show and hundreds of commercials, all while continuing Ernest's many public appearances. He told one reporter that 16 commercials alone had been filmed in the week leading up to the "Scared Stupid" press junkets.

But during press tours he did express excitement about a role he had just been offered in the film "Wilder Napalm," screenwriter Vince Gilligan's first feature film. The romantic comedy, starring Dennis Quaid and Debra Winger, is about estranged brothers who possess pyrokinetic powers. Jim was offered the role of Rex, a heavily tattooed traveling carnival operator and partner of Quaid's character, Wally. "I'm finally breaking out," Jim told one reporter. But he was not planning on turning his back on Ernest. To reassure thousands of fans, he said, "I expect we'll keep making these movies as long as people want to come see them." (Little did Jim

"HEY VERN!"

know that Gilligan would go on to have an outstanding career as a writer/director/producer in film and television, including creating and producing the acclaimed TV series "Breaking Bad.")

The stage also continued to call to Jim. A year earlier, a scheduling conflict had prevented him from reading for a part in "Twelfth Night" in Dallas. Now his sights were set on winning the part of Nathan Detroit in "Guys and Dolls" on Broadway. Although Jim was confident about winning the role he had played in his dinner-theater years, Nathan Lane was eventually cast and earned a Tony nomination for his portrayal. The play ran for about three years. It's interesting to imagine the impact landing the role might have had on Jim's career. Although it surely would have been satisfying professionally, he would have missed out on playing Jed Clampett in "The Beverly Hillbillies," a part that would mark one of his biggest thrills as an actor and become a favorite among fans.

In March 1992, Jim was honored by the Tennessee State Senate for outstanding contributions to the state, with special consideration for his work with children's charities. A resolution was passed commemorating his achievements. The 33 senators in attendance donned Ernest masks while trading jokes with Jim. He grabbed one of the masks, placed it right next to his face and proclaimed, "I'm beside myself."

As many commercials as Jim made, it seemed as if there had to be clones of him to keep up. It was around this time that Jim mentioned in an interview that he had starred in a whopping 2,700 commercials. He always took pride in throwing out the constantly growing number. He was well aware that a prominent West Coast car dealer named Cal Worthington had actually made more. Worthington, who had been parodied by Johnny Carson, had been shooting thousands of crazy commercials with exotic animals for his many dealerships since the '60s. But one detail Jim often mentioned was that Ernest commercials were shot on film while Worthington's were not.

Also during this time, Carden & Cherry decided to resurrect one of Jim's former characters for the Ernest commercials. Jim had created Bunny Jeanette while at the Third Masque Theatre in Chattanooga and later included her in his stand-up act. Bunny shared little in common with Ernest in terms of appearance, but her unsolicited advice and aggressive approach were similar. Her heavily made-up face, dangling jewelry and red beehive gave the beauty consultant an unforgettable look. Her professional background consisted of a diploma from Vo-Tech Beauty College. With that coveted degree, she began operating "Bunny Jeanette's Beauty World" out of her home. Her slogan was "Beauty is Bunny's Business." To say she used unconventional methods is an understatement. She operated an electric bench grinder to file nails and used a chisel for facials. The fact that she was usually more involved in dispensing advice than concentrating on her work made these tools all the more hazardous to clients.

In May 1992, TV viewers from Los Angeles to Knoxville watched in amusement as Bunny began to show up in regional TV commercials. She was not a replacement for Ernest; he was still airing in around 20 regional markets. She was just another character in the vast Jim Varney arsenal that Carden & Cherry thought they could make work as a commercial "pitchwoman."

On June 28, 1992, Jim's family and hometown fans were treated to a special performance. Jim made a rare stand-up comedy appearance in the Grand Ballroom of the Marriott Resort Griffin Gate in Lexington. The occasion was Lexington's "Comic Relief for the Homeless." The money raised went to such charities as the Hope Center and the Salvation Army. Jim shared billing with another talented comedian, Stuart Mitchell, better known as the comic character Heywood Banks, who is still around today. Heywood's energetic act is almost as loud as the colors of his mismatched tie and sport coat. Although he is hardly balding, his hair is combed over on one side, and he wears big horn-rimmed glasses. His goofy, oddball look warrants laughter before he even opens his mouth. The character is famous for his clever, hilarious songs. One of the most popular, "Toast," is sung while Heywood uses a metal toaster (tied around his neck) as a drum with two forks for drumsticks. (He is currently a regular on "The Bob & Tom Show," which is nationally syndicated.)

Unlike Jim's appearances on HBO's "Comic Relief" specials, Jim was not dressed as Ernest for the Lexington show, and few references were made to the character. This was often the case for Jim in smaller venues. Since Bunny Jeanette was back in the public eye, Jim decided to bring out one of his oldest Bunny routines, where she rolls hair with frozen orange-juice cans. Despite how little stand-up he had been performing, he seemed at ease onstage. He smoothly went on to the next bit, where he imitated country music singer Mel Tillis in a fictional story about the two of them visiting the local Keeneland racetrack years earlier. The bit consisted of Tillis betting on a horse that jumped over the fence during the race, never to return. Tillis got so upset that he questioned the trainer who claimed that he had tried everything to prevent what had been a recurring problem. Tillis then suggested that the trainer place a little piece of metal behind the horse's ear. When the trainer asked how he was to keep it in there, Tillis replied, "with a gun!" It was a short set, but the crowd loved it.

CHAPTER TWENTY-ONE

BLUE JEANS AND T-SHIRT MAN

Just a few years into the Ernest phenomenon, John Cherry observed, "None of that prima donna stuff has set in on ol' Jim." Throughout the fame and fortune that Ernest brought him, Jim's overall lifestyle changed very little. He resided in the same house he had purchased before becoming wealthy, preferring the mostly unpretentious appearance of his comfortable surroundings. White House was a down-home environment, and although most everyone in town knew where Jim lived, they respected his privacy and desire for as normal a life as possible.

Few changes were made to his residence over the years with the exception of his constantly expanding inventory of watches and knives.

Jim had been paid $300 for his first Ernest commercial. By now he was making millions. But he took more pride in telling someone how rare or well made an item was instead of bragging about how much he had paid for it. He knew it was all too easy to pick out something from a catalog. He preferred the thrill of searching for something unusual, something with significance. He browsed through jewelry and knife shops as an adult just as he had wandered the school playground searching for coins as a kid.

THE IMPORTANCE OF BEING ERNEST:
THE LIFE OF ACTOR JIM VARNEY

Jim had learned the value of hard work as a child. When he would do odd jobs for his parents and aunts, the coins went directly into a chalkware piggy bank in the shape of a dog. These chalkware, or molded gypsum, figurines first gained popularity during the Great Depression. Jim named his "Gentleman J." He also used it to collect "donations" after performing for relatives in the family room. When Jim started school, his mother helped him crack it open, revealing over several dollars in change, a lot of money for a kid at the time.

As an adult, instead of spending money on an expensive new house, Jim made investments in properties such as a Nashville condo and a farm in Sand Gap, Ky. One of the few indulgences he allowed himself was a DeLorean sports car, made famous by the movie "Back to the Future." The car reflected how Jim stayed true to his own desires instead of trying to impress others. If he had really wanted to be "flashy," he could have bought a top-of-the-line Cadillac or Mercedes. Instead, he preferred something James Bond might drive. Plus, the stainless-steel DeLorean matched his stainless-steel Rolex.

Once when Jim was visiting family in Lexington, his young niece Elaine was inspecting the DeLorean's interior. She looked in the back seat and asked Jim where the flux capacitor was (the hardware that enabled the car in "Back to the Future" to travel through time when the speedometer hit 88 mph). I got a thrill myself as a 13-year-old in 1986 when Uncle Jim offered to take me for a ride in the car. We drove to a nearby gas station. When we pulled up to the pump, Uncle Jim raised both doors, letting the classical music he was blasting fill the air. To say that we drew attention is an understatement.

Another sports car Jim owned that was a rarity in the mid-1980s was a Dodge Conquest. Its electronic dash and voice-alert features likely fascinated the teenage Bond fan inside Jim. Of course, not even Jim's cool cars could escape the reach of his humor. On the back of his DeLorean, one bumper sticker read, "As A Matter Of Fact I DO OWN THE ROAD!" On the Conquest, another read, "YES I AM A MOVIE STAR." Another bumper sticker on the Conquest had been edited. It had originally read, "IT'S ME, IT'S ME, IT'S ERNEST T." This was the line made famous by Ernest T. Bass – the troublemaking mountain-man character from "The Andy Griffith Show." Jim found a letter "P" to cover up the "T" to represent Ernest Worrell's peculiar middle name: "Power Tools."

When interviewed, Jim was often asked about all the money he was making. He was never comfortable with the question, always deflecting it. Sometimes he told reporters tall tales, such as how he had bought a string of small towns in Ohio. Another time, he said he owned "a fleet of pastel Ferraris." No amount of wealth brought him more pleasure than his down-home existence in the rural outskirts of Nashville. "I'm a blue jeans and T-shirt man," he'd say.

CHAPTER TWENTY-TWO

BUCKMASTERS & BUBBA

Jim loved to hunt, everything from bear to deer. He also became proficient with the long bow. Coke Sams remembers how proud Jim sounded when he talked about hunting with "two strings and a stick." He probably envisioned himself as Robin Hood in Sherwood Forest. It would have thrilled Jim to no end if he had known that his fifth-generation great grandfather on his mother's side was Edward Boone, brother of Daniel Boone. I uncovered the family connection during research for this book.

Jim's interest in deer hunting led him to become a fan of Jackie Bushman's "Buckmasters" hunting show on the Nashville Network. Bushman had started the Buckmasters deer-hunting association in 1986 and began his long-running hunting show in the summer of 1989. Jim met Bushman through country music singer Eddie Reasoner and his manager, Wilson Frazier. The two became fast friends, and Jim was soon making regular appearances on Bushman's show.

Jim's association with Buckmasters reached a whole new level after he spoke to Bushman about getting young people more involved in the sport. Jim created an Ernest-type character for the show, Bubba, a bumbling hunter (Jim told Bushman every hunter has a buddy named Bubba). Bubba had been a buffoon Jim had occasionally used in his stand-up, a nameless supporting player. Joe Liles remembers Bubba being a spoof of a character from an early stand-up routine of actor and comedian Tim Thomerson's in the 1970s. Thomerson's character had the dubious distinction of growing up on a mayonnaise farm. As had Thomerson, Jim gave the character a distinctive look by snarling both sides of his upper lip and exposing the top row of his teeth when he spoke.

Before Bubba was complete, he needed the right look. Bushman remembers going with Jim to a local outdoors store in Alabama where Jim picked out a large orange hat with earflaps. He turned one flap up and the other down. Then he said to Bushman, "I'm gonna take this front flap right here and I want you to go get some cardboard, and I want you to write 'BUBBA' on it and we'll duct tape it on there." Along with props such as a rifle with an oversized scope, Bubba was ready for the great outdoors.

The first year or so that Jim was on the show playing Bubba, Bushman paired him with a puppet named Shotgun Red, voiced and operated by comedian Steve Hall. With his well-worn straw cowboy hat, bushy gray moustache and plaid shirt, coupled with Southern charm and a quick wit, Shotgun Red remains a beloved figure for fans of all ages today. The puppet debuted on Ralph Emery's "Nashville Now" TV show in 1982. The combination of Jim and Shotgun Red was an instant hit. Young fans of Bushman's show soon began sending in pictures and questions. A segment was created for Jim to answer selected questions. The only problem was that the cast couldn't stop laughing long enough for Jim to make it through his answers.

Bubba gained a following. "Hey Bush, you know when I go out they don't talk about Ernest, they talk about Bubba," Jim would say to Bushman.

Before long, Bubba was teaching safety to young hunters. Three half-hour safety videos were also created for the organization's Young Bucks Club. In the first, called "The Misadventures of Bubba," Jim – as himself – introduces segments where Bubba and his unseen hunting partner, Billy Bob, break all the rules of hunting. Bubba talks into the camera to Billy Bob in the same way Ernest talks to Vern. Then Jim, again as himself, follows up with an explanation of what rule had been broken and why that rule is critical for safety. The next two videos, "The Misadventures of Bubba II" and "Bubba Goes Hunting," focus on Bubba's over-the-top hunting antics. According to Bushman, the kids loved it, and every fish–and-game department in the country wanted copies. Many stated that it was the only educational video they had encountered that kids wanted to watch repeatedly.

For much of the '90s, Jim participated in the annual Buckmasters National Deer Classic. He always looked forward to the four-day celebrity deer hunt, held for years at the Southern Sportsman Hunting Lodge just west of Montgomery, Ala. Created in 1987, it brought together stars from sports and entertainment along with top whitetail deer hunters from across the country. Bushman was surprised at just how popular Jim was at the Classic; people lined up for his autograph. Apart from entertaining as Bubba, Jim portrayed other characters such as a buffoonish football player who wore black high-tops and a 1960s-style helmet with the face mask removed. Although his equipment wasn't permitted on the football field, it gave him the upper hand when facing off in matches against pro wrestlers also participating in the event. As serious as Jim was about entertaining, he was also fully invested in the hunting competitions. One year he even won the hatchet-throwing contest for his team.

THE IMPORTANCE OF BEING ERNEST:
THE LIFE OF ACTOR JIM VARNEY

Perhaps the most important contribution Jim made to the Buckmasters was his ability to help foster a relationship between the organization and terminally ill children. One year Bushman invited an 11-year-old boy suffering from cystic fibrosis to the Buckmaster's Classic. The boy was thrilled to meet and hunt alongside celebrities like Jim and Atlanta Braves third baseman Chipper Jones. The experience led Bushman to create a program called Life Hunts in 1998 to give disabled and seriously ill children the opportunity to participate in a real hunt. Jim's experiences visiting young hospital patients through the years made him a natural at using his popular characters to bring happiness to many of these brave kids.

One of Bushman's favorite memories of Jim is the time Jim invited him to the premiere of "The Beverly Hillbillies." Bushman had arrived just before the premiere and happened to be walking up when Zsa Zsa Gabor was making her entrance. It appeared as if the two might be together. Reporters and photographers were asking each other, "Who's the guy in the cowboy hat?" Jim, close by, replied, "That's the Buckmaster!" which drew a response of, "Who's the Buckmaster?" Jim said, "That's my hunting consultant."

CHAPTER TWENTY-THREE

A HILLBILLY OF AN OZARK KIND

In the early '90s, vintage TV shows were being resurrected by major movie studios and turned into feature films. Just as comic-book characters are in vogue today, old TV classics such as "Dennis the Menace" and "The Brady Bunch" were finding new life in the hands of Hollywood screenwriters. Toward the end of 1992, 20th Century Fox green-lit the production of "The Beverly Hillbillies." Penelope Spheeris, hot off the success of "Wayne's World," seemed like the perfect choice to direct the beloved TV classic. She had shown the ability to direct a comedy adapted from TV – in this case "Saturday Night Live" – for the big screen. She also related to the material, being a transplanted Arkansan living in California. Her own family had moved there from Hot Springs when she was 8.

The casting was vital in capturing the flavor of the original show, and no character was more important than that of the patriarch, Jed Clampett. After going through close to 50 actors, Spheeris set her sights on Jim. The studio then echoed the sentiment that Jim had feared for years: He was too identified with Ernest to effectively portray a reserved and comparatively sensible character such as Jed. Too much money was on the line for the studio to take the risk.

THE IMPORTANCE OF BEING ERNEST:
THE LIFE OF ACTOR JIM VARNEY

But at Spheeris' insistence, the studio agreed to let Jim do a screen test. One advantage that Jim had was that the look of Jed, with his graying mustache and wide-brimmed hat, gave him a much different appearance.

Jim did not disappoint in the screen test. He landed the role and was thrilled about the opportunity to prove himself in a major film. He said, "I've been waiting a long time for a breakaway character," adding, "But hey, that's Hollywood!" His fans were also anxious to see him in a new role, especially one as iconic as Jed Clampett. He rounded out a talented cast that included Lily Tomlin, Dabney Coleman, Cloris Leachman, Lea Thompson and Rob Schneider. Diedrich Bader and Kevin Connolly, though not stars at the time, gained fame later in popular TV shows. Bader found success on "The Drew Carey Show" and Connolly on the HBO series "Entourage."

Playing the character forced Jim to tone down the physical style of comedy to which he was accustomed. Jed was the quietest member of the Clampett clan. Even though he had his share of funny scenes, Jim was essentially playing the straight man to the more zany members of the Clampett family. Spheeris had to restrain him many times, saying, "No, no mugging. No, no big smile. Pull it back, pull it back."

The difficulty of playing a character familiar to so many people was made all the more challenging with the original Jed close by. Buddy Ebsen was offered a cameo in "Hillbillies," reprising his popular television detective character Barnaby Jones. Miss Jane Hathaway calls upon his services when Granny goes missing. He discovers that she is being held against her will in a nursing home; she was placed there by one of Mr. Drysdale's bank employees and his criminal girlfriend. The girlfriend has been trying to woo Jed into marrying her so the pair can steal his fortune.

When asked what he thought of Jim's portrayal, Ebsen was complimentary, even philosophical. He said, "There are 100 people who have played Hamlet, but only two to play Jed Clampett." Ebsen's only criticism, if you could call it that, was that Jim didn't enunciate Jed's famous exclamation "We-l-l-l-l-l doggies" all that convincingly. It's likely that most people, including Jim, would agree that no one could ever top Ebsen's delivery of the trademark line.

Jim shared the studio's concern about keeping audiences from seeing any Ernest mannerisms in his performance. He spoke of his nervousness when watching the movie for the first time in a theater. "I was sitting through a screening, and I thought, 'Oh God, the first person that yells, "Hey Vern" I'm just gonna shrivel.'" Fortunately that did not happen, and many reviews of Jim's performance were favorable. He hoped that the role might open new doors in his quest to land a dramatic part. "I think it showed a few different facets of things I could do," Jim said.

An Orlando Sentinel newspaper article from a year earlier, headlined "The Character Curse," had examined the question of Jim's ability to ever break out his Ernest shell. It quoted him saying, "It's a blessing and a curse because it's as hard to escape from it as it is to get into it." The article mentioned other famous actors and their iconic characters such as Paul Reubens (Pee-wee Herman), Adam West (Batman), Henry Winkler (Fonzie) and Robin Williams (Mork). All the actors mentioned had varying degrees of success breaking the "curse" – but only after putting space between themselves and their characters. Without Jim doing the same, it seemed that his fate might be sealed.

Soon after the movie's release, Spheeris admitted that she had come close to choosing Sam Elliott for the role of Jed. Along with Elliott's acting ability, his deep voice, and slow Southern-type drawl made him a real contender. Elliott, being five years older than Jim, was even closer to Ebsen's age on the TV series. Although he didn't have the Southern roots that Jim possessed (which Spheeris revealed actually meant very little to her), in the end it was Jim's comedy background that made him the more appealing choice.

In addition, Jim's mountain heritage helped him get inside Jed's head. He illustrated this point following the movie's release. When talking to one reporter he claimed, "One of the best squirrels I ever ate was one my dad ran over on the turnpike." He added, "I've even got wild boar in my freezer."

The soundtrack for "The Beverly Hillbillies" finally provided Jim with an opportunity to record a song for a major label. The song, "Hot Rod Lincoln," was made famous by the country rock band Commander Cody and His Lost Planet Airmen in the '70s. Jim's version was placed over the closing credits. "It was actually kind of a last-minute thing," Jim said. "Ricky Skaggs did the track, and they hadn't chosen anybody to sing it. So, (20th Century) Fox asked me if I'd like to try it, and I said, 'Sure!' And I headed to RCA before they changed their minds." Jim also had the opportunity to shoot a video for the song that included his good friend Buck Finley as a passenger of the Lincoln Jim drives. Finley had been one of many to collaborate with Jim through the years writing songs and composing music. Jim once joked that in Nashville, every lease stated, "I will write country songs and pay my rent on time."

Looking at Jim's life, it was incongruous that despite his best efforts to record in Music City, he had mostly found work there as an actor. Yet it was through his participation in a Hollywood film that he achieved his biggest success in music.

The song was the icing on the cake in Jim's entire experience with "The Beverly Hillbillies." He had finally come to Hollywood and starred in a major film with other big-name actors. Even with his previous success, it was the type of experience the young kid asking about the "Hollywood Bus" had dreamed of so long ago in Lexington, Ky.

During the filming, Jim was also enjoying a new relationship. Early in 1992, Jim was spending time in Lexington thanks to a lull in his schedule. One of his favorite haunts was a restaurant named Charlie Brown's. The cozy and casual dining establishment remains open today. Located close to downtown and the University of Kentucky campus, it has always had an eclectic clientele. It was just the kind of place where Jim could relax and talk to people he thought were interesting. One night hanging out at Charlie Brown's, he met Beth Harper. She worked for a flooring store in Lexington and was sitting at the bar with some of her girlfriends. She was unfamiliar with Ernest and really didn't know who Jim was when they met. This allowed the conversation to go to more interesting places for Jim instead of the usual questions about his career. She remembers how much of a gentleman Jim was that first night, including walking her to her car. The two soon began dating. With Jim off from work for a while, they were able to see quite a bit of each other over the next year.

As was Jim's pattern, he bought Harper a nice watch for her 34th birthday, which occurred just days after they met. Not long after that, he bought her a bloodstone ring from Farmer's Jewelry store, one of his favorite places to browse in Lexington. Of course, with the ring came a free lesson from Jim on the gem's supposed mystical powers. Jim even instructed Harper as to the exact finger on which to wear it to receive its desired benefits. Another gift he purchased for her was a gun he thought necessary for self-defense. Harper was impressed with how accurate a shot he was. Once filming began on "Hillbillies" in California, Jim flew Harper out. She remembers what a thrill it was when he took her to dine at The Ivy. Unfortunately, the relationship ended after a year although the two remained good friends. Harper believes Jim never stopped loving his first wife, Jacqui, and perhaps that was one of the reasons behind his failed relationships.

Soon after shooting on "Hillbillies" started, Jim also traveled to Florida to film scenes for "Wilder Napalm." Although they barely shared any screentime, Jim and M. Emmet Walsh were reunited after nearly three decades following their appearance in "A Midsummer Night's Dream" at the University of Kentucky. Even though Jim's role in "Wilder Napalm" was small, working on another film with such established actors was a promising sign toward breaking away from Ernest. Even so, he remained committed to the character, now running for 13 years. Along with "Wilder Napalm," Jim shot two Ernest movies around the same time.

At some point after the release of "Scared Stupid," the fourth Ernest movie, John Cherry and Disney ended their relationship. A couple of years earlier, things were going so well that Cherry had told a reporter he expected at least four more pictures would be made. Cherry didn't give specifics on what had brought about the end of the partnership other than saying, "They had some problems with me and I had some problems with them, but that's what happens in a marriage. It was a good experience." Cherry's production company, Emshell Producers Group, financed the remaining Ernest movies.

The next two films, "Ernest Rides Again" and "Ernest Goes to School," took Cherry's film crew thousands of miles beyond their home base of Nashville to the Canadian city of Vancouver in British Columbia. The favorable Canadian exchange rate helped keep the budget low. Vancouver actually served as the location for simultaneous movie shoots. Pre-production took place on "School" while

"Rides Again" was shooting. This enabled Cherry to limit the time between the successive shootings of the movies to a mere week.

Originally titled "Ernest Goes Boom," "Rides Again" finds Ernest working as a janitor at a small college. Ernest's professor friend, Dr. Abner Melon, is a Vern-type character the audience actually sees. The plot revolves around Ernest uncovering a Revolutionary War cannon and finding jewels inside it that Dr. Melon believes to be crown jewels from the Tower of London. Ernest eludes the bad guys for most of the movie while being chased along the countryside sitting atop the cannon. Jim thought the chase theme of the film would give children the kind of action they enjoyed from the Indiana Jones movies. He spent the better part of a month riding on top of that cannon. What made it worse was the cold weather in Vancouver, even in July.

The plot of the next movie, "Ernest Goes to School," is similar to the 1968 film "Charly" starring Cliff Robertson. Ernest plays a high school janitor with a low IQ who suddenly becomes brilliant after taking an experimental drug. It is the only Ernest movie that Cherry did not direct; writer/producer Coke Sams took the reins on this production. The movie was the first to be released straight to video.

The movie is notable for being one of actor Sarah Chalke's first feature-film roles. The actress was a familiar face by the time "School" went to video after she replaced the actress playing Becky, the oldest daughter on the hit show, "Roseanne," in the fall of 1993. Years later, Chalke starred on another hit TV comedy, playing Dr. Elliott Reid in "Scrubs."

Always looking for new ways to connect kids to Ernest, Carden & Cherry's Emshell Producers Group teamed up with a home-video company to create an educational video called "Brain Drain Challenge" to promote "Rides Again." The game was comprised of questions related to scenes in the film. Jim managed to make a few appearances at schools to demonstrate the game. He had students in stitches as he answered questions sounding more like one of the snobbish characters in his arsenal, Aster Clement, than the lowbrow Ernest.

"Ernest Rides Again" hit theaters just a few weeks after the release of "Hillbillies" on November 12, 1993. It was the last theatrical release of an Ernest film. With an estimated budget of $7 million and a box-office take of less than $2 million, it was apparent that life without Disney made the now-aging franchise a tough sell.

No matter how successful Jim may have been at making audiences forget about Ernest when playing Jed Clampett, "Rides Again" was an instant reminder of his alter ego. Getting the part in "Hillbillies" was a step forward, but continuing to play Ernest was two steps back from the broader career Jim always claimed he wanted.

CHAPTER TWENTY-FOUR

SLINKY DOG

In 1991, Pixar signed a three-picture movie deal with Disney. The company had morphed over many years from a computer hardware company to one now focused on animation. Pixar's Academy Award-winning animated shorts were so impressive and cutting-edge that it seemed inevitable a major motion picture would someday feature their exciting new animation process. In addition to shorts, Pixar had also found some success producing animated commercials for companies such as Tropicana and Life Savers.

The first feature-length movie that Pixar made was "Toy Story," and Jim was fortunate to be offered a role. Despite the broken partnership with Carden & Cherry, Disney saw Jim's potential for playing something besides Ernest. A few years prior, Disney had been working with Beetle Bailey creator Mort Walker to develop a live-action movie version of his famous comic-strip character. The two sides had come close to working out a deal until Walker balked at Disney's insistence on Jim playing Beetle. Walker appeared to be one more in a growing list of people who could not envision Jim playing anything other than an Ernest-type character. But with "Toy Story," Disney (and perhaps Pixar, too) showed they felt otherwise and wanted him to voice the character of Slinky Dog. "Toy Story" was for Pixar what "Ernest Goes to Camp" had been for

THE IMPORTANCE OF BEING ERNEST:
THE LIFE OF ACTOR JIM VARNEY

Carden & Cherry. Little did Jim, or anyone else, know just how successful "Toy Story" would become, or what kind of impact it would have on animation.

Jim spent the next two years making numerous trips from his home in Tennessee to Pixar's Bay Area studios to record dialogue for Slinky Dog. He described the process as one of the oddest in his film experience, much like putting a large puzzle together. Animators used the mannerisms of each actor to give each toy more human qualities. One coincidence was that at the time, Jim's mother owned a miniature dachshund named Gretchen that looked identical to Slinky Dog.

In a sense, voicing Slinky Dog brought Jim's career full circle. He had started out doing voice work on radio ads for John Cherry in the early '70s. Jim's voice was now in the hands of animators translating it into the personality of the character. Decades of smoking had given Jim's voice a deep, raspy sound that provided well-worn Southern warmth to the coil-bellied dog.

But despite Jim's happiness at being part of "Toy Story," tragedy was on the scene for him again. In August 1994, Jim's mother lost a seven-year battle with leukemia. Jim was able to visit her in the hospital in Lexington in the days before she died. At 45, he had now lost both parents and his oldest sister.

Work, as always, was a salve to Jim's grief. He continued to stay busy by returning to Vancouver once again to shoot another Ernest film. It seemed fitting that being from Kentucky, Jim would someday portray a basketball star. In "Slam Dunk Ernest," Ernest is a mall janitor trying to fit in with his basketball-playing co-workers. Things begin to look up when he is asked to join their city-league team.

Ernest soon receives a big helping hand when the Archangel of Basketball, played by Kareem Abdul-Jabbar, pays Ernest a visit and bestows upon him magical sneakers. Soon Ernest has the ability to perform gravity-defying moves on and off the court. John Cherry provides his own comic relief with a cameo portraying a fan in the stands who creates a minor brawl over a spilled drink.

Ernest's moves eventually propel his team to capture the city-league title, earning them a chance to play against an actual NBA team. In addition to all the usual slapstick silliness, Cherry included a morality subplot as he had done with previous movies such as "Camp" and "Christmas." Ernest teaches the impressionable young son of one of his co-workers that there is more to life than a pair of new basketball sneakers. Although "Slam Dunk" went straight to video, it still satisfied hard-core Ernest fans.

Apart from "Toy Story," few of Jim's next movies gave him the momentum he had built up from "The Beverly Hillbillies." The next non-Ernest movie in which Jim was cast was "The Expert," an action flick filmed in Nashville. Action star and martial artist Jeff Speakman stars as a man out to avenge his sister's murder. Jim plays the role of his longtime friend, a weapons expert named Snake.

Prolific crime author Max Allan Collins wrote the film's screenplay. His resume includes everything from comic strips to short stories. In 1998, he wrote the graphic novel "Road to Perdition," which was made into the 2002 film by the same name starring Tom Hanks and Paul Newman. When speaking of the role of the sadistic warden played by James Brolin in "The Expert," Collins said he had originally written it with Rip Torn in mind. After seeing Jim audition for the role, Collins changed his mind. "I lobbied for him," Collins once said, "and when he didn't get the part, I wrote a new scene, a new character (Snake), especially for him, as a cameo."

THE IMPORTANCE OF BEING ERNEST:
THE LIFE OF ACTOR JIM VARNEY

One highlight in the short list of Jim's mostly forgettable non-Ernest films of the mid '90s brought him back to Lexington; "100 Proof" is based on the true story of two troubled women who together committed five murders in a single day in Lexington, Ky. First-time movie director Jeremy Horton used the 1986 murders as the inspiration for his fictionalized screenplay. He had become interested in the story after moving into an apartment building where one of the convicted murderers, Tina Hickey Powell, once lived. It wasn't so much the crime that intrigued Horton but the thought of what possibly could have led two people to go on such a rampage.

Once Horton had the financing in place, he began casting. He could rely on talented local theater actors he knew for many of the roles but had specific people in mind for central characters. (One wasn't an actor at all. Horton had convinced one of his idols, Southern novelist Larry Brown, to play a drug-dealing storeowner.)

Horton tried to get such accomplished actors as Harry Dean Stanton, M. Emmett Walsh and Dennis Hopper for the part of Rae's father (Rae is one of the two main female characters). When efforts fell through, Jim's name came to his mind.

Horton had met Jim years earlier when Jim attended a stage production he had directed for the Studio Players in Lexington. Remembering how highly the Lexington theater community had spoken of Jim's acting, Horton contacted Jim's management and soon found out that Jim was interested. Even though Jim's character would appear in only one scene, those moments would play a large part in exposing the unrelenting despair that penetrated Rae's life.

In October 1995, shooting started at some of the less-appealing locales in Lexington in order to portray the gritty setting. Horton recalls Jim being the consummate professional. Jim made sure that his performance captured the rhythm Horton intended. At one point, Horton left Jim and actor Pamela Stewart, who plays Rae, alone for about an hour to work on their scene. He says the two even came up with a back story for their father/daughter relationship to help them get more into the heads of their characters. Jim also helped choreograph the brief physical confrontation that takes place between them.

After finishing up work on "100 Proof," Jim continued accepting roles in non-Ernest films. In February 1996, he traveled to Quebec to shoot a comedy called "Snowboard Academy." The movie stars Cory Haim and Brigitte Nielsen. Former SCTV regular Joe Flaherty plays the owner of a ski resort whose two sons try to convince their father how to run the family business. At the time, snowboarding was still building its popularity. The movie does address in a comedic way the problem of snowboarders wanting to ride the ski slopes. Jim plays the part of Rudy James, a jack-of-all-trades maintenance man. Jim pulled from his real-life comedy-club experiences in scenes where Rudy performs stand-up at the resort's clubhouse. Even though Jim isn't playing Ernest, his character displays many of the same slapstick antics. In Rudy's first scene, he gets tangled up in a phone cord, then attempts to use his hands to contain the flowing hot coffee from a malfunctioning coffee maker. Unfortunately, the movie flopped, even inhabiting for many years the "Bottom 100" list on the Internet Movie Database.

As busy as Jim was accepting film roles for non-Ernest characters, he was still shooting commercials as everyone's favorite neighbor for clients such as Louisiana Gas Service. Jim told one Canadian reporter during this period that he planned to continue playing Ernest "until I'm on crutches or too old to actually fall off a ladder."

Jim's next project was set for the spring. It was another independent film that, like "100 Proof," was far removed from Ernest and comedies altogether. The title, "Blood, Friends, and Money" involves a group of horror-movie buffs who gather one weekend to party and watch horror flicks. The film was the project of long-time Ernest assistant camera operator, Armanda Costanza. She had worked on every movie project of Jim's, from "Family Album" to "Scared Stupid." She was now trying her own hand at directing and hoped the film would be successful enough to fund future projects. Jim played the Old Mariner in a few scenes.

The script was written by Tim Ormond, whose family has sometimes been referred to as Nashville's first family of film. Ormond's parents (Ron and June Carr Ormond) had been making independent, B-movie exploitation films in Nashville since the 1960s. Some of the clips from those films were even used in Costanza's picture. Tim's mother, June Carr Ormond, was cast as a restaurant manager. Since Jim and the Ormond family had become synonymous with film making in Nashville, it was fitting that they shared credits on a project.

Around this time, Jim was branching out into computer-software games. In the past, he had always talked about wanting to write stories in the spirit of the original English and Appalachian tales that center around a character named Jack – "Jack and the Beanstalk" being the most popular of these "jack tales." Jim never got around to writing any of his own jack tales, but he did become involved in the production of a computer game for kids called "Jack's Adventures: Beyond the Beanstalk." Despite all the work Jim put into it, the game was never released.

In the fall of 1996, Jim was on location in Denver for the children's comedy, "3 Ninjas: High Noon at Mega Mountain." Jim was cast as Lothar Zogg, his first villain since playing Ernest's evil twin in "Ernest Goes to Jail." The film, starring Hulk Hogan as a retired TV action star turned superhero, failed at the box office. Like "Snowboard Academy," it made the Internet Movie Database's "Bottom 100."

But during this time, Jim did shine in a small-screen hit. He guest-starred on two episodes of "Roseanne," playing Prince Carlos of Moldavia. The storyline involves Roseanne's sister, Jackie, falling for his character after he visits the diner where she and Roseanne work. The two enjoy a short-lived romance that includes a trip to New York and an eclectic family gathering at Roseanne's house.

More good fortune fell upon Jim when "100 Proof" was selected for the Sundance Film Festival in January 1997. Director Jeremy Horton had hoped that Jim would attend and join other cast members in promoting the film. Despite all the obvious reasons for Jim to want to be there, including a chance to rub elbows with Hollywood executives, he decided to participate in the Buckmasters Whitetail Classic with his friends in Alabama. As committed as Jim was to selling hundreds of products as Ernest, he wasn't always as dedicated when it came to selling himself. He lost a major opportunity to capitalize on his small but memorable performance in "100 Proof" and his ability to truly play dramatic roles.

After its screening at Sundance, "100 Proof" went on to receive positive reviews in such publications as the New York Times. Joe Leydon of Variety wrote, "But even Stewart and Bellando are briefly overshadowed by Jim Varney's ferociously nasty cameo as Rae's sleazy father. It's hard to believe this is the same guy who's gained fame as the doltish Ernest P. Worrell in TV commercials and low-budget comedies. More villainous character roles may be in his future."

THE IMPORTANCE OF BEING ERNEST: THE LIFE OF ACTOR JIM VARNEY

The film's producer, George Maranville, told the press how pleased he was with Horton's directing efforts, comparing the film to others in the same genre such as "Badlands" and "In Cold Blood."

In January 1998, the movie was given a special premiere at the historic Kentucky Theatre in downtown Lexington. Jim traveled to Lexington to join his family in attending the event. Although his family had always enjoyed Ernest as much as Jim's biggest fans, they were excited about Jim taking on the type of role he had wanted for so long.

But apart from "100 Proof," few of the movies Jim starred in after "Hillbillies" brought box-office or critical success. That's in large part why he returned once again to making movies as Ernest. A few years earlier when promoting "Rides Again," Jim speculated on how many years of Ernest he might have left. "I'm gonna let it kinda die a natural death, I think," he said. The fact that the movies were now going straight to video reflected that Ernest was already living on borrowed time.

The next two Ernest movies took the film crew all the way to South Africa. The first, "Ernest Goes to Africa," involves Ernest making a long-distance trip to rescue a kidnapped girlfriend to whom he unknowingly has given stolen diamonds.

The second film, "Ernest in the Army," was shot in Cape Town. It would be the ninth and final Ernest movie. In addition to directing, John Cherry plays the part of Ernest's old friend, Sarge, who talks Ernest into joining the Army Reserves. After being promised that the Reserves would be easy, Ernest is shipped out for combat, and calamity ensues. During the shoot, Cherry noticed how his normally energetic star was having a particularly difficult time handling some of the hilly terrain. At the time, no one was aware of the extent to which Jim's health had begun to deteriorate.

In early 1998, Jim was also writing country music and collaborating with two talented musician friends. Bobby Boyd had lived with Jim for a short while in the '90s. After starting out in a country band called The Castaways, Boyd moved into songwriting, doing extremely well. Conway Twitty, George Jones and Jimmy Dean are just a few of the country artists who recorded his songs. His biggest success came from a song he co-wrote in the '80s called "Two of a Kind, Workin' on a Full House." It later became a No. 1 hit for Garth Brooks.

Boyd, Jim and country singer Vern Gosdin gathered on Sunday mornings in Jim's kitchen, a place where Jim often found inspiration, to write and play music. Gosdin, then in his mid-'60s, had first achieved success in the 1960s singing in a band with his brother Rex. He later began a solo career that brought him a long string of mainstream country hits in the 1980s as well as the impressive nickname: "The Voice." In 1984 he landed his first No. 1 hit on the country chart with the song "I Can Tell by the Way You Dance (You're Gonna Love Me Tonight)." Gosdin was working on a new album and was excited about the melodies created during these sessions. One of the many songs the three worked on was called "Maybe Then I'll Be Over You." The lyrics describe a man so wounded over a past relationship that he doesn't believe his heart will recover until he is "six feet under." Gosdin recorded the song for his 1998 album "The Voice." Jim received a writing credit.

The time at home was a nice break for Jim, who was still going as hard as ever. On the heels of the two Ernest movies he had just shot in South Africa, he was traveling to California to record dialogue for "Toy Story 2" and reading over a number of scripts being sent his way.

CHAPTER TWENTY-FIVE

THE END OF A "GREAT ADVENTURE"

In the summer of 1998, Jim was in Los Angeles shooting another children's comedy movie. He was cast as small-time counterfeiter Carl Banks in "Treehouse Hostage." In the movie, Carl manages to escape from jail but is soon strung up by a young boy's booby trap while cutting through backyards. When the boy and his friends discover that Carl is the escapee cops are looking for, they decide to keep him as their hostage. Apart from a few Ernest-type facial expressions and a scene where he appears in drag, Carl is probably the only movie role where Jim played a character "straight," that is, in a way closest to his true personality and mannerisms.

During the shooting, Jim began to experience severe coughing attacks. Before long, he was coughing up blood. He thought he may have contracted something in South Africa. After returning home from California he had chest x-rays at a hospital in Nashville. The news was not good. A mass was found on his lungs, and the doctor wanted Jim to have a bronchoscopy – where a piece of the mass is removed for testing.

As soon as he got the results, Jim called his sister Jake, a nurse, to find out just how worried he should be. He knew her schedule, and the phone rang just as she got home from work. Jake was an operating-room nurse at the time and had actually assisted in bronchoscopies. Jim filled her in, and Jake outlined what was involved, including the need to be put under anesthesia. Jake could tell Jim was worried.

Jake called Sandy soon after, and they both realized that their brother probably had lung cancer. As sad as the probable diagnosis was, it was something for which they had been preparing. Jake and Sandy had observed a noticeable change in Jim's appearance the past few times they had seen him in person. He looked as if he had aged 10 years in the last two. Throw in the fact that Jim had been a lifelong smoker, and the conclusion was not a pretty one. No matter what the news was they were going to do everything they could to get him through it.

With the added reassurance he received from Jake, Jim proceeded with the bronchoscopy a few days after talking to her. The results of the biopsy confirmed everyone's worst fears: The mass was a malignant tumor. Doctors wanted to schedule surgery as soon as possible to remove it. Knowing that the recovery time could be lengthy, Jim quickly began tying up loose ends. One was an exciting new project with Billy Bob Thornton.

Jim's last onscreen performance was in "Daddy and Them," directed and written by Thornton. The Southern-flavored comedy is set in Arkansas and tells the story of a struggling musician named Claude (Thornton), his wife, Ruby (Laura Dern), and the episode that drives their already-dysfunctional family into chaos. Claude's Uncle Hazel, played by Jim, is arrested and jailed in Little Rock for assaulting a man with an iron doorstop. Claude and Ruby go to Little Rock to rally around him and the rest of the family while helping to hire a defense team. The only problem is, the family doesn't get along any better than Claude and Ruby do.

THE END OF A "GREAT ADVENTURE"

By now, Thornton and Jim had been friends for a decade. Even though their busy careers kept them from getting together much, they kept in touch by phone, with Jim often entertaining Thornton for hours. Along with the fact that they both loved to act and sing, they were also unapologetic Southerners who loved the humor that came with the stereotypes of the region. Thornton has admitted borrowing phrases of Jim's through the years, including "How 'boutcha?" and "Getcha a knock off that steak." Thornton used to stay at Jim's house every so often. He recalled once how during a visit he saw Jim's DeLorean up on blocks in the front yard. That prompted a warning from Thornton: "Never give a hillbilly money."

With his recent diagnosis, Jim likely knew "Daddy and Them" could be his last movie. Perhaps his optimistic side hoped to use the performance to break away from Ernest for good. Thornton was giving Jim a shot at the type of dramatic movie role he had been yearning for since he had first come to Los Angeles. Not even cancer was going to stop Jim from pursuing this opportunity. Thornton, being the good friend he was, moved production around to allow Jim to film his scenes before his surgery.

In addition to Dern, the all-star cast includes such actors as Jamie Lee Curtis and Ben Affleck. The unfortunate thing is that Jim's most memorable scene actually ended up on the cutting-room floor. It has been included, deservedly, in the deleted scenes of the DVD release.

In the scene, Jim barges into the house during a family meal. He immediately begins to loudly lecture everyone sitting at the table on how poorly they and other family members have been treating each other. With every word he becomes increasingly enraged until he is worked up into such a fury that he begins to smash furniture in an adjacent room. Never had Jim shown such raw emotion onscreen. It must have taken every ounce of his weakened body to bring forth the passion and physicality the scene required. He dug deep. Perhaps his performance was fueled by the years of being typecast, the elusive roles on Broadway, bad Ernest movie reviews and now the unfairness of a cancer diagnosis. If this were to be his final act, to borrow a phrase from his father's world of boxing, he was determined to "go down swinging."

"Daddy and Them" producer Bruce Heller spoke highly of Jim. "It's amazing what Jim does in the film. It's something different than you've ever seen from him before. He's got the dramatic center of the movie."

Just a few days after filming his scenes, Jim was back in Nashville undergoing a major operation. A large tumor piercing his heart was removed, along with almost two-thirds of his right lung.

Jim's sisters traveled down from Lexington to visit him, as did a nephew, Brad Kelly, the son of Jim's late sister Jo Gail. They were relieved the surgery was a success and hopeful the cancer would not return. Jim's sense of humor gave them added confidence that he would weather this storm. Right before surgery, Jim had told his doctors that if they pulled him through he would give them a handsome tip.

In no time, Jim was using the missing portion of his lung as the butt of his "one lung" jokes. He found out his old friend Johnny Cash was staying in a nearby Nashville hospital undergoing treatment for pneumonia. He called Cash's room and began joking with him: "There you go bragging about having double pneumonia when you know the best I can do is single pneumonia." He also said one advantage to having the extra space in his chest was that it might be a good place to carry a knife.

Jim was curious about all the different machines he was wired to in his hospital bed. One, the pulse oximeter, measured the

THE END OF A "GREAT ADVENTURE"

oxygen in his blood. Jake explained that a desirable reading ranged from 96 percent to 100 percent. Jim's reading was between 88 and 90. He admitted that it was better than most of his high school grades.

During this time, a movie set to feature Jim called "Pirates of the Plain" was announced. John Cherry had written the screenplay and was set to direct. It was the first non-Ernest movie Cherry would direct since "Dr. Otto." The movie is about an 8-year-old Nebraska farm boy who is befriended by pirate Jezebel Jack (Jim) after a storm creates a vortex in time allowing the salty sea captain to be deposited into the future. Right before passing through time, Jack was being forced to walk the plank of his ship by his mutinous crew. Jack helps the boy find a treasure buried underneath a toolshed just before the rest of his crew arrive via another time vortex. Jack and the boy successfully fight off the crew, keeping the treasure out of their hands.

The movie was scheduled to start shooting that fall in Cape Town, but Jim had to pull out because of his health problems. Tim Curry ended up playing Jezebel Jack. The movie has remained a never-ending source of confusion for Ernest fans. It somehow became news that a movie called "Ernest the Pirate" was nearing completion when Jim passed. That was not true. Online petitions have actually demanded Disney release "Ernest the Pirate."

Now not only was cancer affecting Jim's health, it was having a major impact on his acting career. Luckily, he had already finished his voice work for "Toy Story 2" and another animated Disney feature, "Atlantis: The Lost Empire." Jim was the voice of the cook, Jebidiah Allardyce "Cookie" Farnsworth.

Ever since the first "Toy Story" film, Jim had enjoyed a new niche in animated voice work. In 1997, he voiced a character named Walt Evergreen in an episode of "Duckman," an animated sitcom on the USA Network that followed the adventures of a duck private detective. That same year, he portrayed Mr. Gus Holder in the animated Christmas film "Annabelle's Wish," about a calf that aspires to be one of Santa's reindeer. Jim also voiced a carnie named Cooter on an episode of "The Simpsons" in 1998. Five years earlier, the show paid tribute to Jim in an episode where the Simpson family heads out to see a fictional movie called "Ernest Goes Somewhere Cheap."

Meanwhile, Jim was still recovering from his surgery. Jim's sisters Jake and Sandy continued to drive down from Lexington to his home in Tennessee to visit when they could. They would stay over for a night or two and fix him meals.

Another family member who spent a great deal of time with Jim during his recovery was his niece Andrea (Sandy's daughter). Andrea was 25 at the time and able to take time off from her waitress job in Lexington to visit him. Andrea also cooked for Jim and provided welcome company. Jim loved her stir-fry with pineapple chunks. It was one of the few meals he would finish. During a few visits, Jim actually cooked for Andrea, once making his chili with chocolate syrup. She found it quite good.

When Andrea stayed at Jim's she would fix him a pot of coffee in the morning. He wasn't much for breakfast but usually drank most of the coffee. He occasionally talked about his dreams and tried to interpret them.

Then they would hang out on the couch in his den for much of the day and talk. They discussed such things as history, jewelry, politics and Jim's career. Andrea remembers him talking about the Carter family album he had played on with his dulcimer.

Jim was not into technology and told Andrea he thought he wasn't tech-savvy enough for the 21st century. He did not own a computer and had shelves full of VHS movies that he enjoyed watching on his VCR. Andrea remembers a conversation where Jim said he thought children were not as creative as when he was young, and he blamed technology (but remember, this was in 1999, years before such developments as the iPhone and Facebook).

Around March 1999 Jim suffered a seizure, and it turned out the cancer had spread to his brain. After receiving radiation, he lost most of his hair. He decided he might as well have the rest shaved. Ever the comedian, he talked about how much he enjoyed his "Mr. Clean" look. Andrea remembers Jim calling himself "Yul Bummer." Sandy recalls how his bald head made his eyes look "electric and intensely blue." Andrea also remembers her visits to the hospital and the positive outlook that carried Jim through some of his darkest periods:

"In the 18 months of Jim's illness, he was hospitalized several times. He had pneumonia and (a major) seizure. I would sit up in his room the entire time he was there. He liked to watch the national news. He referred to it as "eye dope," and it made him fall asleep. He chewed Nicorette like crazy, chewing twice the amount recommended, a total slave to the nicotine. He didn't want to be left alone in the hospital for a minute while he was there, so I stayed. When he had the seizure, he couldn't talk for a few days. He had to write everything left-handed.

"He got so frustrated so easily. He really had little patience. It was frustrating for me too. I wanted so bad to understand him. We got so close though; I could almost read his mind.

"He never acted the victim of his disease. I think deep down he knew he was going to lose, but he stayed so positive that he was going to beat it. He was a true inspiration. He absolutely never thought smoking would kill him; he said he (always) thought it would be the alcohol.

THE IMPORTANCE OF BEING ERNEST:
THE LIFE OF ACTOR JIM VARNEY

"Jim was religious. He read the Bible many times during the last year of his life, and he told me he grasped much of it. He never lost his creativity, his sense of humor or his hope."

Andrea is my sister, and I was able to accompany her on one of her visits to Jim's home in September 1999. I was 27 years old at the time. We arrived around dinnertime, and we all quickly made ourselves comfortable on the couches in his den. I cannot recall what we began talking about, or to be more specific, what Jim began talking about. What I do remember is that I had a front-row seat to a 12-hour one-man show. Aside from taking a few minutes to eat Andrea's stir-fry, Jim touched on many things, including countless stories of his past. Andrea hung in there for the first few hours, and then it was just my uncle and me.

The conversation took us from Bowie knives and swordfight demonstrations (using a Wiffle Ball bat) to recollections of Lafayette High School. At one point, we moved into the kitchen. Jim retrieved a large bullet from a kitchen drawer and began a lesson on its uses. If only I had known the treat I was going to be in for that night, I would have brought along a tape recorder or video camera.

Jim gave the last major interview of his life in November 1999 with Beverly Keel of the alternative weekly Nashville Scene. She sat down with him in his home; during the conversation Jim showed himself in a way he had rarely done before.

He admitted self-medicating for years with alcohol to deal with his lifelong struggle with depression. Said Jim, "But that wears off in a few hours, and you're back to square one again. I didn't know that there weren't super highs and lows in everybody's life." He even admitted to believing his depression was a contributing factor in his failed marriage to first wife, Jacqui.

As usual, Jim injected humor when speaking of the pressure to be funny in a crowd where he was almost always the center

THE END OF A "GREAT ADVENTURE"

of attention. He joked about how he often wished during those times he could take a raincheck: "We'll do lunch, a very depressing lunch." Then he talked about how he had visited a psychiatrist three years earlier who had prescribed Wellbutrin. After taking it, he admitted, "I found out what normalcy was."

One of the many things that kept Jim going during the trials of his illness was his excitement over the upcoming release of "Daddy and Them." Its original release date had been scheduled for December 1999, just a month after "Toy Story 2." His career was still very much on his mind, and he couldn't wait to get back to work. He told his sisters to make sure not to tell anyone he was sick. He was afraid that it might cause him to get overlooked for future roles.

By November 13, 1999, Jim had regained enough strength to attend the premiere of "Toy Story 2" at the El Capitan Theatre in Hollywood, the site of the first "Toy Story" premiere four years earlier. This time, however, the man walking that same red carpet looked much different. The cancer medication caused swelling in Jim's face, a contrast to his frail frame. His cheeks were fuller and his complexion appeared smooth and pale, making his blue eyes more noticeable. Having lost all his hair, he was now sporting a goatee that was almost completely gray. But he didn't let his looks affect his unique sense of style. Wearing a dark-green silk shirt, stylish black fedora and dangling gold earring, he conveyed the message that he was still the same unconventional Jim.

Just a month earlier in Nashville, Jim had received a special tribute at the Nashville Filmmakers Conference. Now, this big Hollywood premiere was icing on the cake. Janie and his attorney, Hoot Gibson, helped Jim walk through the photographers and crowds of onlookers as he made his way into the theater.

THE IMPORTANCE OF BEING ERNEST:
THE LIFE OF ACTOR JIM VARNEY

Up until that point, Jim had done a good job up keeping his battle with cancer concealed. But with so many media outlets in attendance, his appearance quickly brought up questions about his health. Following the event, news outlets reported on Jim's battle with cancer and what Jim had described to them as an encouraging prognosis.

A few months later, I drove my mother, Sandy, down to see Jim. It was February 9, 2000. We arrived in the early evening, and right away I could tell things were very different than the last time I had visited the previous fall. A hospital bed had been set up in his living room. I could not believe how frail Jim was. It was obvious that he did not have much time. When my mother walked up with me to his bedside she said, "Look who I brought here with me; it's Mistake," referring to the dim-witted son of his Lloyd Worrell character. I managed a smile as I tried to remain as calm and collected as my mother. It seems very much a Varney trait to find humor during the most trying moments.

The hospice nurse came and went, and we all went to sleep. My mom checked on Jim throughout the night. Jim wasn't talking much, but he did manage at one point to ask my mother if the window was open by his bed. She told him it was. Hours later, as we all slept, Jim passed on. My mother tried to make sense of his question about the window in the days that followed, and she wondered if he was preparing his spirit to depart the house.

About 100 people attended Jim's funeral in Lexington; many were close friends and family members. Country singer Vern Gosdin came up from Tennessee and sang "Amazing Grace" during the service. Jim's cousin Ed McChord spoke eloquently about his memories of Jim. He closed by saying, "Jim ran too fast and got there too soon."

THE END OF A "GREAT ADVENTURE"

A public memorial was held for Jim at the War Memorial Auditorium in Nashville on February 16, 2000. Many of his close friends and family, including myself, also gathered there to share stories and listen to touching performances of some of his favorite songs such as "The Old Rugged Cross." One of the people who spoke that day was Dan Butler, a good friend of Jim's and a longtime Ernest writer. It is perhaps Butler's speech, more than anything, that has inspired and challenged me to do the best job possible in writing this biography. The speech was as moving as it was funny. I have watched it many times in the videotape I made that day. Here are selected excerpts:

"I was one of the guys who wrote for Jim, and I went on the State Fair Circuit with him, and late one night, eight years ago, in a room at the Ramada Inn in Springfield, Ill., Jim made me swear that whichever one of us was still standing – survivor – would publicly, at the other one's funeral, confess that together, Jim and I, on movie sets, out on location, plotted the murders of several caterers (much applause). Whew … it was us. It was us.

"… I just want to give you snapshots of one day on the road with Jim Varney at a state fair. Number one, you're on the airplane, and the stewardess said, 'No, you can't be that Ernest guy. He's real stupid.' I saw 20 different comebacks going through Jim's face, and he finally just said, 'Yeah, you're right.'

"We get to the airport in Minneapolis, and a 60-year-old African American shoeshine guy screams out from across the airport, 'Ernest! My man! Get over here!' Now Jim looked more un-Ernest than I had ever seen him look. He had an earring, long suede coat and an Armani suit, and this guy recognized him and had to talk to Jim and get his autograph. And we're just to the airport, right.

"Now we're in a parade in Minneapolis-St. Paul. Jim's sitting up in the back of this convertible, and I'm sitting down front, and a woman breaks through the barricade and runs up to the car with a baby outstretched and says, 'Ernest, kiss my baby!' ... He takes the baby, looks down at me and said, 'I'm kissin' her baby. What a wonderful way of tellin' her how much I love her.' And, uh, we ain't halfway through the day yet. And then another woman ran up and said, 'Ernest, Ernest, I'm 42 and I'm just divorced; will you marry me?' Jim said, 'I'm not havin' *her* baby.' After the show Jim sits there, and he signs probably 600 autographs and takes like 600 photos. It was amazing; I was just wore out.

"And we go back to this Ramada Inn and the phone rings in my room, and it's Jim and he's had about 2 pounds of chocolate and some coffee and he wants to work on his sequel to Hamlet. Now, first thing I said to Jim was, 'In Hamlet everybody died, buddy.' And he said,'Nooo Mr. Butler, there was an antidote.' And I mean, in that Ramada Inn room this guy had written the most beautiful soliloquies and did them, and it was unbelievable, and it went on all night.

"Then there was a day in my life, I don't know about you, but if you can remember one day in your life where you laughed more than any other, and I can tell you to the minute (it was) sitting in the conference room at Carden & Cherry ... before the movie, I think it was 'Scared Stupid,' sitting with John Cherry and Jim. Somehow, Botswana came up, as it will in conversation, and Jim, he just, he went off, and the next thing I knew Jim was the only lumberjack in Botswana. And we were just laughing until we cried. And he was just going off. After 45 minutes you think Botswana is gonna get a little old, right? And I went to the restroom and I came back, and I said, 'All right, I'm not going to laugh anymore. You know, I got work to do.' And I went back in there, and he said, 'Man, there ain't no trees in Botswana!! I should know, I'm the only lumberjack in Botswana, and I haven't worked in 32

THE END OF A "GREAT ADVENTURE"

years!' Then he starts off on the popsicles. 'We don't have the little wooden sticks for the popsicles; we have little steel rods 'cause they ain't no trees ... and the children's tongues adhere to the little steel rods 'cause they're so cold!' My head hurt. It went on for five hours. He taught me to say 'area rug' without closing my mouth. He taught me all sorts of stuff.

"But I tell you the one day that came back to me, and that was 16 years ago. I got to sit in on maybe two Ernest writing sessions; I was the junior member of Glenn, Leasure and Gil (Ernest writers for Carden & Cherry), and I'd been in, like, two sessions, and I hadn't written squat. I had contributed one phrase that I stole from my father-in-law in Oklahoma, which was 'Golly Bob Howdy'... and I had met Jim one time on the Ernest set. I had greatly embellished my role to my family and my in-laws. ... I was big time, I was a writer for Ernest. Well, two weeks later, my family goes out to Oklahoma City to visit my mother and father-in-law, who always said 'Golly Bob Howdy' to me when I told him how much I paid for something. 'Golly Bob Howdy!' And there he was, and he said, 'I want you to introduce me to your ol' buddy Ernest,' and I said, 'Oh, no problem, next time you come to Nashville I'll introduce you.' He said, 'No, in two hours he's gonna be down here at Braum's doin' a personal appearance.' And I said, 'Really? Right here in Oklahoma City? I didn't know he was coming to town.' And man, I'm sweatin' bullets for two hours thinkin' gosh, man, he isn't gonna know me. He didn't even know who I was when I met him on the set. And, ah, oh man, I was dyin'. So we get in the car and we go down, and there was 500 people at this Braum's, and the line is going all the way out to the street, and I said, 'Ah, it's too crowded, I'll get you an autograph back in Nashville.' He said, 'No, no, I'm meeting Ernest buddy, c'mon, he'll recognize you, and we'll get through this line in no time.' And we get in that line and we're way back in the back, and (producer) Lynn Johnston sees me and Jim sees me, and she whispers in Jim's ear. Jim gets up and yells, 'Mr. Butler, what are you doin' in Oklahoma City? Get your butt up here!' And he brings me up there with my son and my father-in-law, and I said, 'Hey man, this is the guy that said "Golly Bob Howdy,"' and Jim said, 'Man, that's my favorite phrase, and Ernest is always gonna say that and you're the guy!' My father-in-law just glowed, and he talked about that day till the day he died, and Jim saved my ass that day. He didn't just save my ass, buddy, he made me think I was something special. Next thing I knew he was telling my father-in-law, this was 1984, 'Oh yeah, Butler here's gonna write movies for Disney, and we're gonna be big Hollywood stars!' And (before that) my father-in-law (had) thought I was a bum, but not after that day. I saw Jim do that, make people feel special; it didn't matter if they were a plumber, a truck driver or a Purity driver. He had that ability, man, to make you think you were something.

"He made me laugh more than any other person in my whole life, and I was the one that was supposed to be writing funny stuff for him. And I know God prepared a room for Jim, and I'll betcha it's got a real fine area rug." (Author's note: Here, Butler said "area rug" without closing his mouth).

Jim's attorney, Hoot Gibson, also spoke at the memorial. Gibson mentioned their recent trip to the "Toy Story 2" premiere in Hollywood. He described how they had made their way through the crowds into the theater and how Jim was greeted by celebrities and big names in the industry, including Disney CEO Michael Eisner.

The two eventually found their seats. As the lights dimmed, and the curtains were about to go up, Jim leaned over to Gibson. "Hoot," Jim said, "it's been a great adventure."

NOTES

Author's note: Many Web sites are continuously changing, updating and evolving their databases. A handful of the Web-site links below are no longer working (and I was unable to access substitutions), however, I have provided them as verification of my original research. – J.L.

Chapter One: Shotgun Wedding

Two young bridesmaids ... Description of McChord family film "Shotgun Wedding" (1956).

Chapter Two: The Beginning

Andrew Varney's first cousin ... Ancestry.com.

Jim's sister Jake vividly remembers ... Author interview with Jake McIntyre.

That day finally came in the summer of 1934 ... Postcard belonging to Louise Varney.

Opened in 1938 ... From newspaper article: "Bluegrass Park and Aspendale 100 percent occupied since opening in 1938," *Lexington Herald-Leader* (Dec. 29, 1940).

THE IMPORTANCE OF BEING ERNEST: THE LIFE OF ACTOR JIM VARNEY

Dr. A. J. Whitehouse ... Jim Varney's birth records.

Sandy swears that Jim ... Author interview with Sandra Varney Spoonamore.

From *Despite the extra* ... to ... *dulcimer he purchased*: Author interview with Jake McIntyre.

Years later, Jim credited Sonny ... Skip Press, "Hey Vern, It's Varney," *Boys' Life* (September 1992).

The absurdity of Jim's character ... "Hey Vern, It's My Family Album" television special (1983).

From *In addition* ... to ... *punish him*: Author interview with Jake McIntyre.

Chapter Three: Watching TV

As an adult, Jim referred to comedian ... Jerry Morse, "Lexington's Own Jim Varney," *Views of Lexington* (March 1995).

From *After the family* ... to ... *was growing up*: Author interview with Jake McIntyre.

Chapter Four: Discovering the Theater

Sandy remembers Jim surprising ... Author interview with Sandra Varney Spoonamore.

In no time Jim was consistently ... Jim Varney resume.

NOTES

From *She was a high* ... to ... *of actors onstage*: Author interview with Mary Polites.

From *Jack Pattie* ... to ... *to recite it*: Author interview with Jack Pattie.

Even though the neighboring ... Author interview with Sandra Varney Spoonamore.

Even at a young age ... Author interview with Jake McIntyre.

From *Soon after moving* ... to ... *from their door*: Author interview with Sandra Varney Spoonamore.

Chapter Five: Anne, Her Mother and the Finer Things

When Jim was around 13 ... Author interview with Jake McIntyre.

Anne Lambert remembers Jim ... Author interview with Anne Lambert.

Along with stories ... Author interview with Jake McIntyre.

Anne Lambert and Jim dated ... "E! True Hollywood Story Ernest Goes to Hollywood: Jim Varney" television special (2000).

From *Jim also loved* ... to "... *Hall Of Fame*": Author interview with Jake McIntyre.

Jim was deeply concerned ... Author interview with Mary Polites.

From *Jake once asked* ... to ... *of his personality*: Author interview with Jake McIntyre.

THE IMPORTANCE OF BEING ERNEST:
THE LIFE OF ACTOR JIM VARNEY

Chapter Six: The Varney Parkers

From *To bring in … to … larger than life*: Author interview with Jake McIntyre.

Ed would later recall … Author interview with Ed McChord.

Chapter Seven: High School Years

Her long tenure … Jennifer Hewlitt, "Thelma Beeler, teacher for 70 years, dies at 91," *Lexington Herald Leader* (January 03, 1996).

One such episode … Cynthia DeMarcus, "Hey Vern! Looka There!" *Bluegrass Magazine* (December 1988).

Jim later recalled … Merlene Davis, "Lessons in life teacher instills self-confidence in her students," *Lexington Herald-Leader* (May 29, 1988).

The University of Kentucky's Centennial Players' Summer Theatre … "Shakespearean Comedy Is Set for Friday Opening," *Lexington Herald-Leader* (July 24, 1966).

The play's director went through … Author interview with Mary Polites.

He later confessed … Skip Press, "Hey Vern, It's Varney," *Boys' Life* (September 1992).

One of the professional actors in the play … "Shakespearean Comedy Is Set for Friday Opening," *Lexington Herald-Leader* (July 24, 1966).

NOTES

Critic Mary Agnes Barnes ... Mary Agnes Barnes, "'Shakespeare's Dream' Takes Honors at UK," *Lexington Herald-Leader* (July 30, 1966).

But when Jim's parents ... Author interview with Jake McIntyre.

He later joked ... Ronni Lundy, "Ernest Goes to Camp," *The Courier-Journal* (Oct. 26, 1986).

Jim's thirst for performing ... Author interview with Jake McIntyre.

Much of this material ... Lafayette Marquis (1968 Yearbook).

Another local performer ... Jerry Morse, "Lexington's Own Jim Varney," *Views of Lexington* (March 1995).

One of his favorite accessories ... Cynthia DeMarcus, "Hey Vern! Looka There!" *Bluegrass Magazine* (December 1988).

His father and Ford ... Author interview with Mary Polites.

He could see what he later called ... Cynthia DeMarcus, "Hey Vern! Looka There!" *Bluegrass Magazine* (December 1988).

It was no different with Jim ... Linda Miller, "Jim Varney's Loud Mouth Turns Him Into Celebrity," *The Daily Oklahoman* (Feb. 26, 1984).

Once, Jim even posed as a student ... Cynthia DeMarcus, "Hey Vern! Looka There!" *Bluegrass Magazine* (December 1988).

Along with cutting up in class ... Don Edwards, "This Harlequin Was Never Taken Seriously," *Lexington Herald-Leader* (Feb. 17, 2000).

THE IMPORTANCE OF BEING ERNEST:
THE LIFE OF ACTOR JIM VARNEY

One of the few extracurricular ... Author interview with Jake McIntyre.

Ford had seen signs ... Author interview with Mary Polites.

From *During this time* ... to ... *large silver bowl*: Author interview with Jake McIntyre.

At the state drama festival ... Western Kentucky University's Web site, http://www.wku.edu/pcal/festival-awards (Accessed May 15, 2010).

During research for this book ... Author interview with Kathy Jansen.

From *Watkins did not* ... to ... *gold convertible Corvette*: Author interview Clay Watkins.

From *Watkins took Jim* ... to ... *a few jobs*: Author interview with Joe Liles.

Chapter Eight: Leaving Lexington

Liles remembers Big Jim ... Author interview with Joe Liles.

Oldest sister Jo Gail admitted ... Jim Warren, "He's A Star – Know Whut Uh Mean?" *Lexington Herald-Leader* (Feb. 6, 1984).

As Jim's final year at Lafayette ... Author interview with Clay Watkins.

He knew of Barter's excellent reputation ... Author interview with Mary Polites.

From *Out of the 370* ... to "... *must be developed*": "Varney to Act in Summer Stock"

NOTES

The Lafayette Times (high school newspaper) (May 14, 1968).

Jim's mother was angry ... Author interview with Jake McIntyre.

The Barter Theatre ... Barter Theatre's Web site, http://www.bartertheatre.com/about/history.php (Accessed March 17, 2013).

When Jim arrived in the spring of 1968 ... Mal Vincent, "'Hey Vern! I'm in Jail'" *The Virginian-Pilot* (April 11, 1990).

"The Company" was the roster ... Author interview with Walter Williamson.

Jim regularly sent letters home ... Jim Varney letter to his parents (1968).

Along with acting ... Author interview with Jake McIntyre.

Actor Walter Williamson ... Chris Willman, "The Importance of Being Ernest," *Los Angeles Times* (Nov. 16, 1993).

He has since written ... Walter Williamson bio on Internet Movie Database, http://www.imdb.com/name/nm0932174/bio (Accessed Oct. 31, 2011).

From *Jim made an* ... to "... *guarded art inside*": Author interview with Walter Williamson.

Walter also spoke ... Chris Willman, "The Importance of Being Ernest," *Los Angeles Times* (Nov. 16, 1993).

He had been keeping in touch ... Author interview with Joe Liles.

THE IMPORTANCE OF BEING ERNEST: THE LIFE OF ACTOR JIM VARNEY

Watkins let Jim stay ... Author interview with Clay Watkins.

He later referred to the auditioning experience ... Jim Warren, "He's A Star – Know Whut I Mean?" *Lexington Herald-Leader* (Feb. 6, 1984).

From *One of Jim's* ... to ... *his mother*: Author interview with Ed McChord.

Despite X-rays ... Author interview with Jake McIntyre.

From *By the summer* ... to ... *"Bye, Bye Birdie."*: Author interview with Julieanne Pogue.

The director of "Birdie" ... Author interview with Jim Hazlett.

Jim broke his contract ... Author interview with Julieanne Pogue.

Jim's cousin Ed McChord ... Author interview with Ed McChord.

Unfortunately, Jim didn't get ... Carole Kass, "Hey Vern! Ernest P.'s a Film Star," *Richmond Times-Dispatch* (May 24, 1987).

From *During Jim's short* ... to ... *remaining good friends:* Author interview with Julieanne Pogue.

Meanwhile, Jim found time ... Author interview with Jake McIntyre.

Jim received rave reviews ... Mary Agnes Barnes, "Studio Players Production Lauded By Reviewer," *Lexington Herald-Leader* (December 1969).

NOTES

Another local critic ... Richard Schwein, "Studio Players Celebrates Anniversary with 2 Plays," *Lexington Herald Leader* (December 1969).

In the summer of 1970 ... "'Boeing, Boeing!' Lands At Playhouse Wednesday," *Lexington Herald-Leader* (June 1970).

At the time ... Robert Cooper, "'Fire on Mountain' at 3rd Masque is a Hilarious Hillbilly Musical," *Chattanooga Times* (Sept. 23, 1970).

There he starred in ... *Harlan Daily Enterprise* (May 24, 1970).

Although actors such as ... "E! True Hollywood Story Ernest Goes to Hollywood: Jim Varney" television special (2000).

Henson was also involved ... Robert Cooper, "'Fire on Mountain' at 3rd Masque is a Hilarious Hillbilly Musical," *Chattanooga Times* (Sept. 23, 1970).

At the Third Masque Dinner Theatre ... Robert Cooper, "'Fire on Mountain' at 3rd Masque is a Hilarious Hillbilly Musical," *Chattanooga Times* (Sept. 23, 1970).

From *One of Jim's* ... to ... *was not returned:* Author interview with Charles Edward Pogue.

Jim's sister Jake ... Author interview with Jake McIntyre.

Headquartered in ... "High Schools Will See 'Antigone' This Week," *Kingsport Times* (Feb. 27, 1972).

THE IMPORTANCE OF BEING ERNEST:
THE LIFE OF ACTOR JIM VARNEY

The actors would meet ... "Fantastick Takes Snow White and Seven Dwarfs to School," *Kingsport Times* (March 29, 1972).

As the tour wound down ... Bart Mills, "Actor won't minimize the importance of being Ernest," *Daily Breeze (Torrance, Calif.)* (May 22, 1987).

In one of the Opryland folk ... Jerry Morse, "Lexington's Own Jim Varney," *Views of Lexington* (March 1995).

From *Yet despite the* ... to ... *it even more:* Author interview with Jake McIntyre.

Chapter Nine: Finding Glory with Cherry

From *Jim soon caught* ... to "... *replied 'Yes, Sir!'*": Author interview with Thom Ferrell.

Years later when being interviewed ... Beverly Keel, "The Importance of Being Ernest," *Nashville Scene,* (Nov. 11, 1999).

In addition to Sergeant Glory ... Jerry Morse, "Lexington's Own Jim Varney," *Views of Lexington* (March 1995).

It was the car salesman ... Bart Mills, "Actor won't minimize the importance of being Ernest," *Daily Breeze (Torrance, Calif.)* (May 22, 1987).

From *He decided* ... to ... *around their bed*: Author interview with Joe Liles.

NOTES

Jim's family didn't see much of him: Author interview with Jake McIntyre.

From *Liles' efforts* ... to ... *asked him to*: Author interview with Joe Liles.

The grim look on Jim's face ... "Johnny Cash – Ridin' The Rails: The Great American Train Story" television special (1974).

From *During the taping* ... to ... *him additional bookings*: Author interview with Joe Liles.

One of Jim's early influences ... John Kiesewetter, "Jonathan Winters Loosens Up," *Cincinnati Enquirer* (August 13, 2000).

Maude Frickert was based ...Archive of American Television's Web site, http://www.emmytvlegends.org/interviews/people/jonathan- winters (Accessed Nov. 17, 2012).

Elwood P. Suggins was a hillbilly ... John Kiesewetter, "Jonathan Winters Loosens Up," *Cincinnati Enquirer* (Aug. 13, 2000).

In one popular routine ... "Whistle Stopping With Jonathan Winters," album (1964).

Jim used various small towns ... Audiotapes of Jim performing at Exit/In, provided to the author by Joe Liles (1975).

From *Soon after Liles* ... to "... *but it worked*": Author interview with Joe Liles.

Also attached to the bio ... Excerpt from Jim Varney's 1975 William Morris bio.

From *After signing with* ... to ... *way they could*: Author interview with Joe Liles.

Thom Ferrell had left ... Author interview with Thom Ferrell.

In addition to polishing material ...Author interview with Joe Liles.

In October ...Milford Reid, "Los Angeles-Bound Varney Looking for Break in Show Business," *Lexington Herald-Leader* (Oct. 9, 1975).

Jim sent a letter home ... Jim Varney letter to his parents (1975).

Chapter Ten: Striking It Rich in California

From *By February 1976* ... to ... *in college*: Author interview with Joe Liles. (Additional author interview with Ed McChord also contributed to information cited here.)

Club owner Mitzi Shore ... Tom Robinson, "Hey Vern! I'm a Celebrity," *Nashville!* (September 1982).

Jim later talked ... Bob Thomas, "Jim Varney Is No Clod," *Associated Press* (April 25, 1990).

From *Along with helping* ... to "... *Morris closed it*": Author interview with Joe Liles.

NOTES

The show, "Johnny Cash and Friends"... Marshall Fallwell Jr., "Nashville Beat," *Photoplay* (September 1976).

From *Liles remembers Martin* ... to ... *invited him back:* Author interview with Joe Liles.

Even though the four-episode ... Marshall Fallwell Jr., "Nashville Beat," *Photoplay* (September 1976).

From *Now that Jim* ... to ... *Jim's sensitivity:* Author interview with Joe Liles.

On October 19, 1976 ... Official Web site for Johnny Carson, http://www.johnnycarson.com/carson/search.do?singleDateMonth=10&singleDateDay=19&singleDateYear=1976 (Accessed Sept. 9, 2008).

From *Jim had just* ... to ... *to his career:* Author interview with Joe Liles.

Jim was also continuing ... Author interview with Joe Liles.

John Cherry later admitted... "Personality Sells," Sellingpower.com, http://www.sellingpower.com/article/display.asp?print=TRUE@aid=SP8826606 (Accessed July 26, 2009).

He later recalled ... Beverly Keel, "The Importance of Being Ernest," *Nashville Scene* (Nov. 15, 1999).

One reporter interviewing ... Tom Robinson, "Hey Vern! I'm a Celebrity," *Nashville!* (September 1982).

THE IMPORTANCE OF BEING ERNEST:
THE LIFE OF ACTOR JIM VARNEY

Liles recalls the Virgil Simms character ... Author interview with Joe Liles.

Virgil also entertained with stories ... "Fernwood 2 Night" television show (1976).

Jim also landed a part ... This book provided excellent background material on "Riding High": Lee Goldberg, "Unsold TV Pilots: The Almost Complete Guide to Everything You Never Saw on TV 1955-1990." *(An Author's Guild Backprint Edition, iUniverse.com).*

Jim's agent at William Morris ... Author interview with Joe Liles.

"Operation Petticoat" was a comedy ...EPGuides.com, http://epguides.com/OperationPetticoat/ (Accessed Aug. 9, 2009).

In the summer of 1978 ... Marilyn Beck, "Pink Subs Crew Gets Pink Slips," *United Feature Syndicate* (Aug. 8, 1978).

Liles visited Jim on the set ... Author interview with Joe Liles.

In the fall ... "Alice" television show (Nov. 5, 1978).

Actress Zsa Zsa Gabor ... "Norm Crosby's Comedy Shop" television show (1979).

Jim also landed an appearance ..."Alan King's Third Annual Final Warning" television special, Baseline Research, http://www.inbaseline.com/project.aspx?project_id=39404 (Accessed Aug. 9, 2009).

From *Even though Liles* ... to ... *Hocker, among others*: Author interview with Joe Liles.

NOTES

The proposal said ... "Jim Varney's Family Album" television proposal, provided to the author by Joe Liles.

Meanwhile, in the summer of 1979 ... Author interview with Joe Liles.

In describing Jim's act ... Gregory Curtis, "Theater In Brief," *Texas Monthly* (October 1979).

Comedian Lonnie Shorr ... Author interview with Lonnie Shorr.

From *Liles accompanied Jim* ... to ... *over the years*: Author interview with Joe Liles.

He continued to do stand-up ... "What's Doing in San Diego County," *Los Angeles Times* (Sept. 7, 1979).

Pink lady was not an actual lady ... Alan Sepinwall, "'Pink Lady' so bad it was spectacular." *The Star-Ledger* (Dec. 8, 2001).

Even though the girls struggled ... Author interview with Jake McIntyre.

Chapter Eleven: Becoming Vern's Favorite Neighbor

In July 1980 ...Robert A. McLean, "Ad-ventures," *Boston Globe* (Aug. 20, 1980).

"There we were ..." Tom Robinson, "Hey Vern! I'm a Celebrity," *Nashville!* (September 1982).

From *Liles always thought* ... to ... *as an artist*: Author interview with Joe Liles.

THE IMPORTANCE OF BEING ERNEST: THE LIFE OF ACTOR JIM VARNEY

With no real paying acting ... Author interview with Jake McIntyre.

John Cherry and Thom Ferrell ... Cathy Darnell, "Ernest a Good Work for Beech Bend," *The Tennessean* (Aug. 20, 1980).

"We developed Ernest coming back ..." Cathy Darnell, "Ernest a Good Word for Beech Bend," *The Tennessean* (Aug. 31, 1980).

After getting the premise down ... Beverly Keel, "The Importance of Being Ernest," *Nashville Scene*, (Nov. 11, 1999).

Ernest also promoted ... Cathy Darnell, "Ernest a Good Work for Beech Bend," *The Tennessean* (Aug. 20, 1980).

Since Ernest had been tailored ... Paula Wade, "Ernest: KnowwhutImean?" *The Commercial Appeal* (April 21, 1985).

Ernest seemed destined for the same fate ... Lou Gaul, "Advertising whiz created Jim Varney's character," *The Intelligencer/Record* (Nov. 27, 1988).

In the latter part of 1981 ... Walt Potter, "From chance to instant hit," *Nashville Banner* (Jan. 26, 1983).

In Raleigh, N.C., Pine State ... Ben Steelman, "Earnest fans know what Ernest Means," *Star-News* (June 5, 1983).

In April 1982 ... Baseline Research, http://www.inbaseline.com/project.aspx?project_id=61174 (Accessed Aug. 9, 2009).

After Purity and Pine State ... Lew Powell, "Hey Vern ...," *The Charlotte Observer* (Feb. 8, 1986).

NOTES

Jerry Carden, John Cherry's partner ...Walt Potter "From chance to instant hit," *Nashville Banner* (Jan. 26, 1983).

He had spent most of his career ... Author interview with Roy Lightner.

One was teaming up ... Author interview with Thom Ferrell.

In the fall of 1982 ...Tom Robinson, "Hey Vern! I'm a Celebrity," *Nashville!* (September 1982).

But before the 26 taped episodes ... Ed Cromer, "Chancellor Says 'Ernest' TV Ads Can Continue," *The Tennessean* (Nov. 13, 1982).

Mayhew countersued ... "Ernest actor settles contract lawsuits." *Nashville Banner* (Feb. 18, 1983).

Both sides eventually settled ... "Ernest actor settles contract lawsuits." *Nashville Banner* (Feb. 18, 1983).

Meanwhile, Jim continued ... Mary Ann Hea, "Varneys to do their comic routines," *Nashville Banner* (Feb. 15, 1983).

According to Jo Swerling Jr.: ... Mary Jane Brown, "NBC expects Ernest figure to really soar in a new series," *Nashville Banner* (July 6, 1983).

The "Rousters" pilot ... Diane Bartley, "'Ernest' Headed for Hollywood – YaknowwhutImean?" *The Tennessean* (May 11, 1983).

During the show's short run ... Joe Edwards, "Recognition Catches Up to Versatile Varney," *Daily Intelligencer* (May 27, 1984).

The demands of filming ... Homer Brickey, "Hey Vern," *Toledo Blade* (March 12, 1989).

In one piece, Jim spoke ... Jim Warren, "He's A Star – Know Whut Uh Mean?" *Lexington Herald-Leader* (Feb. 6, 1984).

Jim's mother was interviewed ... Don Edwards, "Being Ernest May Make Lexington Native a Millionaire," *Lexington Herald-Leader* (July 29, 1984).

Les Bosse, advertising director ... Jim Warren, "He's A Star – Know Whut Uh Mean?" *Lexington Herald-Leader* (Feb. 6, 1984).

In March 1984 ... *The Woodford Sun* (March 29, 1984).

Jim's father carried a copy ... Author interview with Jake McIntyre.

Many had themes ... Janet Patton, "Anita Madden honored as trailblazing businesswoman," *Lexington Herald-Leader* (April 9, 2012).

In May 1984 ... Beverly Fortune, "Diamonds Add Glitter to the Maddens' Gala Derby Parties," *Lexington Herald Leader* (May 5, 1984).

A Tulsa, Okla., TV station ... Linda Franklin, "Varney was the talk of the town," *The Journal Record* (Feb. 14, 2000).

NOTES

Customers at a Braum's ... Cynthia Foley, "Store becomes filming site for commercials Vern!?" Choctaw loves that," *The Daily Oklahoman* (May 10, 1983).

Originally referred to ... Diane Bartley, "Old Ernest Goes to National TV," *The Tennessean* (March 6, 1984).

Consisting of six sketches ... "Hey Vern, It's My Family Album" television special (1983).

Charlie Chaplin had explored ... "The Gold Rush" film, Charles Chaplin Productions. (1925).

From *Meanwhile, after getting*... to ... *into the wall*: "Hey Vern, It's My Family Album" television special (1983).

In Nashville, Ernest's home base ... Diane Bartley, "Ole Ernest Gets His Own TV Show: KnowhutImean?" *The Tennessean* (July 13, 1984).

In the second piece ... "CBS Evening News" (December 06, 1985).

In March 1985 ... "NBC Nightly News," (March 22, 1985).

Chapter Twelve: The Secret of Ernest's Success

Jim said once ... "Varney's Idols," *Orlando Sentinel* (Nov. 5, 1988).

Another time Jim said ... "Jim Varney, 50, comedian who starred in Ernest films," *Atlanta Journal Constitution* (Feb. 11, 2000).

THE IMPORTANCE OF BEING ERNEST:
THE LIFE OF ACTOR JIM VARNEY

John Cherry admitted later: John Cherry's speech at Jim Varney's memorial service, witnessed by the author (Feb. 16, 2000).

In a 1987 television interview ... Mike Randall, *WKBW News* (Buffalo, NY) (1987).

Ernest writer Glenn Petach said ... Homer Brickey, "Hey Vern," *The Toledo Blade* (March 12, 1989).

Another Ernest writer ... Josh Armstrong, "Hey Vern, It's Ernest collaborator Coke Sams," Knowtheartist.com, http://knowtheartist.com/hey-vern-it%E2%80%99s-ernest-collaborator-coke-sams/ (Accessed Oct 30, 2011).

Jim told the Daily Oklahoman ... Tony Frazier, "Hey Vern! Ernest Goes to Camp Today," *The Daily Oklahoman* (May 22, 1987).

Jim once offered a simplified ... Bruce Cook, "Great American Goofball Leaps From Commercials to Films," *Los Angeles Daily News* (May 22, 1987).

Even before the success ... "Personality Sells," Sellingpower.com http://www.sellingpower.com/article/display.asp?print=TRUE@aid=SP8826606 (1987). (Accessed July 26, 2009).

No matter how much praise ... Mike Randall, *WKBW News* (Buffalo, NY) (1987).

As discussed earlier ... "E! True Hollywood Story Ernest Goes to Hollywood: Jim Varney" television show (2000).

NOTES

Perhaps there was no better ... Mark Dawidziak, "'Heyyy Vern' Crazy Character Brings Fame to Actor," *Akron Beacon Journal* (May 19, 1985).

As far as Ernest's last name ... Lou Gaul, "Advertising whiz created Jim Varney's Character," *Intelligencer Record* (Nov. 27, 1988).

Writer Coke Sams recalled ... Josh Armstrong, "Hey Vern, It's Ernest Collaborator Coke Sams," Knowtheartist.com, http://knowtheartist.com/hey-vern-it%E2%80%99s-ernest-collaborator-coke-sams/ (Accessed Oct. 30, 2011)

In one instance ... "E! True Hollywood Story Ernest Goes to Hollywood: Jim Varney" television show (2000).

Coke Sams once said... Josh Armstrong, "Hey Vern, It's Ernest collaborator Coke Sams," Knowtheartist.com, http://knowtheartist.com/hey-vern-it%E2%80%99s-ernest-collaborator-coke-sams/ (Accessed Oct. 30, 2011)

Luckily, he never suffered ... Homer Brickey, "Hey Vern," *The Toledo Blade* (March 12, 1989).

As Cherry once said ... William Greer, "Jim Varney: The importance of being Ernest," *Advantage Magazine* (July 1988).

Studio was founded ... Valerie V. Hansen, "Roll'em! Nashville's video production is booming," *Nashville Business and Lifestyle* (May 1, 1991).

Cherry was aware that a commercial ... Cynthia DeMarcus, "Hey Vern! Looka There!" *Bluegrass Magazine* (December 1988).

THE IMPORTANCE OF BEING ERNEST: THE LIFE OF ACTOR JIM VARNEY

Jim said once … Mark Dawidziak, "'Hey Vern' Crazy Character Brings Fame to Actor," *Akron Beacon Journal* (May 19, 1985).

Jim said that there was … Carole Kass, "Hey Vern! Ernest is Spending His Third Movie in Jail," *Richmond Times-Dispatch* (April 8, 1990).

In Ernest's early years … Timothy K. Smith, "Abominable Ernest of TV Commercials Noses Out Everyone," *Wall Street Journal* (Nov. 20, 1985).

Cherry admitted … Bethany Kandel, "Varney's 'Ernest' Pops Up in Big Apple," *Lexington Herald-Leader* (Jan. 10, 1986).

One aspect that Cherry mentioned … "Raucous television huckster pays off," *Alton Telegraph* (July 24, 1984).

In a 2009 appearance … "Inside the Actors Studio" television show (Ricky Gervais) (Jan. 19, 2009).

The commercial … Ronni Lundy, "Ernest Goes to Camp." *The Courier-Journal* (Oct. 26, 1986).

Cherry also said once … "Personality Sells" Sellingpower.com http://www.sellingpower.com/article/display.asp?print=TRUE@aid=SP8826606, (Accessed July 26, 2009).

Cream o'Weber … Jim Erickson, "Hey Vern!" *Anchorage Daily News* (April 17, 1986).

When Carden & Cherry … William Greer, "Jim Varney: The importance of being Ernest," *Advantage Magazine* (July 1988).

NOTES

California car dealership owner ... Mike Dunne, "Something Strange Happening in Television Land, Vern," *Sacramento Bee* (March 13, 1986).

Cherry once said ... "Personality Sells" Sellingpower.com http://www.sellingpower.com/article/display.asp?print=TRUE@aid=SP8826606, (Accessed July 26, 2009).

Cherry would laugh about ... Kevin Nance, "Varney, 'Ernest' creator, dies at 50," *The Tennessean* (Feb. 11, 2000).

Cliff Cummings saw how Ernest ... Kathy Kalafut, "Hey Vern, I'm A Star," *Entertainment Weekly* (April 13, 1990).

Cummings once described ... "NBC Nightly News" (March 22, 1985).

He further explained ... Kathy Kalafut, "Hey Vern, I'm A Star," *Entertainment Weekly* (April 13, 1990).

Meanwhile, in Indianapolis ... Paula Wade, "Ernest: KnowwhutImean?" *The Commercial Appeal* (April 21, 1985).

And according to Roy Lightner ... Roy Lightner's speech at Jim Varney's memorial service, witnessed by the author (Feb. 16, 2000).

Lightner laughed about the time ... "E! True Hollywood Story Ernest Goes to Hollywood: Jim Varney" television show (2000).

When Ernest first became popular ... Paula Wade, "Ernest: KnowwhutImean?" *The Commercial Appeal* (April 21, 1985).

THE IMPORTANCE OF BEING ERNEST:
THE LIFE OF ACTOR JIM VARNEY

In one Cleveland newspaper article ... Ken Gottlieb, "There may be life after Ernest P. KnowwhutImean," *Chronicle-Telegram* (Dec. 15, 1984).

In New Mexico ... Hollis Engley, "Hey, Vern! I'm sellin' KOB," *The New Mexican* (May 30, 1985).

In the spring of 1986 ... Ed Bark, "Shaping The Image of TV News," *Dallas Morning News* (April 17, 1986).

Said Coke Sams ... Josh Armstrong, "Hey Vern, It's Ernest collaborator Coke Sams," Knowtheartist.com, http://knowtheartist.com/hey-vern-it%E2%80%99s-ernest-collaborator-coke-sams/ (Accessed Oct 30, 2011).

Jim did once say ... Cynthia Foley, "Store becomes filming site for commercials Vern!?" *The Daily Oklahoman* (May 10, 1983).

Jim, who was always ... Associated Press, (May 21, 1984).

In realizing what a hot commodity ... William Greer, "Jim Varney: The importance of being Ernest," *Advantage Magazine* (July 1988).

As far as Ernest's appearance ... Glen Phillips, "Ernest snared by Channel 4," *The Daily Oklahoman* (April 28, 1985).

Said Jim ... Deborah Garrett, "Hey Vern! I'm a movie star," *The Tennessean* (Dec. 5, 1988).

He said that the plain khaki ... Lew Powell, "Hey Vern ..." *The Charlotte Observer* (Feb. 8, 1986).

NOTES

Product merchandising began ... William Greer, "Jim Varney: The importance of being Ernest," *Advantage Magazine* (July 1988).

Braum's Dairy ... Linda Franklin, "Varney was the talk of the town," *The Journal Record* (Feb. 14, 2000).

Jim often stayed ... "Ol' Ern Really Loves His Ice Cream," *The Galveston Daily News* (March 9, 1983).

Perhaps no appearance ... *The News and Observer* (Nov. 24, 1985).

Chapter Thirteen: Gloom Beams, Heartbreak and a Little Luck

The movie was titled ... Rick Bailey, "Jim Varney Breaking Into Movies," *Lexington Herald-Leader* (Aug. 2, 1985).

It was filmed ... Don Edwards, "Hey, Vern, It's a Silver-Screen Debut for Actor Jim Varney," *Lexington Herald-Leader* (Dec. 11, 1985).

The entire production ... Rick Bailey, "Jim Varney Breaking Into Movies," *Lexington Herald-Leader* (Aug. 2, 1985).

One of the interviews ... Arch Campbell, *WRC-TV News* (Washington, D.C.) (1984).

This time he was in Houston ... "Willie Nelson's New Years Eve Party," HBO Special, (Dec 31, 1984).

He co-hosted ... Jon Anderson, "HBO spending $1 million for live country special," *Chicago Tribune* (Dec. 31, 1984).

THE IMPORTANCE OF BEING ERNEST: THE LIFE OF ACTOR JIM VARNEY

Jim was scheduled for ... "TV Talk," *The Tennessean* (March 7, 1985).

Jim spent the spring of 1985 ... Mark Dawidziak, "Heyyy, Vern Crazy Character Brings Fame to Actor," *Akron Beacon Journal* (May 19, 1985).

The busy commercial shooting ... Don Edwards, "Being Ernest Has Been Important to Varney's Career," *Lexington Herald-Leader* (Feb. 12, 1985).

"Otto" was released ... "The Importance of Being Ernest," *Los Angeles Times* (June 2, 1987).

Cherry planned ... Rick Bailey, "Jim Varney Breaking Into Movies," *Lexington Herald-Leader* (Aug. 2, 1985).

Even Lexington-Herald Leader writer ... Don Edwards, "Varney's Movie Lands With a Thud," *Lexington Herald-Leader* (Aug. 3, 1985).

He said at the time ... Rick Bailey, "Jim Varney Breaking Into Movies," *Lexington Herald-Leader* (Aug. 2, 1985).

Looking back at the failure ... Kathy Kalafut, "Hey, Vern, I'm A Star," *Entertainment Weekly* (April 13, 1990).

The Indianapolis area had become ... Roy Lightner's speech at Jim Varney's memorial service, witnessed by the author (Feb. 16, 2000).

"I was at the Indianapolis 500 ..." Rita Kempley, "Big Cheese of the Mouse Factory," *Washington Post* (Jan. 8, 1989).

NOTES

By June 1985 ... Don Edwards, "Lexington Native Making It Big 'Know Whut I Mean?'" *Lexington Herald Leader* (June 14, 1985).

Jim explained ... Adam Bernstein, "Comic Jim Varney Dies at Age 50," *Washington Post* (Feb. 11, 2000).

In the fall of 1985 ... Tina Bodine Fain, "Varney To Head Benefit Style Show," *Lexington Herald-Leader* (Oct. 18, 1985).

He and Jake would debate ... Author interview with Jake McIntyre.

He talked to Sandy ... Author interview with Sandra Varney Spoonamore.

After signing with Coca-Cola ... Keith Herndon, "Plain-folks character helping Coke hawk Mello Yello and Sprite on TV," *Atlanta Journal Constitution* (Dec. 9, 1985).

The commercial opens with ... Description of Ernest Sprite commercial from YouTube video at http://youtu.be/VM3QqTcM55k.

From the beginning... Cathy Darnell, "Ernest a Good Word for Beech Bend," *The Tennessean* (Aug. 31, 1980).

The American Bed Co. ... Bethany Kandel, "Varney's 'Ernest' Pops Up In Big Apple," *Associated Press* (Jan. 11, 1986).

CNN filmed Jim ... *CNN Headline News* (1986).

Of all the interviews ... Bobbi Woloch, "Lexington native Jim Varney making his mark Earnestly,'" *Kentucky Kernel* (May 1, 1986).

269

Another person quoted ... Author interview with Lianne Mize Russell.

Through the years ... Author interview with Jake McIntyre.

In April of 1986, just months after ... "Charlie Daniels 'tunes up' with the Symphony," *Associated Press* (April 5, 1986).

Larry Speakes ... "An Economic Expert? Not Hardly," *Associated Press* (April 22, 1986).

Chapter Fourteen: Ernest in the Movies

Nashville residents were soon ... Greg Bailey, "Disney scouting possible sites for Varney Film," *Nashville Banner* (July 9, 1986).

That fall, the "Camp" movie crew ... Randy Brison, "Ernest Movie Begun," *The Dickson Herald* (Sept. 12, 1986).

There were around 26 ... Michael Spies, "Know what he means?" *Houston Chronicle* (May 22, 1987).

Jim filmed his entire ... Susan Spillman, "He knows the importance of being Ernest," *USA Today* (May 28, 1987).

He had actually told the Atlanta ... Lee Walburn, "Old Ernest P. is doing OK," *Atlanta Journal Constitution* (Nov. 26, 1985).

In a 2005 interview ... Ken Beck, "Know what I mean, Vern?" *The Tennessean* (Aug. 24, 2005).

NOTES

He had studied at ... Jerry Morse, "Lexington's Own Jim Varney," *Views of Lexington* (March 1995).

As Jim was preparing to take Ernest ... Diane Bartley, "The importance of being Ernest," *The Tennessean* (Sept. 24, 1986).

"Where else can you get paid..." Ronni Lundy, "Ernest Goes to Camp," *The Courier-Journal* (Oct. 26, 1986).

In a Nashville Banner article ... Pat Embry, "Ernest mugs on big screen," *The Nashville Banner* (May 21, 1987).

Jim thought with the late-spring ... Jamie Reno, "Varney gets a break during actor's strike," *Winnipeg Free Press* (Nov. 22, 1988).

On the film's opening day... "If Vern Could See Me Now," *The Nashville Banner* (May 23, 1987).

Realizing that critics ... Aljean Harmetz, "Hollywood Hopes for Long, Hot Summer," *New York Times* (June 21, 1987).

With an estimated budget of $3 million ... Internet Movie Database, http://www.imdb.com/title/tt0092974/business?ref_=tt_dt_bus.

Cherry took the poor reviews ... Lisa Belkin, "Ernie: A Commercial Success Story," *New York Times* (June, 8, 1987).

In 2009, Steve Martin ... "Steve Martin brings new 'Panther' to Berlin fest," *Associated Press* (Feb. 13, 2009).

THE IMPORTANCE OF BEING ERNEST: THE LIFE OF ACTOR JIM VARNEY

One critic took his bashing… Doug Brode, "'Ernest' Belongs in Trash Heap," *The Post Standard* (May 22, 1987).

Funny enough, some radio ads … "Varney takes Ernest to camp," *Houston Chronicle* (May 22, 1987).

While working on "Camp … Talk-show host Peter Anthony Holder interview with Jim Varney, on Holder's Web site, http://peteranthonyholder.com/cjad28.htm (Accessed June 7, 2013).

During the musical's successful run … Singer and entertainer Roger Miller's official Web site, http://www.rogermiller.com/bio4.html (Accessed Feb. 1, 2010).

In a 1996 interview … Talk-show host Peter Anthony Holder interview with Jim Varney, on Holder's Web site, http://peteranthonyholder.com/cjad28.htm (Accessed June 7, 2013).

In November 1999 … Beverly Keel, "The Importance of Being Ernest," *Nashville Scene* (Nov. 11, 1999).

He joked … Tony Frazier, "Hey, Vern! Ernest Goes to Camp Today," *The Daily Oklahoman* (May 22, 1987).

He often reminded reporters … Lawrence Toppman, "That face, that IQ, the DeLorean," *Knight-Ridder Newspapers* (April 16, 1990).

Another actor Jim mentioned … Cynthia DeMarcus, "Hey Vern! Looka There!" *Bluegrass Magazine* (December 1988).

NOTES

Around 1988, Jim and Betty Clark ... Homer Brickey, "Hey Vern," *The Toledo Blade* (March 12, 1989).

Walden rose to prominence ... Maria Saporta, "Signs right for Capricorn Records," *Atlanta Journal Constitution* (March 22, 1999).

Two years after ... Phillip Ramati, "Stepson pushes for Frank Fenter's inclusion in music hall," The Georgia Telegraph's Web site, http://www.macon.com/local/story/952458.html (Accessed Dec, 14, 2009).

Along with the help ... "Jerry Wexler, Visionary Music Producer, Passes Away at 91," Marketwired, http://www.marketwire.com/press-release/jerry-wexler-visionary-music-producer-passes-away-at-91-890217.htm (Accessed Aug. 15, 2008).

But in 1979 ... Maria Saporta, "Signs right for Capricorn Records," *Atlanta Journal Constitution* (March 22, 1999).

Throughout that time ... Phil Walden's speech at Jim Varney's memorial service, witnessed by the author (Feb. 16, 2000).

Martin Mull, an actor ...Tom Popson, "Capricorn Records and Phil Walden back in the game," *Chicago Tribune* (July 19, 1991).

But one of Jim's first ventures ... Author interview with Joe Liles.

Jake had originally written ... Author interview with Jake McIntyre.

One rainy night I met a man ... Lyric from "Born in a Boxcar," written by Jake McIntyre (1973).

THE IMPORTANCE OF BEING ERNEST:
THE LIFE OF ACTOR JIM VARNEY

Shortly before Jim hired Walden ... Pat Embry, "Ernest mugs on big screen," *Nashville Banner* (May 21, 1987).

The song was eventually recorded ... "Freedom" album Neil Young, liner notes (1989).

He was asked to play ... Carlene Carter Fan Club Web site, http://forum.carlenecarterfanclub.com/music-12.html (Accessed Aug. 12, 2010).

Walden traveled to Los Angeles ... Swampland.com, Russell Hall, "Capricorn Records," http://swampland.com/articles/view/title:capricorn_records (Accessed Jan. 28, 2011).

Years later, drummer Todd Nance ... James Calemine, "Down in the Groove With Widespread Panic's Todd Nance" Swampland.com, http://www.swampland.com/articles/view/title:down_in_the_groove_with_widespread_panics_todd_nance (Accessed (Dec. 22, 2010).

Chapter Fifteen: Pluvio

Jim said you should always ... Author interview with Jake McIntyre.

From *Coke Sams was* ... to ... *have surprised him*: Author interview with Coke Sams.

Jim occasionally told stories ... Author interview with Jake McIntyre.

Chapter Sixteen: Hobo Stew

A letter Jim wrote ... Jim Varney letter to his parents (Sept 19, 1984).

NOTES

Jim welcomed the chance ... "Florence Henderson's Country Kitchen" television show (1987).

His sister Sandy remembers visiting ... Author interview with Sandra Varney Spoonamore.

Jim's father always said ... Author interview with Jake McIntyre.

He laughed off ... Dixie Reid, "The Importance of Being Ernest P. – Movies, Records, Television – If Vern Could See Him Now," *Sacramento Bee* (May 2, 1987).

Chapter Seventeen: Handgun Wedding

Jane Hale ... Brad Schmidt, "Hey, Vern! You drive a milk truck or what?" *The Tennessean* (Feb. 17, 2000).

Janie was a travel agent ... Homer Brickey, "Hey Vern," *The Toledo Blade* (March 12, 1989).

She actually had no idea ... Brad Schmidt, "Hey, Vern! You drive a milk truck or what?" *The Tennessean* (Feb. 17, 2000).

Chapter Eighteen: Saving Christmas

Carden & Cherry had declined ... Patricia Duarte, "Ernest May Be a Redneck, But He's a Hot Property, Too," *The Miami Herald* (July 21, 1985).

The Ernest TV series ... "Hey Vern, It's Ernest" TV Series (1988).

THE IMPORTANCE OF BEING ERNEST: THE LIFE OF ACTOR JIM VARNEY

The network originally wanted … Karleena Tuggle; Diane Biebo; Dana Mangiacapre; Julieann Ulin, "Kidsday 'Talking With' Jim Varney," *Newsday* (Nov. 16, 1988).

From Gailard Sartain, no … *to "… what I mean?"*: "Hey Vern, It's Ernest" TV Series (1988).

Spin Magazine was one … Bart Bull, "Ernest P. Worrell Talks to Vern and Us," *Spin* (February 1989).

As CBS children's programming … Ed Bark, "'Ernest! Gives New Meaning to Weird," *The Dallas Morning News* (Sept. 24, 1988).

Jim thought too many cartoons … Lou Cedrone, "Actor Varney Comfortable As Ernest," *Baltimore Evening Sun* (April 10, 1990).

Although it was a busy time … Kathy Hogan Trocheck, "Jim Varney Working Ernest-ly," *Atlanta Journal Constitution* (Sept. 30, 1988).

That same year … Bart Mills, "Actor won't minimize the importance of being Ernest," *Daily Breeze (Torrance, Calif.)* (May 22, 1987).

The budget was double … Internet Movie Database, http://www.imdb.com/title/tt0095107/business?ref_=tt_dt_bus.

The reindeer used in the movie … Anne Paine, "Reindeer will be ….reindeer," *The Tennessean* (June 9, 1988).

Sounding like an angry Santa Claus … Michael McCall, "Hey, Vern-director-writer is the man who makes Ernest," *The Nashville Banner* (Jan. 30, 1989).

NOTES

But filming the movie ... Joan E. Vadeboncoeur, "Ernest emerged from weeds," *Syracuse Herald Journal* (Nov. 20, 1988).

As shooting was wrapping up ... Ed Bark, "Cleaning Up 'Reunion' Won't Be Easy," *The Dallas Morning News* (Aug. 2, 1988).

During the week of the movie's ... Christopher Hicks, "Tapping Stooge Tradition, 'Ernest' Goes to Hollywood," *The Deseret News* (Nov. 11, 1988).

Cherry said later ... "E! True Hollywood Story Ernest Goes to Hollywood: Jim Varney" television show (2000).

The box-office total ... Internet Movie Database, http://www.imdb.com/title/tt0095107/business?ref_=tt_dt_bus.

In addition to the new children's TV show ... Greg Baily, "Jim Varney's now winning in 'Ernest,'" *The Nashville Banner* (Nov. 4, 1988).

Despite a letter-writing ... Stephanie DuBois, "Jim Varney moves beyond commercials," *Austin American-Statesman* (July 7, 1989).

Cherry thought the show ... Kathy Kalafut, "Hey, Vern, I'm A Star," *Entertainment Weekly* (April 13, 1990).

Chapter Nineteen: The Line Blurs Between Jim and Ernest

He once recalled his reply ... Chuck Davis, "The Importance of Being Ernest," *The Daily Oklahoman* (Nov. 11, 1988).

THE IMPORTANCE OF BEING ERNEST: THE LIFE OF ACTOR JIM VARNEY

Jim said that he made a point ... "Varney Scared Stupid Of Being Typecast," *Daily News of Los Angeles* (Oct. 10, 1991).

At the 1986 Music City News Country Awards ... "20th Annual Music City News Country Awards" television special (June 9, 1986).

He wore the same formalwear ... CBS' "Happy New Year, America" television special (Dec. 31, 1988).

In 1989, Jim participated ... HBO's "Comic Relief III" television special (March 18, 1989).

In September 1988 ... Kathy Hogan Trocheck, "Jim Varney Working Ernest-ly," *Atlanta Constitutional Journal* (Sept. 30, 1988).

Film critic Richard Roeper ... Richard Roeper, "'Fast Food' goes nowhere – slowly," *Chicago Sun-Times* (June 7, 1989).

He was negotiating a new contract ... Ed Gregory, "Ernest's TV ads may end," *The Tennessean* (Aug. 24, 1988).

By mid-1989, Jim eventually received ... "Hey, Vern, Ernest is Coming Back to Series," *Chronicle-Telegram* (July 6, 1989).

One idea under serious ... Richard Schweid, "Jim Varney minus Ernest," *The Tennessean* (April 26, 1989).

The basic plot ... Buzz McClain, "Hey, Vern! Jim Varney's for real. KnowhutImean?" *Annapolis Capital* (April 20, 1990).

NOTES

At some point ... "Ernest goes to jail in Nashville," *The Tennessean* (July 25, 1989).

One Tennessee Baptist church ... Wayne Lee, "Hey Ern: Yer Really Making a Spectacle of Yerself," *The Seattle Times* (Oct. 28, 1985).

In August 1989 ... Hillary Saperstein, "Importance of Being Ernest Apparent to Varney at Fair," *The State Journal-Register* (Aug. 11, 1989).

Jim was familiar with the role ... Bob Carlton, "The Importance of Being Ernest," *St Louis Post-Dispatch* (April 27, 1990).

Jack Turner ... Jack Turner, Ph.D., "Jim Varney understood his role in the real world," *Delaware State News* (March 6, 2000).

He said during the time ... Bob Carlton, "The Importance of Being Ernest," *St Louis Post-Dispatch* (April 27, 1990).

As Jim prepared for his dual-role ... "Creator Varney Revels in Slapstick," *Rocky Mountain News* (April 7, 1990).

From *The dog became...* to ... *the action sequences*: Mal Vincent, "Hey Vern! I'm in Jail!" *The Virginian-Pilot* (April 11, 1990). Author's personal knowledge also contributed to information cited here.

As he is flying ... "Ernest Goes to Jail," Touchstone Pictures (1990).

Letterman writer Bill Scheft ... Bill Scheft, "Take My Quarterback, Please," *Sports Illustrated* (Jan. 26, 2009).

THE IMPORTANCE OF BEING ERNEST:
THE LIFE OF ACTOR JIM VARNEY

In addition, one little-known fact ... Author interview with Joe Liles.

Comedian Jeff Altman ... "Pink Lady and Jeff" DVD (2001).

Elrod always got ... Author interview with Joe Liles.

In February 1990 ... "Ernest's new pitch: Hey Vern: How 'Bout Them Atlanta Braves," *The Tennessean* (Feb. 7, 1990).

An open house ... Marcia Dick and Cheryl Charles, "Hey Vern, have you seen Ernest lately?" *The Boston Globe* (March 16, 1990).

Two years later ... Gary Laden, "Varney Now Pitching Hunting Safety," *Atlanta Journal Constitution* (July 12, 1992).

Undeterred, Carden & Cherry ... Jennifer Mann Fuller, "Chiefs are going for comic relief in new round of television ads," *The Kansas City Star* (Aug. 20, 1991).

In the early spring of 1990 ... John F. Rhodes, "Ernest goes to the hospital," *The Dallas Morning News* (March 28, 1990).

Chapter Twenty: "Hey Vern!"

In the "E! True Hollywood Story" ... "E! True Hollywood Story Ernest Goes to Hollywood: Jim Varney" television show (2000).

Before deciding on the name ... Cindy Pearlman, "Ernest's not too scared to think of future," *Chicago Sun-Times* (October 20, 1991); Dann Gire, "Movie Review: 'Ernest Scared Stupid,'" *Daily Herald (Chicago, Illinois)* (Oct. 11, 1991).

NOTES

With "Scared Stiff" ... Dann Gire, "Movie Review 'Ernest Scared Stupid,'" *Daily Herald (Chicago, Illinois)* (Oct. 11, 1991).

Jim joked ... Cindy Pearlman, "Ernest's not too scared to think of future," *Chicago Sun-Times* (Oct. 20, 1991).

Gene Siskel and Roger Ebert ... "Siskel & Ebert" television show (1991).

When Jim was doing interviews ... "Ernest No Blarney for Actor Jim Varney," *Daily Herald* (Oct. 18, 1991).

He told one reporter ... "The Mouth That Roared," *Daily Breeze (Torrance, Calif.)* (October 16, 1991).

"I'm finally breaking out ..." "Ernest No Blarney for Actor Jim Varney," *Daily Herald* (Oct. 18, 1991).

To reassure thousands ... Gene Wyatt, "Varney believes Ernest maturing," *The Tennessean* (Oct. 11, 1991).

A year earlier ... Dick Kreck, "Beneath Ernest's Comic Side Lurks a Shakespearean Actor," *The Denver Post* (March 31, 1990).

Now his sights ... Margaret Dick, "Varney's talent stretches beyond wacky comic," *The Nashville Banner* (Oct. 10, 1991).

In March 1992 ... Tom Humphrey, "Legislature Pauses For 2 Weeks of R R," *The Knoxville News-Sentinel* (March 15, 1992).

It was around this time ... "The Mouth That Roared," *Daily Breeze (Torrance, Calif.)* (Oct. 16, 1991).

Jim had created ... Author interview with Joe Liles.

Bunny shared little in common ... "Jim Varney says he's earnest about Ernest's hip, new image," *Associated Press* (May 15, 1992).

Chapter Twenty-One: Blue Jeans and T-Shirt Man

Just a few years into the Ernest ... Patricia Duarte, "Ernest May Be a Redneck, But He's a Hot Property, Too," *The Miami Herald* (July 21, 1985).

Jim had been paid $300 ... Lou Cedrone, Baltimore Sun (May 05, 1990).

When he did odd jobs ... Author interview with Jake McIntyre.

Sometimes he told reporters ... Don Edwards, "Hey Vern, It's a Silver-Screen Debut for Actor Jim Varney," *Lexington Herald-Leader* (December 11, 1984).

Another time ... Tony Frazier, "Hey, Vern! Ernest Goes to Camp Today," *The Daily Oklahoman* (May 22, 1987).

"I'm a blue jeans and T-shirt man ..." Homer Brickey, "Hey Vern," *The Toledo Blade* (March 12, 1989).

Chapter Twenty-Two: Buckmasters & Bubba

Bushman had started ... Tom Fegely, "RV, White-Tailed Deer Shows Join Growing List of Outdoor TV Selections," *The Morning Call* (July 8, 1990).

NOTES

Jim met Bushman ... Author interview with Jackie Bushman.

From *Bushman remembers going ...* to *"... my hunting consultant":* Author interview with Jackie Bushman.

Chapter Twenty-Three: A Hillbilly of an Ozark Kind

She also related ... Joe Rhodes, "So they loaded up the truck and moved to Beverly," *Newsday* (June 15, 1993).

The casting was ... Luaine Lee, "Director talks about 'Beverly Hillbillies' and 'Wayne's World,'" *Knight Ridder/Tribune News Service* (Oct. 4, 1993).

After going through ... Joe Rhodes, "So they loaded up the truck and moved to Beverly," *Newsday* (June 15, 1993).

But at Spheeris' insistence ... Dayton Daily News (November 7, 1993).

He said, "I've been waiting ..." Chris Hicks, "Varney Takes a Chance at Not Being Ernest," *The Deseret News* (Nov. 11, 1993).

Spheeris had to restrain him ... Chris Willman, "The Importance of Being Ernest," *Los Angeles Times* (Oct. 16, 1993).

When asked what he thought ... "Ebsen in Exclusive Jed Clampett Club," *The Pantagraph* (Oct. 21, 1993).

He spoke of his nervousness ... Chris Willman, "The Importance of Being Ernest," *Los Angeles Times* (Oct. 16, 1993).

THE IMPORTANCE OF BEING ERNEST: THE LIFE OF ACTOR JIM VARNEY

An Orlando Sentinel newspaper ... Phil Rosenthal, "The Character Curse: Actor, Role Seen As One," *Orlando Sentinel* (Oct. 27, 1991).

Soon after the movie's release ... Luaine Lee, "Director talks about 'Beverly Hillbillies' and 'Wayne's World,'" *Knight Ridder/Tribune News Service* (Nov. 4, 1993).

When talking to one reporter he claimed ... Barry Koltnow, "The Story of a Man Named Jed Has 'Em Packin' Theatres," *Orange County Register* (Oct. 29, 1993).

"It was actually kind of..." Chris Hicks, "Varney Takes a Chance at Not Being Ernest," *The Deseret News* (Nov. 11, 1993).

Jim once joked that ... Talk-show host Peter Anthony Holder interview with Jim Varney, on Holder's Web site, http://peteranthonyholder.com/cjad28.htm (Accessed June 7, 2013).

From *During the filming...* to ... *his failed relationships*: Author interview with Beth Harper.

At some point ... "Jim (Ernest) Varney drops Disney to ride alone this time," *The Hamilton Spectator* (Oct. 22, 1993).

This enabled Cherry to limit ... RoughEdge.com, R. Scott Bolton, "Goodbye, Ernest" www.roughedge.com/videoverdicts/features/varney.htm, (Accessed December 6, 2011).

Always looking for new ways ... Wendy Wilson, "The Education of Seeing 'Ernest,'" *Video Business* (April 1, 1994).

NOTES

With an estimated budget ... Internet Movie Database, http://www.imdb.com/title/tt0106827/business?ref_=tt_dt_bus

Chapter Twenty-Four: Slinky Dog

In 1991, Pixar ... Joss Langdale, "A Bug's Life," *Rome News-Tribune* (Dec. 14, 1998).

Pixar's Academy Award-winning ... Lawrence M. Fisher, "Hard Times for Innovator in Graphics," *New York Times* (April 2, 1991).

A few years prior ... Gary Schwan, "He's The Real Sarge," *Palm Beach Post* (March 7, 1996).

Animators used the mannerisms ... Talk-show host Peter Anthony Holder interview with Jim Varney, on Holder's Web site, http://peteranthonyholder.com/cjad28.htm (Accessed June 7, 2013).

When speaking of the role ... Official Web site for Max Allan Collins, Matthew Clemens, "Mommy's Daddy," www.maxallancollins.com/max/interview.php (Accessed Jan. 29, 2013).

He had become interested ... Kevin Nance, "Two Lexington Filmmakers Get Invitation to Sundance," *Lexington Herald-Leader* (Jan. 19, 1997).

One wasn't an actor ... Brandon Griggs, "Brown Most Enjoys Role as Self-Taught Writer," *The Salt Lake Tribune* (February 2, 1997).

Horton tried to get ... Author interview with Jeremy Horton.

THE IMPORTANCE OF BEING ERNEST: THE LIFE OF ACTOR JIM VARNEY

Jim told one Canadian reporter ... Talk-show host Peter Anthony Holder interview with Jim Varney, on Holder's Web site, http://peteranthonyholder.com/cjad28.htm (Accessed June 7, 2013).

She was now trying ... The Weekly Wire's Web site, Jim Ridley, "The Secret Cinema: The Reel-Life Struggles of Independent Filmmaking in Nashville," http://www.weeklywire.com/ww/07-02-97/nash_cover.html (Accessed Jan. 30, 2009).

The script was written ... FilmNashville.org, David Duncan & Jim Ridley, "The Ormonds: The Untamed Story of Nashville's First Family of Film," http://www.filmnashville.org/june/psycotronic01.html (Accessed Jan. 30, 2009).

Jim never got around to writing ... Promotional material for "Jack's Adventures: Beyond the Beanstalk" videogame.

In the fall of 1996 ... "'Show Boat' cast members enjoying life in Denver," *The Denver Post* (April 27, 1997).

More good fortune ... Heather Svokos, "'100 Proof' uses Lexington killing rampage as inspiration," *Lexington Herald-Leader* (Dec. 18, 1998).

Joe Leydon of Variety ... Joe Leydon: "100 Proof," *Variety* (March 1, 1997).

The film's producer ... Heather Svokos, "'100 Proof' uses Lexington killing rampage as inspiration," *Lexington Herald-Leader* (Dec. 18, 1998).

A few years earlier ... Chris Willman, "The Importance of Being Ernest," *Los Angeles Times* (Nov. 16, 1993).

NOTES

In early 1998 ... Official Web site for Bobby Boyd, http://www.bobbyboyd.com (Accessed Aug. 26, 2009).

Boyd, Jim and country singer ... Author interview with Andrea Lloyd.

Chapter Twenty-Five: The End of a "Great Adventure"

From *During the shooting...* to ... *to remove it*: Author interview with Jake McIntyre.

Thornton has admitted ... Hoot Gibson's speech at Jim Varney's memorial service (Feb. 16, 2000).

Thornton used to stay ... Chris Riemenschneider, "Review: Costello not acting his age – and that's a good thing," *Star Tribune* (June 6, 2002).

Thornton, being the good ... Beverly Keel, "The Importance of Being Ernest, *Nashville Scene*, (November 11, 1999).

"Daddy and Them" producer ... Kevin Nance, "Varney, 'Ernest' creator, dies at 50," *The Tennessean* (Feb. 11, 2000).

From *Jim's sisters traveled* ... to ... *high school grades*: Author interview with Jake McIntyre.

During this time ... Marilyn Beck, "Lionel Ritchie Wants To Be in Pictures," *Rocky Mountain News* (Aug. 21, 1998).

Five years earlier ... "Cape Feare" episode, "The Simpsons" television show (Oct. 7, 1993).

THE IMPORTANCE OF BEING ERNEST: THE LIFE OF ACTOR JIM VARNEY

From *Another family member...* to "*... or his hope*": Author interview with Andrea Lloyd.

Jim gave the last ... Beverly Keel, "The Importance of Being Ernest," *Nashville Scene*, (Nov. 11, 1999).

Jim wasn't talking much ... Author interview with Sandra Varney Spoonamore.

"I was one of the guys ..." Dan Butler's speech at Jim Varney's memorial service (February 16, 2000).

Jim's attorney ... Hoot Gibson's speech at Jim Varney's memorial service (February 16, 2000).

ACKNOWLEDGEMENTS

I would like to begin by thanking Joe Liles for his participation and significant contribution. I enjoyed getting to know Joe through the numerous conversations we had by telephone during the writing of this book. His candid recollections of Jim and their experiences together proved invaluable in my efforts to make this an extensive look at Jim's life. I appreciate Joe trusting me with information he has shared with few others.

I would also like to thank the Carnegie Center for Literacy in Lexington, Kentucky. Through their author-mentoring program, I was paired with author Leslie Guttman, who guided me through the many aspects of bringing this book to publication. Her years of experience coupled with her continued support and enthusiasm were extremely important to the process of writing the book. Leslie also served as my editor; while respecting my voice as an author, she did an outstanding job of fine-tuning and polishing every last detail of my manuscript.

I must also give special thanks to the very kind Julieanne Pogue for granting me an interview and assisting me with other important phases of this book.

In addition, this biography could not have been possible without the cooperation of these wonderful people:

THE IMPORTANCE OF BEING ERNEST:
THE LIFE OF ACTOR JIM VARNEY

Lianne Mize Russell, Thom Ferrell, Jake McIntyre, James McIntyre, Elaine McIntyre, Sandra Varney Spoonamore, Andrea Lloyd, Ken Lloyd, Ed McChord, Shannon Kelly, Charles Edward Pogue, Walter Williamson, Mary Polites, Michael Polites, Jeremy Horton, Kevin McMurray, Jackie Bushman, Mark Evanier, Beth Harper, Meg Moye, Rob Neuhauser, Randy Soard, Marshall Fallwell Jr., Anthony Johnson, Kathy Jansen, Coke Sams, Jack Pattie, Roy Lightner, Kevin Lightner, Trevor Wells, Scott Hayes, Bob Singleton, Janet Kinstle, Clay Watkins, Greg Gortman, Lisa Murray, Peg Gaw, Debbie May, R. Scott Bolton, Lonnie Shorr, Janet Isenhour, Neil Chethik, Luisa Trujillo, Anne Lambert, Matthew Conrad, Dan Adkins, Jim Combs, Jim Hazlett, David Griffin, and Christopher Smedley.

Finally, my wife, Keli, was incredibly supportive throughout what became a very long process of putting all of this together. She served as a sounding board and provided valuable input on countless matters. She assisted me with many small tasks too numerous to mention. I am forever grateful for her contribution.

For videos, fan remembrances, little-known facts about Jim and more, check out the Facebook page for this book at:

https://www.facebook.com/beingernestbook

CPSIA information can be obtained at www.ICGtesting.com
Printed in the USA
LVOW06s1813030915

452710LV00020B/997/P